HOW TO RUN YOUR
BUSINESS
WITH
dBASE II®

HOW TO RUN YOUR
BUSINESS
WITH
dBASE II®

BY RICHARD H. BAKER

TAB **TAB BOOKS Inc.**
BLUE RIDGE SUMMIT, PA. 17214

FIRST EDITION

FIRST PRINTING

Copyright © 1984 by TAB BOOKS Inc.

Printed in the United States of America

Reproduction or publication of the content in any manner, without express
permission of the publisher, is prohibited. No liability is assumed with respect to
the use of the information herein.

Library of Congress Cataloging in Publication Data

Baker, Richard H.
How to run your business with dBASE II.

Includes index.
1. dBase II (Computer program)   2. Small
business—Data processing.   I. Title.
HF5548.4.D22B34   1984   658′.022′0285425   84-8534
IBSN 0-8306-0918-0
ISBN 0-8306-1918-6 (pbk.)

Contents

HOW TO RUN YOUR
BUSINESS
WITH
dBASE II®

Introduction

The computer is no longer just a high-priced roomful of machinery, spinning its tapes and flashing its lights in mysterious fashion for the benefit of its blue-chip proprietors. Reasonably priced microcomputers are now available to the small business manager who:

- ☐ Would like to spend more time building the business and less time slaving over the books.
- ☐ Is forced to make critical business decisions without adequate information, and often on the basis of nothing more than educated guesswork.
- ☐ Would do something about slow-moving products and slow-paying customers—if only you had time to identify and correct the problems.

If you're like many small-business people these days, you've probably wondered what a computer really can do for you. You may have stepped into a computer store and been confronted by a bewildering array of high-tech products. You might even have bought one of them.

Still, if you're like most computer customers you probably are a bit unsure exactly what a microcomputer can do for your business. Your common sense tells you it probably can do something. But your business sense tells you at the same time you should not invest in a personal computer unless you have a good idea exactly what it can do for you and how well it will pay off.

This book was written to help you answer those questions. Its purpose is to show you, in a concrete and practical way, just how you can use a personal computer to manage a small business more efficiently, more profitably, and with a better chance of success.

We'll work the same way you should select a computer system: with the program you want to run. We'll want a versatile program that can be applied to a variety of small business problems and that won't demand great gobs of computer capacity to do so. One popular program that fits these requirements is dBASE II, produced (and registered as a trademark) by Ashton-Tate, of Culver City, California.

dBASE is a versatile program that can do a multitude of jobs. Like other database programs, it serves as a central file cabinet full of information you can recall, compare, sort, and calculate. It stores a wealth of information and—much more important—it puts the computer to work to let you *use* that information.

There are other kinds of business programs available. A *spreadsheet* sets up your information much as it would appear on a financial ledger, letting you do most kinds of mathematical calculations, both basic and advanced.

Word processors are also business programs widely used to produce letters and reports. There also is a great variety of specially written programs to do your accounting, prepare your tax returns, and so on.

Among the newest types of software on the market is the *integrated program,* which combines several business programs in a single package. For example, you could retrieve information from a database, evaluate it with a spreadsheet, and use a word processor to report your findings.

That may be a bit much, though, for the typical small business. A multitude of programs, whether you purchase them separately or in an integrated package, can be expensive. They also need more sophisticated computers with larger memory capacities.

To keep the time, the cost, and the learning process within reason, this book will demonstrate how you can use dBASE II to attack some of the most common business problems. Once you understand how it does so, you may want to consider additional programs to serve added purposes. In fact, one chapter of this book will show you how to link dBASE with word processing and spreadsheet programs to create an integrated program of your own.

You should find, though, that dBASE is a versatile and useful program that can meet many of your business needs with a single purchase.

To demonstrate what you can do with dBASE, we'll consider the cases of some fictional small businesses, with many of the needs and problems you also face. We'll take these mythical firms through three major steps:

1) Using the techniques of systems analysis in a simplified way that can help you determine what a computer can do for you.
2) Learning the basic techniques of database operations, including simple, plain-English procedures that can make it easy for even non-programmers to use.
3) Presenting a series of prewritten procedures that you can type, enter your own data, and start using today. As you become comfortable with dBASE, you can customize these programs to meet your own specific needs.

Not only will you have these ready-to-use programs available, but you'll have a better understanding of what a small computer can do to improve your own small business. The computer—and dBASE—can seem confusing at first, but as you progress you can replace your confusion with a growing knowledge of the computer's possibilities and how you can make use of them.

Part 1

Introduction to dBASE

dBASE II is the best-selling and probably the best-known microcomputer application of a *database management system* or *DBMS*. The DBMS is a recent development in computers, and only in the last few years has it spread in any great numbers to microcomputers. The University of Minnesota, whose graduate school of management keeps track of such things, reports that in the fall of 1980 there were 40 systems which might have been described as database management systems for microcomputers; the 1983 count turned up 140.

Many of these are not practical choices for small business use. According to Professor Gordon C. Everest, who heads the Minnesota project, the quality and cost of these programs vary widely. Only about 60 have qualified for listing in the department's latest survey.

Of these, dBASE is by far the most popular, particularly with business users. In one survey, 40 percent of the respondents who already have a DBMS said they have dBASE II. Another 32.4 percent said they were thinking of buying it. The two figures total nearly three-quarters of all respondents. The second-place product was mentioned by only 7.3 percent of the current DBMS users and 9.3 percent of the prospective buyers.

That kind of popularity must have a reason. It also might be significant that dBASE has something in common with MicroPro's WordStar, the nation's most popular word processing program. Both programs use extensive lists of commands that can be intimidating to first-time users. Once you've learned to use them, though, both prove to be high-performance products. And dBASE has achieved much the same kind of dominance among DBMS programs that WordStar has captured in word processing.

The Database You Manage

If you're going to manage a database, the next logical question is to ask exactly what kind of thing you'll be managing. DBMS programs have proliferated in recent years, particularly on mainframes but also on microcomputers.

The main appeal of a DBMS is that you can maintain a single file of information and do a variety of things with it. You don't have to maintain different information files for different purposes. DBMS systems come in several varieties, but for this purpose it's important to describe only two of them.

A *physical* database lists its contents one item after the other, like pages of a book. If you want to look something up in such a system, you must first check page 1, then page 2, and so on. If the information you want is on page 52, you'll first have to check pages 1 through 51. A computer can search its "pages" much faster than you can scan a book, of course, but the principle still is the same.

dBASE is an example of a *relational* system, which you could compare to the same book with a separate index. You could consult the index, then go directly to page 52. That means you must read only the information that's important to you at the moment—you don't have to go through the rest of the book.

Another common description compares a relational system to a table, in which the program can identify the column and row that have the information you need, ignoring everything you don't need. You also might compare it with the isolated replay camera that zeroes in on the pass receiver in a football game.

The main advantage of a program like dBASE is that it can arrange and use your data in a *logical* order. You decide how your files will be organized. In other types, the program makes the decision. You must sort through your data in the order in which it appears.

Everybody Into the Act

dBASE clearly can be more efficient than an older-style database. It certainly can do a better job of serving the main purpose of a DBMS: getting multiple use of the same information file. These advantages have turned "relational" into an industry buzzword, and everyone these days seems to be advertising their systems as "relational." IBM recently introduced a relational system for mainframe use with the double-take title of DB2.

One problem here is that there is no clear, universally accepted definition of a relational database—or for that matter of any system for categorizing the DBMS field. For example, one professorial type suggests that relational databases are one of four basic types, and it's absolutely vital that you understand all four. Then he goes on to admit that there's not a single product on the market that fits neatly into any of his cubbyholes.

In other words, don't get hung up on definitions. dBASE probably doesn't have all the qualities on which this professor would insist, but it does operate primarily as a relational database. IBM's close skirting of Ashton-Tate's trademark should be taken as a compliment. If you're willing to devote some effort to learning what dBASE can do for you, you'll find it will do many things well.

In the Middle

In the full spectrum of microcomputer programs for business, dBASE stands somewhere near the middle. On one flank is the off-the-shelf applications package, such as the many accounting and personnel systems available for small companies. These offer the advantage of plug-and-go use, but they may go nowhere if they aren't well suited to your company and its needs.

On the other side is the high-level computer language, such as BASIC or Pascal, with which you can create your own applications from scratch. The program can be written exactly for your personal needs, but like any kind of custom tailoring, this approach requires time, skill—and money.

dBASE is a compromise. At its heart it is a prewritten program, ready to accept your data, process it, and produce a meaningful report. It also comes with its own programming language. That's the part that can seem intimidating, but it's also an advantage. It gives you the ability to do some useful customizing, without requiring that you start every activity from the discouraging blank sheet of paper.

Ahead of the Game

Actually, dBASE is ahead of many mainframe programs in some respects. For example, IBM's SQL database system operates from a short, simple list of built-in commands, without the added language dBASE provides. If you want to go beyond SQL's immediate capabilities, you'll have to write a program in some standard computer language to do so.

The advantage of dBASE is that it gives you a wide range of possibilities. The first exercises in this book will use the so-called *query language,* a list of commands much like those in SQL. Later, we'll work this language into programs that can make dBASE about as user-friendly as you'd ever like to get. Once you're involved in applications of your own, you're free to work on the level at which you feel most comfortable.

The payoff of all this is that the more programming you're interested in doing, the simpler you can make things in daily use. A dBASE program can generate menus and forms that a novice operator can complete just by picking a menu item and filling in the blanks.

dBASE and You

dBASE users range in skill from rank beginners to veteran programmers. This book will assume that you do know one thing: how to turn on your computer and load the program. These procedures vary among computers and operating systems, so you'll have to refer to your instruction manual for that. Otherwise, we'll assume you know nothing about dBASE except that it makes funny use of capital letters.

This book won't try to teach you to master every dBASE command. There are many, and some are near-duplicates that vary only in small details. Instead, the technique will be to show you what dBASE can do, then explain how it does it. If you understand what the program can do for you, you always can refer to this book or to the dBASE instruction manual for the specific language to execute your intentions.

Keep in mind that as you use dBASE you'll move up the skill ladder. If you're a novice, or if your system will be used by less-than-expert employees, you'll want a menu-driven system that provides plenty of screens, prompts and menus. At a little more advanced level, you may find that the forms and menus tend to get in the way, and you'll want to be free to drive the system by making direct commands in the query language. At an advanced level, you'll know how to write dBASE programs to your personal specifications. One advantage of dBASE is that you can train yourself—and train the program—to work on any of these levels.

dBASE and Hardware

dBASE brings a measure of mainframe flexibility to the microcomputer world. You won't be limited much by the capacity of the program. You could find yourself restricted, though, by the capacity of your hardware, particularly of the disk drives.

The basic single-density, 5¼-inch disk will hold, at most, the records of a few hundred employees, customers, inventory items, and so on. The exact number depends on how long each record is. Once you get into the double-density disks, your capacity probably will extend beyond the thousand-record mark. Double-sided disks, naturally, will hold about twice as many records.

If your needs go beyond that—remembering that you can store employee and customer records on separate disks, for example—you probably could use a hard disk system, both for its capacity and its faster operation.

Beyond this are *shared systems,* in which several micro users can use the programs and data stored in a central system. Multiple users, though, mean multiple complications. Ashton-Tate has announced a multi-user version of dBASE, but the original version should be considered a one-user program. It is possible to adapt it to multiple use, but it probably isn't a good idea.

An Important Technicality

We've gone to great lengths to make sure the programs listed in this book are reliable. Most are based on established dBASE routines, and many were produced by automatic program generators. Several routines originally planned for this volume were thrown out because they did not produce dependable results.

You must understand, though, that you use them at your own risk. No doubt you will encounter several "bugs" as you type and adapt the listings. They are an inevitable part of programming. Neither the author, the publisher, nor anyone but you can take responsibility for them.

We strongly recommend that you maintain a duplicate set of records under your existing system until you are sure that the dBASE routine you wish to use is as reliable as you would like it to be. After every dBASE session, copy your revised records onto a separate disk, and maintain it as a backup copy.

Chapter 1

Learning to Use dBASE

A long-running advertisement for Ashton-Tate's dBASE II shows a user slyly covering the label on his IBM Personal Computer with the model identification of a larger mainframe computer. The copy suggests that you can use dBASE to give a microcomputer much of the power of its larger and more expensive counterparts.

Some reviewers have criticized that ad as overstating the case. After all, even the most powerful micro with the best-designed software can't match a mainframe in such important characteristics as speed, memory and storage capacity. A large corporation that tried to manage itself with a single microcomputer would . . . well . . . would know enough not to try it in the first place.

If you're the manager of a smaller business, the advertised suggestion may indeed make some sense. dBASE does bring much of the flexibility and versatility of a mainframe to smaller computers and smaller companies. It's often described as "powerful," an overused term that means a program is useful and versatile. dBASE can't turn your micro into a mainframe, but on a smaller scale it can give you many of the same advantages.

The big advantage of dBASE II is that once you establish a basic storehouse of information, you can recall and manipulate this information for all kinds of purposes. The *capacity* of your computer may determine *how much information* you can store and process, but with a versatile program like dBASE, there are few limits to *what you can do with it*. These are some of the possibilities:

- ☐ You'd like separate lists of employees who are on salary and those who earn hourly wage rates. If you have a database which lists the employees and their wage rates, dBASE can produce your lists. It can put them in alphabetical order if you'd like. Or, it can list the employees in order of their pay rates.
- ☐ The annual company party is coming up, and you'd like to present awards to employees who have

completed 10 and 25 years with the firm. If your employee database also lists the date each employee was hired, dBASE can tell you who should get the awards.

☐ You can use the basic file of names and wage rates, add information on payroll deductions, and use dBASE to print out the paychecks.

Notice that you're able to do all this with one basic file of information. If the information is in the file in the first place, dBASE can extract it in just about any form that suits your needs. Now, think of what you can do with additional databases on your vendor and customer accounts or your inventory records.

Adam B. Green, who conducts nationwide dBASE seminars for SoftwareBanc of Arlington, Massachusetts, describes dBASE as a "word processor for data." Just as a word processor lets you enter and manipulate words, sentences and ideas, a program like dBASE lets you do much the same thing with names, numbers, and information.

BUT ALL THAT PROGRAMMING!

It's true. If you're going to use dBASE to its full capacity, you'll have to involve yourself with its built-in programming language. You can use dBASE's commands to control the program directly. That's how beginners learn to use it, and even many experienced users (including me) prefer to continue doing it that way. Still, there are things you can do only through the programming language. And if you're preparing a system to be used by inexperienced operators, a well-written program can provide the user-friendliness they will require.

Particularly to a beginning user, dBASE programming can seem discouraging. That has been the major complaint against dBASE. Compared with newer programs that make heavy use of graphics, menus and overlapping "windows" to guide you through the process, dBASE requires a more fundamental approach. In particular, it asks that you gain some passing familiarity, at least, with its programming language.

That may not be as bad as you think. If you've already thumbed through some of the later pages in this book you've probably seen some program listings that look pretty intimidating. They really aren't as bad as they may look right now. Consider these points:

☐ Compared with most other computer languages, and with many packaged programs, dBASE uses a logical, easy-to-follow system. An early version of dBASE was called *Vulcan*, after the super-logical Mr. Spock of *"Star Trek."*

☐ It's a necessary fact of computing life that the more versatile a program is, the more things there are to learn. There are database and integrated programs on the market that might be easier to learn. Generally, though, these programs also have less capacity to do the job. You might prefer them at first, but you'll encounter their limitations later.

☐ dBASE speaks to you in more or less ordinary English. You'll command it to DO something or to FIND this. As your English teachers used to tell you, there are many rules for using the language. In dBASE, though, these are reasonably easy to learn and observe. By comparison, BASIC looks like so much gibberish, and dBASE programmers universally report a minimum number of encounters with the dreaded error message.

☐ The purpose of this book is to guide you through the dBASE procedure. It will do so by taking advantage of dBASE's modular construction. A typical dBASE program is actually a routine that links together several standard procedures. Each procedure is a separate module or building block. For example, there's a module to present a menu, a module to accept data input and a module to produce a particular kind of report. Once you've set up the modules to accomplish a particular group of tasks, writing a dBASE procedure is as simple as assembling them in the right order and making a few small modifications.

GETTING OUT THE NEWS

You're the publisher of a small newspaper, the Submetropolis *Weekly Satellite*. You have a small staff working for this prize-winning publication, and it's divided into several departments.

The news department is headed by editor Lou Asner, who has come to Submetropolis for a change of pace after the rigors of big-city journalism. On the news staff are Ida Rather, who covers City Hall and the County Courthouse; Willie Cronkite, who handles club notices and obituaries; and Bobby Carl Woodstein, who covers the White House. Matt Brady is the staff photographer.

Also under Asner's supervision is the sports department. Frannie Rice is the sports editor. Staff writer Cosell Smith covers roller derby, professional wrestling, and the Tampa Bay Buccaneers.

The business manager is a retired Army food service officer known as General Mills. Chris Barnard takes care of circulation. Frank Tarlek sells advertising, Rocky Feller keeps the books, and Effie Scrooge makes out the payroll.

Down in the production department, Maggie Houlihan presides over Sherrie Brinkley and Chris Teigs, who set the type and make up the pages. Their work then goes to Walter Troll, who runs the press.

The organizational chart for the *Satellite* looks something like Fig. 1-1.

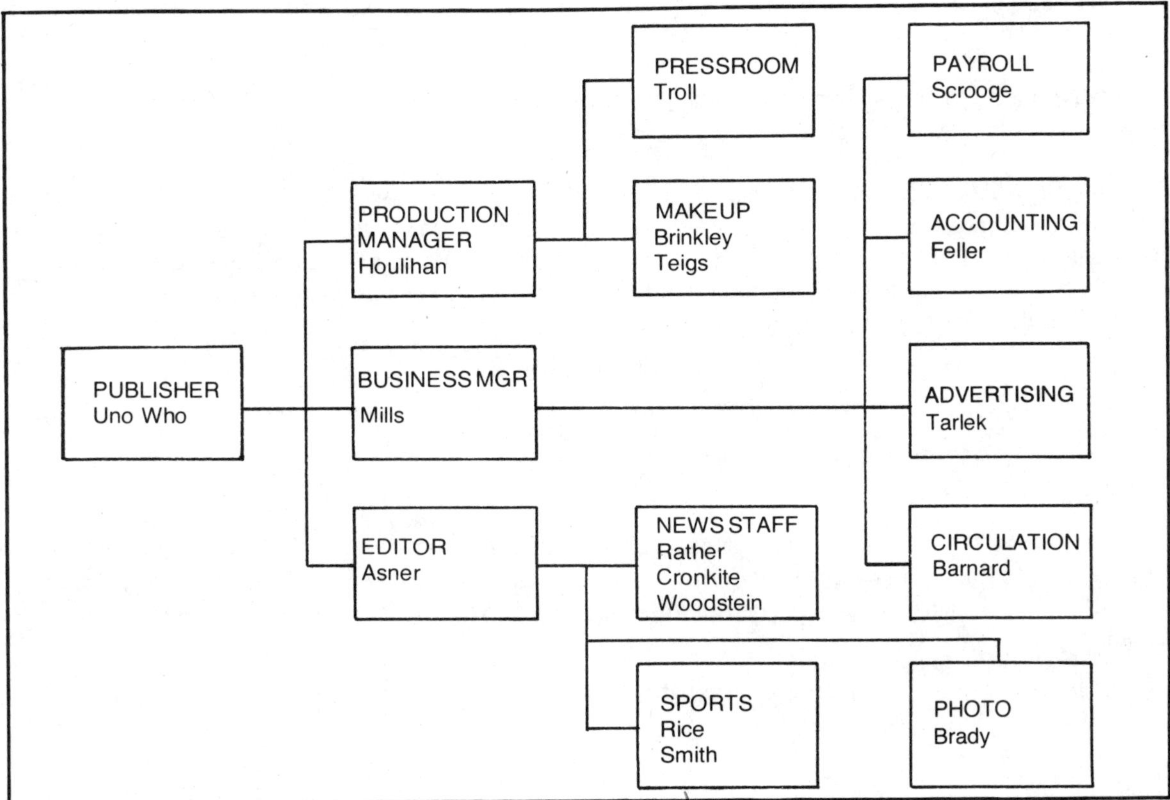

Fig. 1-1. Organizational chart—for a company and a database.

This chart also could outline the organization of a database. It shows every employee in relation to the chain of command. For example, photographer Brady reports to editor Asner, who in turn reports to you. That's important to know, if you don't already, when the time comes for Brady's annual performance evaluation.

In fact, you might want to organize your personnel files in that way. That way, if you want to look up Troll's personnel record, you'll find it filed under the production department, behind Houlihan's and in the same slot with Brinkley and Teigs.

ELECTRONIC FILING

A file drawer full of records is a database on paper. We've organized the personnel records by department. When we set up a dBASE file for these records, we might want to enter them the same way.

In fact, the file drawer is not just a database but it is a *physical* database. Each record is in a fixed physical location in relation to all the rest. If we were to enter these records into a physical type of database they would have the same relationship on the computer disk that they now have in the drawer.

But suppose one day Mills walks into your office and reminds you this is the time of year when you must find out who is newly vested in the *Satellite's* pension plan. Those employees who've had their fifth anniversaries with the company during the preceding year are eligible for this honor.

Your file drawer, or its physical equivalent inside the computer, won't readily tell you this. Oh, you could go through every file to find out who was hired five years ago. The computer could search through the physical database the same way. One big benefit of programs like dBASE, though, is that you can ask it a question like this:

"Give me the names of everyone who joined the company
between the appropriate dates five years ago."

dBASE will happily comply. In fact, if you give it the right commands it will reorganize the database for just this purpose, ranking the employees by hiring date instead of by department. Of course, the necessary information must be in the file in the first place, and that means you must put it there.

To repeat: a physical database itself determines the order in which its information will be filed and used. With dBASE II, *you* make the decisions.

Be Creative

Load up your dBASE disk and look for the standard prompt:

```
Enter TODAY'S DATE as MM/DD/YD
 Or RETURN for none:_
```

Do as it says. As the second line suggests, you can simply press your RETURN or ENTER key to plunge ahead without the date. The date you enter now, though, will be stored for possible future use in your dBASE programs. It also will be recorded as the date your file was last updated—or in this case, begun.

Either way, once you've entered the date or skipped that part of it, the next thing you'll see is:

•

That's it, just

•

The period you'll see at the left side of your screen is dBASE's funny way of saying it is waiting for instructions from you. Your first instruction is one that may give you a sense of omnipotence. After the period you're going to type:

. CREATE

Like all dBASE commands, CREATE is a verb. This verb must have an object. The object is the answer to the obvious question, "CREATE what?"

What we're out to create is a file of basic information on the *Satellite* employees. Every file must have a name, and it must follow the file naming rules of your operating system. For instance, CP/M allows up to eight letters—no spaces or colons allowed. We'd like to call our file **Employees,** because that would be the most descriptive title, but that's a nine-letter word. So we'll settle for the file name **Employee.**

In response to the first dBASE period, we could have combined the verb and object and said:

. CREATE Employee

But we didn't do that. All we said was:

. CREATE

So, dBASE will respond with:

ENTER FILENAME:

Do it, then press RETURN. Your screen then will say:

ENTER FILENAME: Employee

Now, we start to get some action instead of those inquisitive periods. Your screen will look like this:

ENTER RECORD STRUCTURE AS FOLLOWS:
 FIELD   NAME,TYPE,WIDTH,DECIMAL PLACES
 001

How's that again? dBASE is asking what kind of information you want to put into the new file called **Employee.**

Look at the second line. It calls for something called "Field." You may have some thought at this moment of putting the whole thing out to pasture, but don't panic. A *field* is simply *one type* of information you intend to store—like the employee's name, for instance. In fact, **Name** could be the name of one of our fields.

Later, though, we'll probably want to sort this information alphabetically. There are some other applications where the last name is enough, and anything else just wastes disk space and processing time. Most veteran dBASE users, then, separate the first and last names. We might as well start out doing it right. So, we'll enter **First**—for first name—as the name of the field 001.

Field names are a little different from file names. Now, dBASE's own rules take over. The field name can be up to 10 characters long, either capitals or lowercase, and you can use numbers and colons if you do it right. The name must begin with a letter, and it can't end with a colon.

For example, you could use these names for initial field:

First

FirstName
First:Name

But you couldn't use:

First Name (Sorry, no spaces allowed)
First_Name (A more readable version used in some other systems; unfortunately it doesn't work in
        dBASE)
1stName (Begins with a number)
First: (Ends with a colon).

If all these rules sound confusing, here's the one you really should remember:

While setting up and using your dBASE files, you'll constantly find yourself naming things.

In fact, one of the hardest things about dBASE may be to keep track of all the names you've handed out. It helps to jot down the names you assign, with some indication of what you've assigned them to. It helps even more, to use the simplest, most descriptive names you can think of and to avoid cryptic abbreviations—of the kind that make you wonder later, "Whatever did I mean by that?"

Anyway, we've decided on the name **First** for the field. Next, dBASE asks you for something called a "Type." dBASE fields come in three basic types:

☐ *Character* fields are composed of ordinary things you can read—like someone's name.
☐ *Numerical* fields are numbers you can add, subtract, multiply and divide.
☐ *Logical* fields are items that are either true or false.

Indicating the type is a simple one-word entry: C for character, N for numeric and L for logical.

The "Width" specification calls for the maximum number of letters, numbers and punctuation marks you'll allow in any one field. You can specify any number up to 254, but avoid the temptation to make use of that vast outer limit. The number you specify will be the disk space you devote to every entry in that field. If you call for all 254 characters and use only 5 of them, you'll still be charged for the entire 254. Most names will fit into 10 spaces, so that's what we'll specify.

The decimal place specification is used only for numerical fields, so we can skip that.

At this point, we've decided on a field called **First**, of type C, 10 characters long. Following the example of the second line, enter these choices, in order and separate by commas. Check your entries, because they can be hard to change later. Once you've done this, press RETURN. The screen then should look like this:

```
ENTER RECORD STRUCTURE AS FOLLOWS:
 FIELD    NAME,TYPE,WIDTH,DECIMAL PLACES
 001      First,c,10
 002      _
```

Notice that the cursor is there, ready to take your specifications for the second field. The remaining entries should look like this:

```
ENTER RECORD STRUCTURE AS FOLLOWS:
 FIELD    NAME,TYPE,WIDTH,DECIMAL PLACES
```

```
001        First,c,10
002        Last,c,10
003        Street,c,20
004        City,c,10
005        State,c,2
006        Zip,c,5
007        Hired,n,2
008        Dept,c,5
009        Supervisor,c,10
010        <RETURN>
```

Take a look at Field 6. Everyone knows a ZIP code is a number. But here, we've entered it as a character. What gives?

Look at it this way: when was the last time you added or subtracted a ZIP code? If you enter the codes as numerical items, you could ask dBASE to add up a grand total at the end—but why? It's a small thing, but most dBASE experts recommend that you use numerical entries only when you plan to conduct mathematical operations on them.

Field 7 is for the date the employee was hired. To simplify this initial discussion, we'll use only the last two digits of the year. In real-life practice you'd want to enter the entire date in the MM/DD/YY format of the dBASE sign-on message.

This database has nine fields. When the prompt calls for Field 10, simply enter RETURN to indicate that you're through. dBASE then will ask if you want to

INPUT DATA NOW?

Answer Y to this question, and dBASE will switch to its data entry mode and you can start typing in the data on individual employees. Let's answer N right now, though, so we can step back for a moment and see where we are.

In Review

We've CREATEd a database called **Employee.** Our negative answer to the "input data" question led us back to the familiar dBASE period. Remembering that a dBASE command is a verb, which must then have an object, enter:

```
. USE Employee
```

USE is one of the dBASE's most basic commands. dBASE will hardly do anything unless you first specify which database you want to USE. Once you've done that, enter:

```
. DISPLAY Structure
```

dBASE will do just that. You should see:

```
STRUCTURE FOR FILE:   EMPLOYEE.DBF
NUMBER OF RECORDS:    00000
DATE OF LAST UPDATE: 00/00/00
PRIMARY USE DATABASE
FLD       NAME        TYPE WIDTH    DEC
001       FIRST        C     010
```

```
002        LAST           C      010
003        STREET         C      020
004        CITY           C      010
005        STATE          C      002
006        ZIP            C      005
007        HIRED          N      002
008        DEPT           C      005
009        SUPERVISOR     C      010
** TOTAL **                      00075
```

Make one last check of the entries. If you want to change something you can do it with the command:

. MODIFY Structure

As dBASE then will warn you, this command will destroy any data that's already in the file. There's a way around that, but it requires that you do things the hard way. Consider this your last easy chance to make any changes in the basic structure.

Satisfied? If you've made any changes, use CTRL/W to save them. (In case you don't know, use the CTRL key like a shift key, holding it down while you press the W.)

Entering Data

Now it's time for what easily could be the deadliest, most boring job in all computerdom, entering data. There's no way around it. Someone has to sit down and type in all the names, addresses, and other information you want to store about your employees. At least with dBASE you only must do it once. To start the process we must reach deep into the dictionary for the command:

. APPEND

You'll see:

```
RECORD # 00001
FIRST      :                :
LAST       :                :
STREET     :                          :
CITY       :                :
STATE      :    :
ZIP        :        :
HIRED      :    :
DEPT       :          :
SUPERVISOR:                :
```

This is a blank form. You can fill it in with information on yourself. The colons indicate the field lengths you've selected; dBASE won't let you go beyond them. Then press RETURN to move on to the next field or, when you're done with this record, to Record 2, where you can enter the same information for another employee. Once you've finished, CTRL/W will again save your work.

To alter a record already on file, use the command:

. EDIT

Control Key	Effect	Control Key	Effect
X	Next field		
E	Previous field	**In APPEND mode:**	
D	Ahead one character		
S	Back one character	R	Next record
V	Toggle between insert and overwrite modes.	Q	Erases record
G	Delete individual character	<RETURN>	Moves to next field or record. If entered at the top of a blank record, it will return to dBASE operations.
P	Toggles printer on and off		
Q	Quit. Returns to dBASE program WITHOUT saving changes.		
W	Writes new and revised entries on disk.	**In MODIFY mode:**	
		T	Deletes field
In EDIT mode:		Y	Deletes data only, leaving a blank for inserting a new field
C	Next record	N	Inserts space for a new field
R	Previous record		

Fig. 1-2. dBASE II editing commands.

followed by a record number.

In either the APPEND or EDIT modes, WordStar-like cursor commands will let you move around, and from record to record. A full list of the cursor commands is in Fig. 1-2.

There are some limits on the records as well as on the fields. A record is limited to 32 fields of 1,000 characters, whichever comes first. A file can have no more than 65,535 records. If you even come close to these outer limits, though, you've probably created a monster.

For the purposes of this lesson, the data already has been entered. To see what we've done (and later to see what you've done) enter the command:

`. LIST All`

Everything you've entered should appear on the screen, something like Fig. 1-3.

The command DISPLAY will do just about the same thing as LIST, with this difference: DISPLAY will stop every screenful of listings to let you examine them. Press RETURN when you want to continue. LIST will just scroll through the files until it reaches the end.

As you can see from the listing, your **Employee** database really is just a simple table. The fields are columns, and the individual records are the lines.

00001	Uno	Who	2107 Main St.	Submetro.	NM	87654	63	Publ.	None
00002	Lou	Asner	1600 Leisure Dr.	Carcasonne	KY	41806	82	Edit	Who
00003	Ida	Rather	2881 Cathy La.	Purdy Sta.	NY	10578	80	Edit	Asner
00004	Wallace	Cronkite	23 Allweather Slip	Westport	CT	06880	70	Edit	Asner
00005	Bobby Carl	Woodstein	1150 15th St. NW	Washington	DC	20071	81	Edit	Asner
00006	Francis	Rice	606 Limbo Walk	Lucedale	MS	39452	23	Spts	Asner
00007	Cosell	Smith	1267 Mission Cir.	Yamhill	OR	97148	83	Spts	Rice
00008	Matthew	Brady	800 Tripod Dr.	Gettysburg	PA	17325	78	Photo	Asner
00009	Frank	Mills	23 Gun Salute	Ft. Meade	FL	33841	82	Bus.	Who
00010	Chris	Barnard	54 Left Ventricle	Heartland	TX	76543	67	Circ	Mills
00011	Frank	Tarlek	876 Traffic Pattern	Cinc.	OH	45201	83	Adv.	Mills
00012	Rocky	Feller	Goldpaved Way	Palm Sprs.	CA	92262	67	Acct.	Mills
00013	Effie	Scrooge	67 Pudding Lane	Cuttyhunk	MA	02713	80	Pay.	Mills
00014	Maggie	Houlihan	1848 Nursery Rd.	Cloudy	OK	74537	80	Prod.	Who
00015	Sherrie	Brinkley	23 State St.	Limerick	ME	04048	81	Prod.	Houlihan
00016	Chris	Teigs	1868 Greenhill Dr.	Leaksville	NC	27288	80	Prod.	Houlihan
00017	Walter	Troll	15 Underhill St.	Smartt	TN	37378	79	Press	Houlihan

Fig. 1-3. Submetropolis *Weekly Satellite* employee database.

You also might notice that the table appears more or less by department, just as we organized the old file drawer. That's because we entered them that way. The beauty of dBASE is that you're not stuck with this order. You can sort and sift through the files to isolate the information you want.

NOW FOR THE FUN PART

The tedium of entering data is really the worst part of using dBASE II. Don't blame that on the program. It's the same with all of them. You'll be rewarded, though, when it comes time to play around with the data you entered. Let's try a few commands:

```
LIST OFF For Hired=80
```

```
Ida        Rather      2881 Cathy La.       Purdy Sta. NY 10578  80 Edit  Asner
Effie      Scrooge     67 Pudding Lane      Cuttyhunk  MA 02713  80 Pay.  Mills
Maggie     Houlihan    1848 Nursery Rd.     Cloudy     OK 74537  80 Prod  Who
Chris      Teigs       1868 Greenhill Dr.   Leaksville NC 27288  80 Prod  Houlihan
```

This command is a little more complicated than those we've used before. LIST OFF is a command you can use to list the database without the record numbers. We then added a statement which imposed some *conditions* on what we wanted dBASE to list. If people hired in 1980 are soon to be eligible for vested pensions, we could use that command to find out who they are.

```
. LIST Last for Dept='Edit'

00002  Asner
00003  Rather
00004  Cronkite
00005  Woodstein
```

This time we imposed conditions on which fields we were going to report, as well as on the characteristics for which the names are to be selected. This command asked for the last names of people who work in the editorial department.

Note that when we refer to a character field, the entry must be enclosed in quotes. That wasn't necessary in the earlier example when we used a numerical field.

By the way, since we used the term **Edit** to identify that department in the database, we must use exactly the same term to recall the data. "Editorial" won't work, nor will "EDIT" or "edit." Actually, given the limited space we allowed for the departmental field, we probably could have saved some confusion by referring to this department as "News."

We've also discovered a problem with our database. The sports and photography departments are part of the overall editorial operation, but in the database we classified the employees in these departments under separate headings. On the other hand, if we had classified all of them as **Edit,** we would have no way, should we need it, of isolating the members of these specialized units.

```
. LIST All for Supervisor='Mills'

00010  Chris    Barnard   54 Left Ventricle  Heartland   TX 76543  67 Circ  Mills
00011  Frank    Tarlek    876 Traffic Pattern Cinc.      OH 45201  83 Adv.  Mills
00012  Rocky    Feller    Goldpaved Way      Palm Sprs.  CA 92262  67 Acct. Mills
00013  Effie    Scrooge   67 Pudding Lane    Cuttyhunk   MA 02713  80 Pay.  Mills
```

Here we added the idea of the *scope* of a command. In this case, the scope is "All" It also might be "Next" or a record number. Try this version:

```
. LIST Next 5

00017  Walter      Troll       15 Underhill St.      Smartt  .  TN 37378  79 Press Houlihan
```

Wait a minute. This command was supposed to display the next five items in the database. It displayed only the last one. Why?

When we executed the last command, we ended up at the bottom of the file, reading the last record. When we asked for the next five, dBASE tried, but there weren't five more records to LIST. We saw the only one dBASE could find. To correct this situation, enter:

```
. GOTO Top
. LIST next 5

00001  Uno         Who         2107 Main St.        Submetro.   NM  87654  63  Publ.  None
00002  Lou         Asner       1600 Leisure Dr.     Carcasonne  KY  41806  82  Edit   Who
00003  Ida         Rather      2881 Cathy La.       Purdy Sta.  NY  10578  80  Edit   Asner
00004  Wallace     Cronkite    23 Allweather Slip   Westport    CT  06880  70  Edit   Asner
00005  Bobby Carl  Woodstein   1150 15th St. NW     Washington  DC  20071  81  Edit   Asner
```

This time we went to the top of the file, then asked for the next five—and got them.

```
. LIST All for State='DC'

005  dobby Carl Woodstein 1150 15tn St. NW Washington DC 20071  81 Edit
```

```
. LIST ALL FOR HIRED <80

00001  Uno       Who        2107 Main St.       Submetro.    NM 87654  63 Publ.  None
00004  Wallace   Cronkite   23 Allweather Slip  Westport     CT 06880  70 Edit   Asner
00006  Francis   Rice       606 Limbo Walk      Lucedale     MS 39452  23 Spts   Asner
00008  Matthew   Brady      800 Tripod Dr.      Gettysburg   PA 17325  78 Photo  Asner
00010  Chris     Barnard    54 Left Ventricle   Heartland    TX 76543  67 Circ   Mills
00012  Rocky     Feller     Goldpaved Way       Palm Sprs.   CA 92262  67 Acct.  Mills
00017  Walter    Troll      15 Underhill St.    Smartt       TN 37378  79 Press  Houlihan
```

This command asked for everyone whose hiring date was earlier than 1980—"less than 80" in dBASE parlance. dBASE offers several so-called relational operators including:

< : less than
> : more than
<= : less than or equal to
>= : more than or equal to

You also can use what are known as Boolean operators:

.AND.
.NOT.
.OR.

00001	Uno	Who	2107 Main St.	Submetro.	NM	87654	63	Publ.	None
00002	Lou	Asner	1600 Leisure Dr.	Carcasonne	KY	41806	82	Edit	Who
00003	Ida	Rather	2881 Cathy La.	Purdy Sta.	NY	10578	80	Edit	Asner
00004	Wallace	Cronkite	23 Allweather Slip	Westport	CT	06880	70	Edit	Asner
00005	Bobby Carl	Woodstein	1150 15th St. NW	Washington	DC	20071	81	Edit	Asner
00006 *Francis	Rice	606 Limbo Walk	Lucedale	MS	39452	23	Spts	Asner
00007	Cosell	Smith	1267 Mission Cir.	Yamhill	OR	97148	83	Spts	Rice
00008	Matthew	Brady	800 Tripod Dr.	Gettysburg	PA	17325	78	Photo	Asner
00009	Frank	Mills	23 Gun Salute	Ft. Meade	FL	33841	82	Bus.	Who
00010	Chris	Barnard	54 Left Ventricle	Heartland	TX	76543	67	Circ	Mills
00011	Frank	Tarlek	876 Traffic Pattern	Cinc.	OH	45201	83	Adv.	Mills
00012	Rocky	Feller	Goldpaved Way	Palm Sprs.	CA	92262	67	Acct.	Mills
00013	Effie	Scrooge	67 Pudding Lane	Cuttyhunk	MA	02713	80	Pay.	Mills
00014	Maggie	Houlihan	1848 Nursery Rd.	Cloudy	OK	74537	80	Prod.	Who
00015	Sherrie	Brinkley	23 State St.	Limerick	ME	04048	81	Prod.	Houlihan
00016	Chris	Teigs	1868 Greenhill Dr.	Leaksville	NC	27288	80	Prod.	Houlihan
00017	Walter	Troll	15 Underhill St.	Smartt	TN	37378	79	Press	Houlihan

Fig. 1-4. The staff listing again, with one marked for deletion.

Another little dBASE rule is that when you use these they must be embraced by periods. Let's try a few and see how they work:

```
. LIST all for Hired=80.AND.Supervisor='Mills'

00013  Effie      Scrooge     67 Pudding Lane      Cuttyhunk  MA 02713  80 Pay.  Mills


. LIST all for Hired=81.OR.Hired-82


*** SYNTAX ERROR ***
                ?
```

Yikes! The dreaded syntax error. Relax. This was a simple typo, and dBASE will help you correct it. You'll see:

```
LIST all for HIRED=81.OR.HIRED-82
CORRECT AND RETRY (Y/N)?
```

You answer "Y" of course. dBASE will then walk you through the correction process. In full, it looks like this:

```
LIST all for HIRED=81.OR.HIRED-82
CORRECT AND RETRY (Y/N)? Y
CHANGE FROM :-

CHANGE TO   :=

LIST all for HIRED=81.OR.HIRED=82
MORE CORRECTIONS (Y/N)? N
00002  Lou        Asner      1600 Leisure Dr.     Carcasonne KY 41806  82 Edit  Who
00005  Bobby Carl Woodstein  1150 15th St. NW     Washington DC 20071  81 Edit  Asner
00009  Frank      Mills      23 Gun Salute        Ft. Meade  FL 33841  82 Bus.  Who
00015  Sherrie    Brinkley   23 State St.         Limerick   ME 04048  81 Prod  Houlihan
```

There's a list of people hired in either 1981 or 1982. Meanwhile, though, it's decided that everyone who joined the company before 1960 will be eligible for a generous pension bonus in return for immediate retirement. If everyone eligible took us up on the offer, where would we be?

```
. DELETE all for Hired <60
```

dBASE responds with:

```
00001 DELETION(S)
```

Only one? Well, anyway, let's find out who it is:

```
. LIST
```

This produces the staff listing shown in Fig. 1-4.

This is the complete list again, with one small exception. An asterisk(*) has appeared next to Rice's name. That means you've assumed he's going to retire and have ordered his name deleted from the list.

But what if the old warhorse changes his mind and decides to keep on working? No problem. Just enter the command RESTORE, and he'll be a full-fledged member of the database again. Once you're sure he can safely be deleted from the list, you can complete the deletion process with the command PACK.

In other words, deletion is a two-step process. Before you do something irrevocable, dBASE offers you a chance to check up and make sure it's what you really wanted to do. See Fig. 1-5 for more about the Perils of PACK.

PACK is the official command for completing the deletion of a record, but as Ashton-Tate's own customer support people advise, its use can be hazardous to your files. Among the problems:

- You'd expect that when you DELETE a substantial number of records and PACK the file you'd gain some disk space — in fact, that may be the reason you deleted the records in the first place. It doesn't work that way. The operating system has no way to reclaim the space you've "saved," so it still is no good to you. That's not the fault of dBASE, but it still can be a problem.
- PACKING a file with an index in effect is a good way to mess up your indexing system. The effects vary with the complexity of the indexing you are using, but the main point is, it doesn't work very well.
- PACK is a long re-sorting process. Should you bump the ESCAPE key or if there's an electrical glitch in the middle of this proceeding, it can throw off your record count or insert an end-of-file signal somewhere in the middle.

Liberal use of the COPY command is one solution. Most word processing programs automatically create backup files as fresh versions are saved. With dBASE you must do this manually. Before you start, COPY your data to a backup file. If there's an interruption, COPY the backup back to the main file and try again. After a successful PACK, COPYing the finished version will reclaim the disk space.

To avoid the indexing problems, USE the file you wish to PACK without specifying any kind of index. Once the PACK and any necessary COPYing are complete, issue a new command to INDEX the PACKed file on your selected data fields.

Fig. 1-5. The Perils of PACK.

We've found ways to leaf our way through the **Employee** database and selectively pick out information. Even so, what we've been doing so far is the electronic equivalent of pulling out all the files and looking through them for the characteristics we want. Our files still are in the departmental order in which we entered them.

There's a way to change that order—two ways in fact. The first way is to SORT the file. This creates an entirely new copy of the file, arranged in a different order.

The second method is to INDEX it. This process also creates a second file, but it contains only a few "pointers" which help dBASE reach the records you want as fast as possible. Let's give both a try.

For example, you might want to send a mailing to all the employees. In many cases (although not this one) you can get a discount on postage if you sort the mailing in order of the ZIP codes. Better yet, SORT the mailing list and display it in ZIP code order:

`. SORT on Zip to Mail`

When the sorting is finished, dBASE will say so:

`SORT COMPLETE`

Remember, SORTing produces an entirely new database. In this instance we've called it **Mail.** Now we must:

`. USE Mail`

We don't need the supervisors and department entries for the purposes of this mailing list, so we'll just call for the names and addresses by typing

`. LIST Last, First, Street, City, State, Zip`

thus producing the listing in Fig. 1-6.

Notice that Rice did indeed decide to retire, and we have DELETED his name and PACKed the file. Notice, too, that the **Mail** file has been completely rearranged. Everyone now has a new file number, in order of ZIP codes. Now, let's go back to the **Employee** file and create a list of people and departments. We'll use the INDEX command to arrange the names in alphabetical order:

00001	Scrooge	Effie	67 Pudding Lane	Cuttyhunk	MA	02713
00002	Brinkley	Sherrie	23 State St.	Limerick	ME	04048
00003	Cronkite	Wallace	23 Allweather Slip	Westport	CT	06880
00004	Rather	Ida	2881 Cathy La.	Purdy Sta.	NY	10578
00005	Brady	Matthew	800 Tripod Dr.	Gettysburg	PA	17325
00006	Woodstein	Bobby Carl	1150 15th St. NW	Washington	DC	20071
00007	Teigs	Chris	1868 Greenhill Dr.	Leaksville	NC	27288
00008	Mills	Frank	23 Gun Salute	Ft. Meade	FL	33841
00009	Troll	Walter	15 Underhill St.	Smartt	TN	37378
00010	Asner	Lou	1600 Leisure Dr.	Carcasonne	KY	41806
00011	Tarlek	Frank	876 Traffic Pattern	Cinc.	OH	45201
00012	Houlihan	Maggie	1848 Nursery Rd.	Cloudy	OK	74537
00013	Barnard	Chris	54 Left Ventricle	Heartland	TX	76543
00014	Who	Uno	2107 Main St.	Submetro.	NM	87654
00015	Feller	Rocky	Goldpaved Way	Palm Sprs.	CA	92262
00016	Smith	Cosell	1267 Mission Cir.	Yamhill	OR	97148

Fig. 1-6. The *Satellite* staff in mailing-list (ZIP code) order.

dBASE uses several different file types, identified by a period and suffix. Normally, dBASE will assign the proper suffix at the time you create the file.

.DBF	The basic database files used to store information.
.NDX	Index files which guide database searching. These are created by the INDEX command.
.CMD	Used on 8-bit CP/M computers. These are command files which store the text of dBASE programs and procedures.
.PRG	Same as .CMD files. This is the designation used on 16-bit machines with CP/M-86 or MS-DOS.
.FRM	Format files created by the dBASE report generator.
.FMT	Format files, special command files used to lay out forms for data entry, display, and printing.
.MEM	Memory variable files which store information for future use.
.TXT	Text files which store data generated by dBASE in a form that can be used by word processors, spreadsheets, and other non-dBASE programs.

Fig. 1-7. dBASE file types.

```
. USE Employee

. INDEX on Last to Employee.NDX
```

This command sets up the limited separate file. To minimize the number of names we have kicking around in the system, we'll also call this file **Employee,** adding the **.NDX** suffix. (dBASE generally supplies the appropriate suffix to identify types of files, as shown in Fig. 1-7.)

If all goes well we'll soon get the message:

```
00016 RECORDS INDEXED
```

To use the newly indexed data we must call up both files. It's done by first calling the file to USE, then the file on which it will be INDEXed:

```
. USE Employee INDEX Employee

. LIST Last, First, Dept

00002  Asner      Lou       Edit
00009  Barnard    Chris     Circ
00007  Brady      Matthew   Photo
00014  Brinkley   Sherrie   Prod
00004  Cronkite   Wallace   Edit
00011  Feller     Rocky     Acct.
00013  Houlihan   Maggie    Prod
```

```
00008    Mills       Frank        Bus.
00003    Rather      Ida          Edit
00012    Scrooge     Effie        Pay.
00006    Smith       Cosell       Spts
00010    Tarlek      Frank        Adv.
00015    Teigs       Chris        Prod
00016    Troll       Walter       Press
00001    Who         Uno          Publ.
00005    Woodstein   Bobby Carl   Edit
```

Notice that in this example, the record numbers have not been changed. The **Employee** file has not actually been rearranged. The information has been pulled out and reported in the order dictated by the Index file. You can establish more than one Index file to serve different purposes on the same database. You also could do something like this:

```
. INDEX on Last + First to Employee.NDX
```

That command would give you the same list as above, but should you have two employees with the same last names, dBASE would list the two in order of their first names.

Another feature of INDEX is that new additions to your main file automatically are INDEXed. (At least they're supposed to be. In practice it pays to occasionally repeat the INDEX on . . . command.)

The versatility of the INDEX command, plus the limited disk space it requires, make it a better choice than SORT for most purposes. When the time comes to use the list, though, dBASE will process a SORTed list faster than it will an INDEXed one.

SORT can be the better choice, then, when you have a file that doesn't change frequently but which you use often. The SORTed file will then be a special-purpose database for that particular task. For example, you could use such a file to print labels for a standard mailing that goes out once a week.

MAINTENANCE AND MODIFICATIONS

Our database is far from ideal. We've already found one problem: the **Supervisor** field doesn't really do a good job of accurately denoting supervisory relationships. Neither does the **Dept** heading, since it isn't geared to account for subsidiary departments with their own supervisors. These two fields duplicate each other's mistakes. In fact, they really duplicate each other. They take up valuable disk space to provide much the same information, and it's not very good information at that.

We can do better. We can eliminate the supervisor heading. In an organization this small we know who runs what—in fact, we know who *really* runs the place. Instead, we can list individual job specialties. These will give us more useful guidance when we're trying to determine individual areas of responsibility.

To do this, we enter the extremely dangerous command:

```
. MODIFY STRUCTURE
```

To which dBASE will respond:

```
MODIFY ERASES ALL DATA RECORDS ... PROCEED? (Y/N)
```

When we last saw this warning there was no data to be erased. Now there is. Let's thank dBASE for the timely warning, answer "N" and look for a way to alter our database without destroying it completely. Fortunately, there is a way to do it. It involves juggling data around using the COPY and APPEND commands. The first entry in this process is:

. COPY to Temp Structure

This command copies your database to another file which we'll call **Temp** because it's temporary. We won't copy everything, though, just the structure. Then we:

. USE Temp

Now that we're away from our main database we can enter the fateful command:

. MODIFY Structure

MODIFY ERASES ALL DATA RECORDS ... PROCEED? (Y/N) Y

This time when dBASE flashes its warning it's safe to answer yes. **Temp** has no data to be erased.

dBASE then will show us a listing of the structure as it currently stands. Using the cursor commands, we can wend our way through this layout, altering whatever we'd like. We can eliminate fields, change their size or type or rename them as we're going to do now. Go down to the entry that reads **Supervisor** and type **Speciality** instead. Now, to make sure everything has come out all right, type:

. DISPLAY Structure

You should get:

```
STRUCTURE FOR FILE:     TEMP.DBF
NUMBER OF RECORDS:      00000
DATE OF LAST UPDATE: 00/00/00
PRIMARY USE DATABASE
FLD         NAME        TYPE WIDTH      DEC
001         FIRST        C      010
002         LAST         C      010
003         STREET       C      020
004         CITY         C      010
005         STATE        C      002
006         ZIP          C      005
007         HIRED        N      002
008         DEPT         C      005
009         SPECIALTY    C      010
** TOTAL **                    00075
```

That's the structure we want, all right. Right now it has zero records. We can add the data we've already accumulated in the **Employee** file with this command:

. APPEND from Employee

dBASE will bump and grind for a little while and then will issue this confirmation:

00016 RECORDS ADDED

That's the right number. Again, let's make sure everything came through without a glitch:

. LIST

produces the employee table in Fig. 1-8.

00001	Uno	Who	2107 Main St.	Submetro.	NM	87654	63	Publ.
00002	Lou	Asner	1600 Leisure Dr.	Carcasonne	KY	41806	82	Edit
00003	Ida	Rather	2881 Cathy La.	Purdy Sta.	NY	10578	80	Edit
00004	Wallace	Cronkite	23 Allweather Slip	Westport	CT	06880	70	Edit
00005	Bobby Carl	Woodstein	1150 15th St. NW	Washington	DC	20071	81	Edit
00006	Cosell	Smith	1267 Mission Cir.	Yamhill	OR	97148	83	Spts
00007	Matthew	Brady	800 Tripod Dr.	Gettysburg	PA	17325	78	Photo
00008	Frank	Mills	23 Gun Salute	Ft. Meade	FL	33841	82	Bus.
00009	Chris	Barnard	54 Left Ventricle	Heartland	TX	76543	67	Circ
00010	Frank	Tarlek	876 Traffic Pattern	Cinc.	OH	45201	83	Adv.
00011	Rocky	Feller	Goldpaved Way	Palm Sprs.	CA	92262	67	Acct.
00012	Effie	Scrooge	67 Pudding Lane	Cuttyhunk	MA	02713	80	Pay.
00013	Maggie	Houlihan	1848 Nursery Rd.	Cloudy	OK	74537	80	Prod.
00014	Sherrie	Brinkley	23 State St.	Limerick	ME	04048	81	Prod.
00015	Chris	Teigs	1868 Greenhill Dr.	Leaksville	NC	27288	80	Prod.
00016	Walter	Troll	15 Underhill St.	Smartt	TN	37378	79	Press

Fig. 1-8. The staff list with supervisor fields deleted.

Something's missing. The Old **Supervisor** listings are gone, and there's nothing yet in the new **Specialty** field. The reason: when dBASE copies data from one file to another it matches up the field names. Since your modified **Temp** file didn't call for data from the **Supervisor** field, dBASE didn't copy it. The **Specialty** field is blank because you haven't entered anything into it yet. To do that, use the EDIT command.

Actually, there isn't much sense entering specialty data for everyone. For example, as publisher you specialize in being the publisher. And there's nothing about dBASE which absolutely requires an entry in every blank.

The same probably is true of editor Lou Asner, so the first record to enter is Number 3. The command:

```
. EDIT 3
```

You'll soon see before you the file for Ida Rather with a blank space for her specialty. Move the cursor down to that space and type in an appropriate entry. Once you've finished, CTRL/C will take you to the next record; CTRL/R will spool you backward through the file.

When you reach Smith's record, you'll probably want to change two entries. Change the department to **Edit** and add **Sports** as the specialty. You can do this for other employees as well. A RETURN in a blank record will tell dBASE you're through, and you'll be back to the familiar period.

Again, let's make sure everything went right:

```
. LIST
```

should produce the screen display in Fig. 1-9.

Meanwhile, your original **Employee** file has been sitting undisturbed and in reserve. No need to bother this backup resource until you are sure all your changes to the **Temp** file are in order. After you're satisfied, give the order:

```
. COPY to Employee
```

Then:

```
. USE Employee
. LIST
```

Everything all right? If so, you're ready to use **Employee** in its modified form. If not, the **Temp** file now is available as a backup. Once you're satisfied that everything is in order, you can save some file space with the command:

```
. DELETE file Temp
```

ON REPORT

Let's move along now to that wonderful time of year when production manager Maggie Houlihan must ask pressman Fred Troll to produce an inventory of his ink and paper supplies. After much prodding, although a little less than last year, Fred finally produces a list written with a broad-tip felt pen on a dirty shop towel:

25 rolls of mauve paper, 6 of white and 3 goldenrod.
5 Drums red ink, 3 cans pink, 2 bottles black

"That's what we get for buying all this bargain-basement stuff," Houlihan mutters. Even so, she looks up the cost of these odd items and enters it along with the quantities into a file called **Press.**

The pressroom inventory file is structured like this:

```
FIELD      NAME,TYPE,WIDTH,DECIMAL PLACES
001        Item,c,7
002        Color,c,7
003        Package,c,7
004        PerUnit,n,7,2
```

LIST the inventory, and it looks like:

```
00001     PAPER     MAUVE     ROLL          685.43          25
00002     PAPER     WHITE     ROLL          726.77           6
00003     PAPER     GOLD      ROLL          685.43           3
00004     INK       RED       DRUM          185.67           5
```

00001	Uno	Who	2107 Main St.	Submetro.	NM	87654	63	Publ.	
00002	Lou	Asner	1600 Leisure Dr.	Carcasonne	KY	41806	82	Edit	
00003	Ida	Rather	2881 Cathy La.	Purdy Sta.	NY	10578	80	Edit	Govt
00004	Wallace	Cronkite	23 Allweather Slip	Westport	CT	06880	70	Edit	Obits
00005	Bobby Carl	Woodstein	1150 15th St. NW	Washington	DC	20071	81	Edit	White Hse
00006	Cosell	Smith	1267 Mission Cir.	Yamhill	OR	97148	83	Edit	Sports
00007	Matthew	Brady	800 Tripod Dr.	Gettysburg	PA	17325	78	Photo	Photo
00008	Frank	Mills	23 Gun Salute	Ft. Meade	FL	33841	82	Bus.	
00009	Chris	Barnard	54 Left Ventricle	Heartland	TX	76543	67	Circ	
00010	Frank	Tarlek	876 Traffic Pattern	Cinc.	OH	45201	83	Adv.	
00011	Rocky	Feller	Goldpaved Way	Palm Sprs.	CA	92262	67	Acct.	
00012	Effie	Scrooge	67 Pudding Lane	Cuttyhunk	MA	02713	80	Pay.	
00013	Maggie	Houlihan	1848 Nursery Rd.	Cloudy	OK	74537	80	Prod.	
00014	Sherrie	Brinkley	23 State St.	Limerick	ME	04048	81	Prod.	Makeup
00015	Chris	Teigs	1868 Greenhill Dr.	Leaksville	NC	27288	80	Prod.	Makeup
00016	Walter	Troll	15 Underhill St.	Smartt	TN	37378	79	Press	

Fig. 1-9. The staff list with specialty field added.

```
00005    INK      PINK     CANS          7.86       3
00006    INK      BLACK    BOTTLE        1.25       3
```

That's a little better organized than the shop towel report, and it includes some figures from Houlihan's cost records, but it still tells her nothing she didn't know already: the pressroom is overstocked with odd-colored materials and is short on basic black-and-white. What Houlihan really needs to know is how much money is tied up in this multihued fiasco. To wring some useful new information from this file, she can use dBASE's report generator.

This is a dBASE program activated, logically enough, by the command:

```
. REPORT
```

Like nearly everything else in dBASE, this report must have a name. We'll call it **Press,** and dBASE will add the **.FRM** suffix. We could save some time by making the initial command:

```
. REPORT FORM PRESS
```

But we didn't, so dBASE will ask us to enter the name. It will also ask the appropriate questions if we forget to specify a database file before we call for a report. If the report form is brand new, as it is here, dBASE then will ask us to format the report, much like we set up the database structure earlier. The report generator will lead us through a series of questions like these:

```
ENTER OPTIONS, M=LEFT MARGIN, L=LINES/PAGE, W=PAGE WIDTH
```

Unless you specify otherwise, REPORT will format itself for an 8-space left margin, a 57-line page and an 80-column page width. If you want to alter any of these, you can enter the changes in the same format as the prompt. For example, to get a 5-space margin, enter "M=5."

The default settings are good enough for now, though, so let's move on to the next question:

```
PAGE HEADING? (Y/N) Y
```

If you'd like, dBASE will center a heading across the top of the report. We answered "Y," so dBASE now asks what the heading should say:

```
ENTER PAGE HEADING:
```

"PRESSROOM INVENTORY" would be a good answer. Then dBASE moves on to even more questions. With Houlihan's answers they look like:

```
DOUBLE SPACE REPORT?  (Y/N)  N
ARE TOTALS REQUIRED?  (Y/N)  Y
SUBTOTALS IN REPORT?  (Y/N)  Y
ENTER SUBTOTALS FIELD:  ITEM
SUMMARY REPORT ONLY?  (Y/N)  N
EJECT PAGE AFTER SUBTOTALS?  (Y/N)  N
ENTER SUBTOTAL HEADING:
```

You have a choice between single and double spacing. dBASE also will ask whether you will want totals or subtotals in the report. In the case of subtotals you must specify the field. Houlihan would like separate totals on paper and ink, so we'll call for subtotals on the **Item** field, the one which contains that information.

24

If you answer "Y" to the summary report question it will list only the items and subtotals, without the details of each record. We want all the colorful details. We didn't enter a subtotal heading because dBASE already provides one. You can add to it if you wish.

The question about ejecting pages is for a printed report. If you select that option, the paper and ink entries will appear on different pages. Now, the report generator asks for the details of your report. Enter them much as you did the database specifications. In fact, you'll often find yourself using the same field names and lengths. The first prompt calls for:

```
COL        WIDTH,CONTENTS
001
```

Enter your choice, and you'll see:

```
COL        WIDTH,CONTENTS
001        7,ITEM
ENTER HEADING:  ITEM
```

The heading will appear in the final report. It can be the field name, but you are free to choose some other term. Now, fill in the rest of the entries:

```
002        7,COLOR
ENTER HEADING: COLOR
003        7,PACKAGE
ENTER HEADING: PACKAGE
004        5,ONHAND
ENTER HEADING: ON HAND
ARE TOTALS REQUIRED? (Y/N) N
005        7,PERUNIT
ENTER HEADING: UNIT COST
ARE TOTALS REQUIRED? (Y/N) N
```

Notice that when dBASE came to a numerical field it stopped to ask if we'd want totals for that field. To total the **OnHand** field would give us a meaningless sum of various rolls, drums and bottles; a total of the unit cost field would be just as useless.

At this point we've set up the report for all the information that's now in the database, but to give these figures meaning let's add one more item:

```
006        9,ONHAND*PERUNIT
ENTER HEADING: TOTAL COST
ARE TOTALS REQUIRED? (Y/N) Y
```

Here we're able to use dBASE to create new knowledge from existing information. We call for a column headed **Total Cost,** in which we multiply the number of items in stock by the cost per unit. And yes, we do want to add this column. When dBASE calls for Item 7 we can hit RETURN, and dBASE will automatically print the report shown in Fig. 1-10.

There you have it. Houlihan not only knows how much money is tied up in this odd inventory, but can easily see that the vast majority of it is in paper. Should she want a printed report she could command:

```
. REPORT FORM PRESS TO PRINT
```

```
PAGE NO. 00001

                                        PRESSROOM INVENTORY

        ITEM      COLOR     PACKAGE     ON        UNIT      TOTAL
                                        HAND      COST      COST

        *    PAPER
        PAPER     MAUVE     ROLL        25        685.43    17135.75
        PAPER     WHITE     ROLL         6        726.77     4360.62
        PAPER     GOLD      ROLL         3        685.43     2056.29
        ** SUBTOTAL **
                                                            23552.66


        *    INK
        INK       RED       DRUM         5        185.67      928.35
        INK       PINK      CANS         3          7.86       23.58
        INK       BLACK     BOTTLE       3          1.25        3.75
        ** SUBTOTAL **
                                                              955.68


        ** TOTAL **
                                                            24508.34
```

Fig. 1-10. The Pressroom Inventory—from shop towel to dBASE.

To get the total cost figure for this report we made use of dBASE mathematical capabilities. In this case the print file used the "*" command to multiply the contents of two fields. In other applications you could use "+" to add, "−" to subtract or "/" to divide.

LEARNING THE LANGUAGE

Houlihan also would like to know exactly how much of the money tied up in inventory has been invested in odd-colored products. This is where she'll need to know how to use the selective nature of dBASE commands. A full dBASE command answers these questions:

Do what . . .
. . . to how many . . .
. . . of what . . .
. . . under what conditions?

Or to put it in dBASE language:

Verb . . .
. . . Scope . . .
. . . Object . . .
. . . Conditions

A simple dBASE command consists of a verb and an object: USE a database, for example, or DISPLAY its contents. As an advanced exercise in this kind of "sentence structure," dBASE gives you two basic ways to describe the circumstances under which this action is to take place.

The first of these is the *scope* specification. This defines which records you wish to work with. LIST ALL would be a signal to list every record in the file. DISPLAY NEXT 10 would, naturally enough, call up the next 10 records.

The second type of specification lists the *conditions* you wish to impose. These are preceded by the FOR instruction.

For example, Houlihan could decide she wants to see the colors entered in the first three records of her paper inventory. She would structure her command like this:

```
Verb    Scope     Object   Conditions
List    Next 3    Color    For items = 'Paper'
```

The result of such a command would be:

```
00001   MAUVE
00002   WHITE
00003   GOLD
```

Then, see what happens when you enter:

```
. LIST NEXT 2

00003   PAPER   GOLD   ROLL   685.43   3
00004   INK     RED    DRUM   185.67   5
```

A couple of things happened here. First, at the end of the previous command the "pointer" with which dBASE navigates through a file structure was left at Record 3. So, when you asked for the next two records, dBASE did exactly as you said, not necessarily what you meant. The GOTO command is a safety valve for this situation. Unlike its counterpart in BASIC, dBASE's GOTO is a signal to move the pointer to a particular record. You can GOTO TOP, which places the pointer at the first record, GOTO BOTTOM which sends you to the last item or GOTO 5, which directs the pointer to that record number.

The second point is that the latest LIST command had no further specifications for the fields to be listed or the conditions under which to show them. You don't have to specify the scope, object or conditions for every dBASE command, but if you don't, dBASE will take that as a signal to give you everything it has which fits the requirements of what you *did* command.

IMPROVING YOUR MEMORY

There's a fifth possible member of the standard dBASE command sequence. It begins with TO, and it's among the most useful and versatile features dBASE has to offer.

The TO command tells dBASE *where* to act. Earlier, we used it to copy information TO a new database. This command also can establish a *memory variable,* a temporary storage place for information you'll need later in the same procedure, but which you don't want to store permanently in a data file. In its simplest form, you can STORE information to a memory variable:

```
. STORE 1040 to Form
```

dBASE then will verify your action by displaying the stored amount:

```
1040
```

Let's store another memory variable:

```
. STORE 1080 to Newform
  1080
```

Now, let's play around with these two numbers. Using the "?" symbol in dBASE is much like using the PRINT command in BASIC. Enter:

```
. ? Newform-Form
```

That tells dBASE to subtract the two stored numbers and enter the result. Of course, the answer is 40. To get a look at what we've stored so far, enter:

```
. DISPLAY MEMORY
```

The result should be:

```
FORM          (N)      1040
NEWFORM       (N)      1080
** TOTAL **        02 VARIABLES USED   00012 BYTES USED
```

This display says you've stored two numerical variables with given names and amounts. You can store character and logical variables just as easily.

Pay particular attention to the status line at the bottom. You're limited to 64 variables or 1,000 bytes. This will tell you where you stand.

Not that we're in danger of crowding the limit right now, but let's assume we want to get rid of some old but unneeded variables to make room for new ones. We can say:

```
. RELEASE FORM
```

```
. DISPLAY MEMORY
```

This time dBASE will respond:

```
NEWFORM       (N)      1080
** TOTAL **        01 VARIABLES USED   00006 BYTES USED
```

Wouldn't we all like to get rid of a form 1040 this easily?

STORE isn't the only way to put a memory variable into storage. The results of several dBASE commands also can be stored. For example, if Houlihan wants to know how many rolls of paper she has on hand, she could command:

```
. SUM ONHAND FOR ITEM='PAPER' TO ROLLS
  34
```

Checking the memory inventory again we see what now is a small collection of unrelated information:

```
ROLLS         (N)      34
NEWFORM       (N)      1080
** TOTAL **        02 VARIABLES USED   00012 BYTES USED
```

If we're through with these items we can issue the command RELEASE ALL and clean up our 64 slots for more useful data.

LOOKING FOR WORDS

dBASE flexibility is verbal as well as mathematical. Its character search feature—officially called a *string operator*—lets you check for the appearance of a word or any other sequence of letters within a given field of your database.

For example, I maintain a dBASE file which holds an extensive bibliography of law journal articles on freedom of the press. I've also set up a report form to print out the records in a standard bibliographic format.

This is pretty specialized stuff, so I'll avoid most of the details. Let's say, though, that I'd like a list of articles which comment on the famous libel case, *New York Times v. Sullivan*. One of my data fields, called **Cases** it lists the court decisions to which the article refers. I would want to search, then, for articles in which the name "Sullivan" appears in the **Cases** field and print it out in my standard form, which I call **Biblio.** The specific format for these instructions is:

```
. REPORT FORM BIBLIO FOR 'SULLIVAN' $(CASES) TO PRINT
```

I have asked dBASE to report on the named form the contents of any record for which the character string "Sullivan" appears under the heading of **Cases** and to send the results to the printer. All I need do from there is to tear off the printout and head for the library.

This is another example of how dBASE does *exactly* what you tell it to do. I could have searched for the full name of the case, but that is unwieldy and unnecessary. I could have searched under "Times," or even "New York Times." However, *The New York Times* has been a party to several major cases over the years. A search under its name would have given me material on issues like the Pentagon Papers as well as the libel case. It's not likely, though, that within the scope of my database there has been more than one party named Sullivan. This unique character string is all I need to find the articles.

WORKING WITH A SECOND FILE

While we were using the employee data file we found it overloaded with not-too-useful information on departmental assignments and supervisory relationships. We deleted these in favor of information we considered more useful.

Even so, this information is not entirely irrelevant. There are times when we might want to retrieve it. We just don't want it taking up space in the master employee file.

For this purpose we can create a second file—call it **Chain** for chain of command. In it we can include the department name, the name of the current supervisor, the name of any superior department over this one and perhaps some information on whether the employees here are on weekly salaries or hourly wage rates.

The **Chain** file has one field, **Dept,** in common with the **Employee** file. Thus, if we wanted to use dBASE to identify an individual employee's supervisor we could link the material in the two databases. The mechanics:

```
. USE Employee

. SELECT Secondary

. USE Chain

. SELECT Primary
```

Establishing and Maintaining a File

CREATE	Begins a new file structure.
USE	Use an existing file. This command also closes any files already in use unless it is used with the SELECT command.
COPY	Create a backup file. You also use this command to create a duplicate so you can modify an existing file structure without losing the data already on file.
DISPLAY STRUCTURE	Shows the field names, sizes and other specifications of an existing file.
MODIFY STRUCTURE	Alters the structure of an existing file, but destroys any data in that file. If you wish to preserve stored data, you must use it in combination with the COPY command.
DISPLAY FILES	Lets you review the files you have established. DISPLAY FILES ON B gives you the files on that drive. DISPLAY FILES LIKE .CMD would call for the command files on the default drive.
QUIT	Saves all files and exits from dBASE to the operating system.

Entering and Updating Data

APPEND	Displays a blank record for entering data.
DISPLAY or LIST	Lets you examine records already on file.
EDIT	Lets you change a specific record.
BROWSE	Another editing command that displays a group of records and lets you make changes.
DELETE	Tentatively deletes a record.
RECALL	Lets you restore a deleted record to the file.
PACK	Fully removes the deleted record.
REPLACE	Lets you place new data in specified fields.
UPDATE	Adds records from another file.

Organizing and Searching

SORT	Reorganizes the database in a specified order.
INDEX	Lets you search the file in a particular order without altering it.
SKIP	Move to the next record. You can add conditions to move forward or backward, or to move a specified number of files.
GOTO	Moves you to a particular record number, or to the top or bottom of the file.

Fig. 1-11. dBASE commands grouped by function. (Continued on page 31.)

| LOCATE | Moves you to records which fit the conditions you specify. |
| FIND | A rapid form of LOCATE, used only with indexed files. |

Using Memory Variables

STORE	Places information in a variable.
RELEASE	Removes stored information.
DISPLAY MEMORY	Shows the contents of current variables.
SAVE	Places the contents of memory variables into a disk file.
RESTORE	Recalls the contents of a saved memory file.

This sequence starts you in the **Employee** database, sets up **Chain** as a secondary file and then switches you back to **Employee.** You then are able to call for the data in either or both files. There's no way, though, that dBASE will let you add a third file by this means. That's one of its significant limits. Most users prefer to establish a master file with basic information (like **Employee**), and then one or more secondary files to serve special purposes such as writing the payroll or checking the employee's pension status.

You'll make the most use of this feature when we get into dBASE's programming features.

DO YOU REMEMBER ALL THAT?

Of course not. Don't think you have to gain an instant grasp of every dBASE command to start using the program. The purpose of this discussion has been to demonstrate the kinds of things you can accomplish with dBASE and to give you an idea of how to go about it.

Don't try to memorize all the commands we've just gone through. As you move along and decide what you want dBASE to do for you, you can come back to this chapter or refer to the dBASE instruction manual for the commands that will help you do it.

To help, Fig. 1-11 is a list of the major dBASE commands, grouped by the functions they perform.

Chapter 2
Learning to Use It Right

Even people who never have seen a computer before probably have heard one familiar saying. It goes something like this:

Garbage out, garbage in.

Of course, that may not be exactly the way you remember it; the most usual version is just the reverse. Where database planning is concerned, though, our version is the right one. It goes along with a basic principle of planning and organizing a database or any other business program:

Kniht Sdrawkcab

Think backwards. What you put into your database should depend on what you expect to get out of it. Start at the end. Think about the results you'd like to get. Then set up your database to produce those results.

THE VALUE OF DOING IT RIGHT

It's one thing to know the mechanics of using dBASE. It's more important to know how to use dBASE well. If you learn how to do that, you always can go back to a reference source for the procedural details.

For demonstration purposes, we've set up a couple of ridiculous databases. They're not ridiculous because they are made up of people with funny names who commute from impossible distances, or because the inventory has all those odd-colored items in it. They were made up to show how dBASE works, and any similarity with a working, useful database is purely deliberate. The real problem with databases structured like these examples is that they might be totally useless.

For example, would you as the head of the organization really need to know the full home addresses of all your employees, or would it be enough that these be kept in a separate file the payroll clerk could use to mail out the yearly W-2 forms? Is it truly necessary that you have a computerized understanding of the departmental and supervisory relationships of your small organization?

Another thought: was it necessary that so many of our queries into the **Employee** file produced yet another printout of the entire database?

Perhaps you could use this information—and perhaps not. Only you can be the judge. You must determine what you need. Then tell dBASE. Only then can the program respond to your particular needs and desires. If you're going to set up a dBASE file, it's important to do it right.

SYSTEMS ANALYSIS: THE CORPORATE APPROACH

On a corporate scale, the process of determining and meeting the company's data processing needs is known as *systems analysis*. It can be a truly elaborate process, carried out by specialized professionals and involving an entire file drawer full of forms, reports, and memos.

You surely don't want anything that elaborate. You have a business to run, and you barely have enough time to grasp the material in this book, let alone run around generating red tape for yourself. After all, you want the computer to make your firm more efficient, not less.

The systems analysts have the right idea, though, in their general approach to the job. It is they who have recognized the need to approach your challenge from the output side. For the purposes of a small business we can adopt their principles without the paperwork.

Let's say you are a systems analyst with a large mail-order computer supplies company. You sell disks, paper, furniture, ribbons, printwheels—and mailing lists. Like most companies that have compiled extensive mailing lists, yours has developed a profitable sideline selling its customer list to noncompetitors who also would like to reach a list of computer owners.

In fact, this was such a profitable sideline that many years ago it was computerized. Using the technology of the day, your company set up a set of punch cards. These are run through a reader, from which the computer program converts them into a set of mailing labels, in order of ZIP code. It's been a matter of pride that when a buyer asks for a copy of your list, you're able to put a set of labels in the mail the next day.

Business has boomed as more and more potential mailing list users want access to the expanding computer market. Ironically, the boom has cut sharply into your company's profits on the mailing list sideline. To meet the demand, the mailing department has had to go way beyond its overtime budget.

What's more, even with all the overtime, you're continuing to fall behind. Delivery time has slipped into the 10-day bracket, and some customers who had dealt with you because of your previously speedy service canceled their orders when you could not deliver in time. You've spent so much time trying to meet the demands of the new customers you're beginning to lose your established ones.

Investigation and Analysis

This clearly is not a healthy situation, and soon the division manager in charge of fulfilling orders is at your desk, begging you to design some relief.

In a typical corporation setting you'd cite the 2½-year backlog of programming work and tell the manager you'd get to the mailing list problem as soon as you can. You'll also ask for a formal written work order, which you'd duplicate and circulate to top management, asking for permission to conduct a preliminary analysis.

Once you receive a memo giving you the go-ahead for an analysis, you'd prepare another memo assigning a couple of staff members to interview people in the mailing list department, determine what their problems are and suggest ways to improve them.

This study might find, for example, that it takes more than two days to complete the typical mailing list order. You're averaging about four orders per week. The problem is mathematically obvious. As a solution, your assistants recommend that the process be upgraded to a faster, more modern computer system. The alternatives are more overtime or a bigger staff.

Again, a written report is sent to management recommending the new system, and again the reply comes back. Assuming the reply is favorable, you can proceed to the next step.

Designing the System

This is where you determine your input by defining your output. In this case the output is fairly simple: a set of printed mailing labels, with name, address and ZIP code. The input requirement, then, is equally simple: name, address and ZIP code.

There is one thing to consider, though: you'll always be making changes to your list. New customers will join the list, old ones will be dropped and there will be the usual run of address changes. The input side of the system, then, must include some way to make these changes. The process is often called *file maintenance*.

Consider your own needs, too, when you design such a system. For example, you might want to include a trigger that deletes the names of catalog recipients who haven't ordered in the last five years.

Writing the Program

After another round of management review, you prepare a set of specifications for the program that will implement the new system. A staff programmer will write the COBOL code necessary to produce the output and accept the inputs you have specified. Finally the day comes to produce a mailing list with the newly written program.

Implementation

This is the final phase actually putting the program to work. You probably will have to make several test runs and correct more than your share of glitches, though, before the program is ready to go into full-scale operation. At the same time, you will be preparing to document the system for users and for other programmers who might someday have to maintain it. Ideally this is done as the system is developed; in practice, that hardly ever happens—one reason the computer world has been plagued by poorly written instructions.

ON YOUR LEVEL

This was not a particularly major project as corporate data processing activities go, and both the input and output are fairly simple. Large or small, though, the process of developing a computer system should follow these basic steps:

1) An *investigation* and a preliminary *analysis* of the situation, assessing the problem and evaluating possible solutions.
2) *Designing* the system—determining what results you need and what input and processing you will need to achieve them.
3) *Programming* the system.
4) *Implementing* the system, including trial runs, adjustments, and corrections.

For your own purposes you'll be less formal. You'll need fewer memos and reports, and obtaining management approval may be as simple as rechecking your own work. It's still important, though, to follow the same four steps of sound program development.

INVESTIGATION AND ANALYSIS

Before you can improve an operation you must fully understand how it's being done now. This is the basis of your investigation: to study the current operation and determine its shortcomings. The best-written database system will be useless—or worse—if it doesn't address the needs of the operation as it exists in your own operation.

Remember, dBASE is the program that thinks it's a language. It lets you escape the fixed structures of most prewritten business programs, but you need not go so far as writing a custom program from scratch. Make use of that capacity to tailor your dBASE applications to the specific needs of your own business.

What's Your Problem?

Let's go back to the fictional *Weekly Satellite*. You're aware that the ever-faithful Effie Scrooge has been putting in a great deal of overtime getting out the payroll. You're also aware that the Submetropolis area is expected to grow rapidly in the next few years, which means the *Satellite* can expect to grow with it. That's good news in a lot of ways, but growth also can bring problems. In particular, it could mean a growing staff and further strains on Effie's already limited time.

Your mission: to find out what you can do, and particularly what dBASE can do, to process the payroll more efficiently.

Go With the Flow

Start, then, by taking a look at the way Effie now processes the payroll data. She probably uses a process something like the one outlined in Fig. 2-1 and 2-2.

The basic payroll records are kept on a master list of the employees and their basic payroll information. When an employee joins or leaves the company, the new data is used to update the master list.

Each week, Effie uses the updated master list to prepare the weekly time cards, which are distributed to the employees' departments.

At the end of the week, the filled-out cards are collected from the departments. Each employee's time and wages for the week are entered on a payroll register. Effie also takes notes of any changes in the employees' status and enters them on both the register and the master list. She also subtracts the deductions for withholding taxes, medical insurance, the pension plan, and so on.

From this data on the payroll registered she computes and writes the checks, and payday is here at last.

Unplug Bottlenecks

Where are the sticky spots in this operation? The first is the number of manual operations in the process. The employee master list must be filled out and maintained. When an employee leaves, arrives, gets married, or qualifies for a vested pension, these facts must be noted and recorded. A full set of time cards must be made out each week.

When the completed cards are returned, the data is entered on the payroll register along with the deductions and withholding. Any recent changes in status must also be noted here. Then, this information

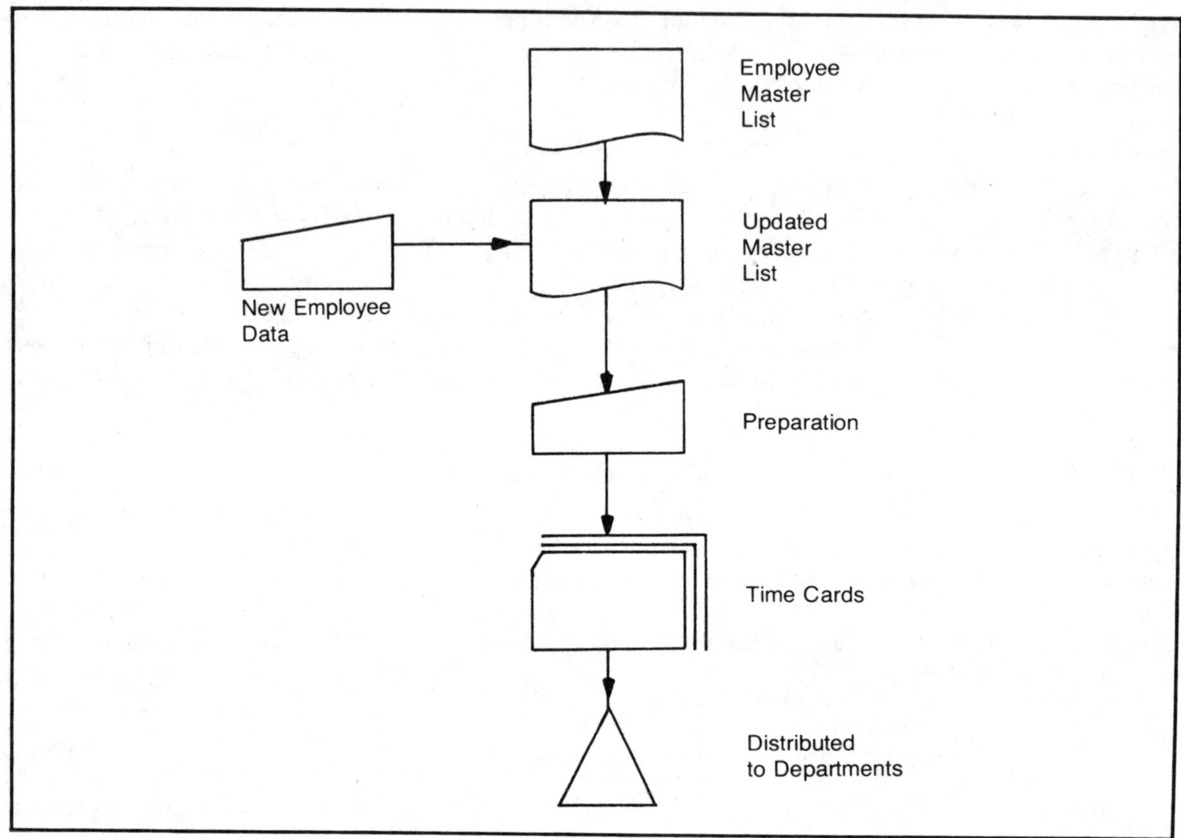

Fig. 2-1. Preparing time cards.

must be transferred again to the paychecks, the only documents in this entire process that we truly value.

Here, then, is a process that seems to cry out for computerization. A program like dBASE can eliminate many of the repetitive manual data entries. One master file, plus a procedure for updating it, should basically be enough for the purpose.

Call In a "Consultant"

Before you plunge ahead with such a plan, though, take time to explore the angles. In particular, it will pay to have a talk with an expert on your payroll system. And no person on earth is more expert in the details of how your system works than Effie Scrooge herself. She has the kind of insight that comes only from active involvement with this system every working day. Take advantage of it.

Remember, too, that once you've installed a new payroll system, Effie is the person who will be called on to operate it. Again, she probably has some useful thoughts on what would or would not work well. And, it's a matter of good employee relations to inform the affected people and listen to their reactions before you inject something new into their lives.

The User's Point of View

Ask Effie, then, what she thinks are the reasons she's been so badly swamped with work recently. She probably has a definite opinion.

"It's those deductions," she complains. "Oh, the income tax part is okay—I can work from a standard table there. But even on a payroll as short as ours, people are always making changes: getting married, having children, claiming new exemptions. Posting the changes is a real chore, particularly since I have to do it once on the master list and again on the payroll register for that week."

"I can see where that would be a problem," you agree.

"That's not the half of it," Effie continues. "We have five different variations on our health and life insurance plan, and as far as the pension contributions are concerned . . . well, let's just say it was a lot easier before the government got involved with all its rules and requirements."

"I'm afraid we can't change that," you point out.

"I know, I know. But you asked me what I thought, and I'm telling you."

"And I hope to do something about it. I'm thinking of putting your operation on the computer."

If that remark brings a sudden gape-mouthed stare from your payroll clerk, don't be surprised. No matter how much trouble they may be having with the present manual system, many employees are afraid of change, and they are particularly afraid of changes that involve computers.

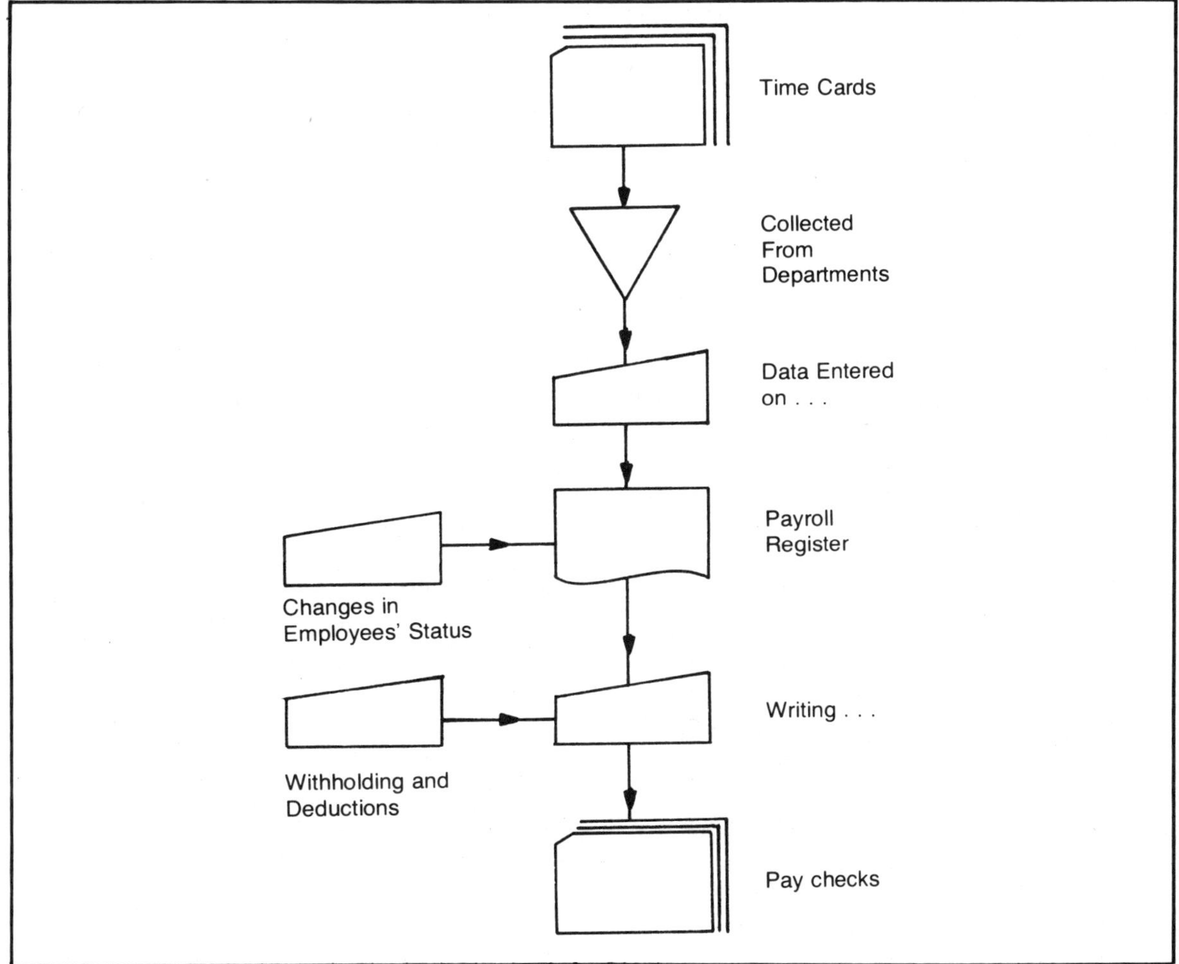

Fig. 2-2. Writing payroll.

Keep this firmly in mind as you plan the new system. Effie hasn't said anything, but her feelings are obvious. You'll need to gently convince her that the system you're planning will be easier to use as well as being more efficient. You'll also have to make sure you design it that way.

It also can sometimes be helpful just to observe the process you're about to commit to dBASE, but use some discretion in doing so. Many employees still have a latent resistance to "efficiency experts," compounded by a fear of computers.

What You Should Know

Young news reporters are taught that their stories should emphasize five basic points: who, what, when, where, and how. In connection with each of these there is an implied sixth point: why? You should conduct your review to answer the same basic questions:

- ☐ *Who* performs each of the operations that make up the process? *Why* are they doing so; would it be better to reassign the job to another employee—or to dBASE? Also: are these people experienced or comfortable with computers?
- ☐ *What* procedures are they following? *Why* is it done in this way? In particular, is there a good reason or is it an old, established procedure that should yield to a better method?
- ☐ *When* are these procedures done? Is this really the best time or frequency?
- ☐ *Where* are they done? Is there a better place?
- ☐ *How* is the procedure performed? *Why* is it done that way? Is there a better method?

These are good things to know about any process in your business, and it's particularly important to learn them before you try to establish a dBASE procedure to handle them. *Computerizing a faulty process won't correct the faults.*

At the same time, the more you know about the process the better you can make use of dBASE to improve it and make it more efficient.

Is This Necessary?

Once you've assessed the current situation, your analysis should take you into the question of how to improve it. Consider all the alternatives, including dBASE, other types of programs—or even no computer at all. Look for the solution that does the job *best*. dBASE will often provide that solution, but even a versatile program like this can't do everything.

PRINCIPLES OF DATABASE DESIGN

"Database design is very much a human problem, not a system problem." That's the view of C. J. Date, who's written several textbooks on the subject. The system doesn't care whether a particular design is good or bad, he points out. But the users do.

From that point of view, even the faulty database we designed in Chapter 1 was not truly a "bad" design. It served a purpose: it was a teaching tool. If you learned something from it, you—the user—found it useful.

From another perspective, that of someone actually trying to manage the personnel and payroll functions of a going business, that database was not at all well designed. It contained too many things we don't really need to know—and lacks some things we do need.

Neither Good nor Bad

In short, a "good" database is in the eye of the beholder. In your business, you're the beholder. After all, the main reason you're preparing to apply dBASE to your business is to improve that business for your benefit.

If you plan to use the system yourself, the consideration ends there. Build a system to satisfy your own needs, and even your own whims. However, if some employees also will be expected to use the system they become an important secondary group of users. You must design the database so it can easily be used by people of their particular skill levels. In fact, if there is one overriding principle of database design it is this:

Never forget the user

Don't forget the needs and fears the users express when you talk with them about their work and your plans for the coming system. Effie Scrooge, you'll remember, talked about the difficulty of keeping up with changes. Any system you design should concentrate on entering those changes more easily and efficiently. She also displayed an unspoken fear of computerization. Your system should be designed to lead her gently through the process, making liberal use of prompts, menus, and "help" resources.

The End Is the Beginning

It's possible, of course, to write a dBASE procedure that simply duplicates the existing system. It is better, though, to make full use of dBASE's power. The real test of a good dBASE procedure is this:

How well does it meet the information needs of your business?

The purpose of dBASE is not just to collect information but to report it in a useful form. Your basic question, then, is what kind of information is useful to you, and in what form it can most usefully be presented.

The answer to this question should give you a basic idea, at least, of the type of output you'll require. This output, in turn, will form the basis of your input requirements. After you have decided on some potential form of output, evaluate it against this checklist:

- ☐ How will I use this report?
- ☐ Is all of the information essential, or is there something I could leave out?
- ☐ Is any—or all—of this information already available from some better source?
- ☐ How often should this report be produced—and in how many copies?

Be careful of the tendency to become an information pack rat. It's not uncommon when you're designing a database to call for every bit of information the present system generates, plus every new kind of information you can persuade dBASE to spit out. There's a tendency to call for information you think you *might* need some day.

Ask yourself instead what would happen if the information wasn't available. If you find you normally can get along without it, perhaps you normally *should* get along without it. If you will need the information only on rare occasions, consider setting up a separate procedure to retrieve it when necessary. That way you won't have it cluttering up your more regular reports.

Some Are Simple

Getting the output you need may sometimes be no more difficult than asking dBASE to LIST the appropriate entries for the conditions you specify—say, for example, employees whose base salary is more than \$300 per week. Or, you might use the subtotal feature of the REPORT command to generate a report of the total payroll broken down by department.

One thing, of course, is necessary. The database from which you try to generate these reports must have the information you desire: the employees' names, their base salaries, and the departments in which they work. Thus, your reporting requirements strongly influence the structure of your database.

Effie Scrooge's problem with the deductions requires a more complicated solution. She needs quick access to the proper figures for each employee's withholding and payroll deductions. Meeting her needs will dictate that you establish a database which includes, or a procedure that can compute, the necessary figures. Ideally, it then should incorporate these figures into the individual payroll records, figure the net pay, and print the stubs and payroll checks. At this last stage you need not only the computed data but an output format to fit a printed form.

In this more complex case it's even more important to look first at the output. Without a firm eye on the information you must produce, it will be easy to set up a database that has too much information, too little or—very often—both.

Going Overboard

For example, here's the wrong way to set up an employee-database for payroll purposes:

```
. CREATE EMPLOYEE
ENTER RECORD STRUCTURE AS FOLLOWS:
 FIELD     NAME,TYPE,WIDTH,DECIMAL PLACES
 001       DEPT,C,5
 002       MANAGER,C,10
 003       PAY:BUDGET,N,8,2
 004       EMPLOYEE1,C,20
 005       JOB1,C,10
 006       GROSS1,N,7,2
 007       WHHOLD1,N,7,2
 008       FICA1,N,7,2
 009       INS1,N,6,2
 010       NET1,N,7,2
 011       EMPLOYEE2,C,20
 012       JOB2,C,10
 013       GROSS2,N,7,2
 014       WITHHOLD2,N,7,2
 015       FICA2,N,7,2
 016       INS2,N,6,2
 017       NET2,N,7,2
 018       EMPLOYEE3,C,20
 019       JOB3,C,10
 020       GROSS3,N,7,2
 021       WHHOLD3,N,7,2
 022       FICA3,N,7,2
 023       INS3,N,6,2
 024       NET3,N,7,2
 025       EMPLOYEE4,C,20
```

```
026         JOB4,C,10
027         GROSS4,C,7,2
028         WITHHOLD4,N,7,2
029         FICA4,N,7,2
030         INS4,N,6,2
031         NET4,N,7,2
```

One thing about a file this large: it offers plenty of room for things to go wrong—as they inevitably will if you try to use it. Here are just some of the worst possibilities:

- [ ] How on earth would you print a report based on this database, or even view it on a normal 80-column screen? All told, it spreads across 301 characters. Your reports will be hard to read and understand, and you cannot truthfully say that the report has provided the information you need if you cannot readily read it.
- [ ] We've provided for the records of four employees from each department. That's adequate for the present staff of the *Satellite*, but what about future expansion? Let's say you expand the news staff to four, then receive an application from a mild-mannered reporter with a national reputation. He's just the kind of superstar your newspaper needs. There've been some reports of strange behavior on his part, but you decide to hire him anyway, taking note that telephone booths aren't what they used to be. That much may be settled, but where do you put him in the database? You've already set up 31 data fields, and dBASE has room for only 32.
- [ ] Most of your departments have fewer than four employees. Remember, dBASE claims disk space for every number and character you specify when you create the file, whether or not you fill in the blanks. In this case, blank characters will take up disk space that you probably could put to good use elsewhere.
- [ ] The dBASE commands for searching, sorting and indexing can organize groups of records, but they cannot rearrange the single record you have set up for this entire department. Should Ida Rather announce her marriage to Chuck Allen, you'll have a choice of rewriting the entire file or leaving it in something other than alphabetical order.

Searching can truly be a chore. Consider the command you'd have to write for a report on all employees who are paid more than $300 a week:

```
LIST Employee1 .OR. Employee2 .OR. Employee3 .OR.
  Employee4 FOR Gross1 > 300 .OR. Gross2 > 300 ... and so on
```

From the problems we've found in this database, we can reach a few conclusions:

- [ ] A database should have only a few fields. The table should be narrow enough to be printed or displayed easily.
- [ ] It should be designed so practical space problems or the limits of dBASE's capacity don't unnecessarily limit the number of entries you can make.
- [ ] You should be able to sort, index, or search the entries in a convenient order without having to rewrite existing records.
- [ ] Inserts, deletions and corrections should be easy to make, and you should have to handle only the record you actually are correcting.

Another Mistake

Let's set up this database again, this time illustrating some other kinds of mistakes. This time we'll correct some of the errors of the first version:

```
.  DISPLAY  STRUCTURE

STRUCTURE  FOR  FILE:      EMPLOYEE.DBF
NUMBER  OF  RECORDS:       00000
DATE  OF  LAST  UPDATE:  00/00/00
PRIMARY  USE  DATABASE
FLD          NAME         TYPE  WIDTH      DEC
001       EMPLOYEE       C      020
002       GROSS          N      007        002
003       WITHHOLD       N      007        002
004       FICA           N      007        002
005       INS            N      006        002
006       NET            N      007        002
007       DEPT           C      005
008       SUPER          C      010
009       PAY:BUDGET     N      008        002
**  TOTAL  **                   00078
```

This is a great improvement. We now are realistically within the limits of an 80-column screen and a standard printer. There is a separate record for each employee. Still, there are some problems.

For example, suppose editor Lou Asner resigns and you appoint Wally Cronkite to replace him. This means you must correct the supervisor entry for every employee in the department, being sure to include Cronkite's. It's all too easy to miss a record and to leave the departed Asner still listed as a supervisor.

In a spate of resignations, Frank Tarlek, the advertising manager, also leaves your employ. He's been a one-man department. Delete his personnel record, and you also delete all your data about the advertising department.

The resignations plus your expansion plans mean you'll have to do some serious recruiting and hiring. You also realize that after that emergency is over your expanded staff will have more recordkeeping needs than you can handle yourself. So, you create a personnel department and assign an appropriate budget for its payroll, but you have yet to hire someone to run it. This would leave you with entries for the department name and the budget, but otherwise a group of blank records. What's more, should you set up a search based on employees' names, there would be nothing to direct you to this record.

The Real Problem

In short, this database is better than the first attempt, but not by much. It still suffers from this basic fault: each record includes information about *two separate subjects*: the employee and the department. Particularly in departments with several employees, information is needlessly duplicated. When you alter or manipulate information about employees, you also get involved in departmental data that should remain unchanged. The reverse is also true.

We can avoid this by observing three basic principles of database design:

1)Each database should deal with a *single subject*.

That could be information about individual employees, for example, or the organizational and budget details of each department. Be careful not to include information on one subject in a database that deals with another.

2) Each record should be identified by a *distinctive key*.

This must be a field which includes a unique value for each record. An employee's name would be one example, although it's not a particularly good one. It's better to assign a distinctive number to each employee, to allow for employees with the same or similar names.

3) The information in the database should pertain *only to the subject* of that database.

In other words, departmental information should not appear in an employee database, or vice versa. Instead, establish fields which can serve as *links* between the employee and departmental files. For example, the employee's file could list a department number, but no other departmental information. Any further details about the department's operation could be found by locating that number in the departmental file.

Let's put these principles into action by creating three separate databases that look like this:

```
STRUCTURE FOR FILE:     EMPLOYEE.DBF
NUMBER OF RECORDS:      00000
DATE OF LAST UPDATE:  00/00/00
PRIMARY USE DATABASE
FLD          NAME        TYPE WIDTH      DEC
001     NO              C      004
002     LAST            C      010
003     FIRST           C      010
004     DEPT            C      005
** TOTAL **                    00030


STRUCTURE FOR FILE:     SALARY.DBF
NUMBER OF RECORDS:      00000
DATE OF LAST UPDATE:  00/00/00
PRIMARY USE DATABASE
FLD          NAME        TYPE WIDTH      DEC
001     NO              C      004
002     GROSS           N      007      002
003     WITHHOLD        N      007      002
004     INS             N      006      002
** TOTAL **                    00025


STRUCTURE FOR FILE:     DEPT.DBF
NUMBER OF RECORDS:      00000
DATE OF LAST UPDATE:  00/00/00
PRIMARY USE DATABASE
FLD          NAME        TYPE WIDTH      DEC
001     DEPT            C      005
002     SUPER           C      010
003     PAY:BUDGET      N      008      002
** TOTAL **                    00024
```

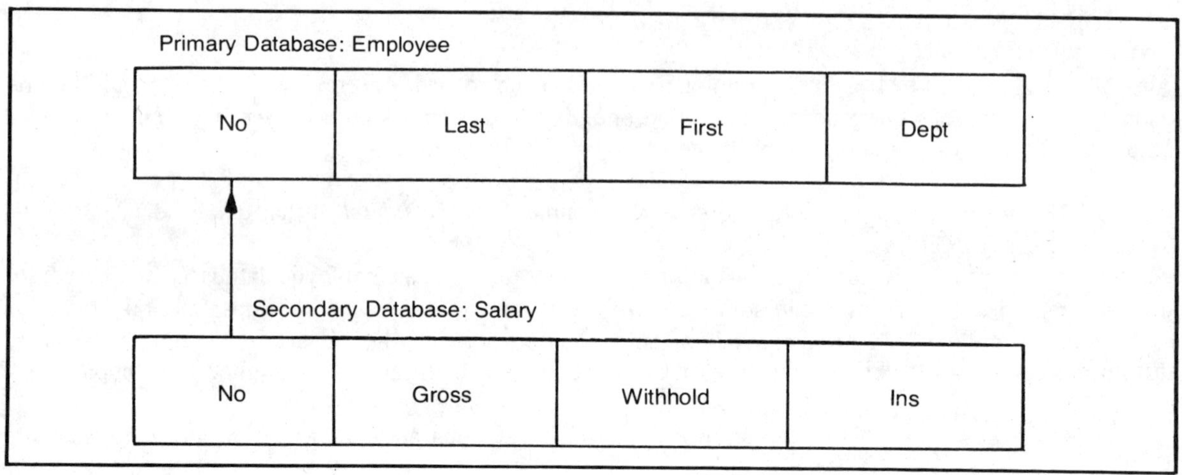

Fig. 2-3. How databases can be linked.

The **Employee** file still is the key to this system, but now it contains only basic personal information about the employees. Each employee also is now identified by a distinctive number.

That same number is provided in the **Salary** file. It now serves as a *link* between the two. Salary information now is listed only by the employee number; if you want to know the employee's actual identity, you can use the SELECT or JOIN commands to report information from both files. These links are illustrated in Fig. 2-3 and 2-4.

The **Employee** file also includes a **Dept** field to serve as a link with the **Dept** file. Using that point of contact you could, for example, call up a report on the departmental budget plus a list of its employees.

We now have a group of databases that has these characteristics:

1) A *primary key* which uniquely identifies each record.

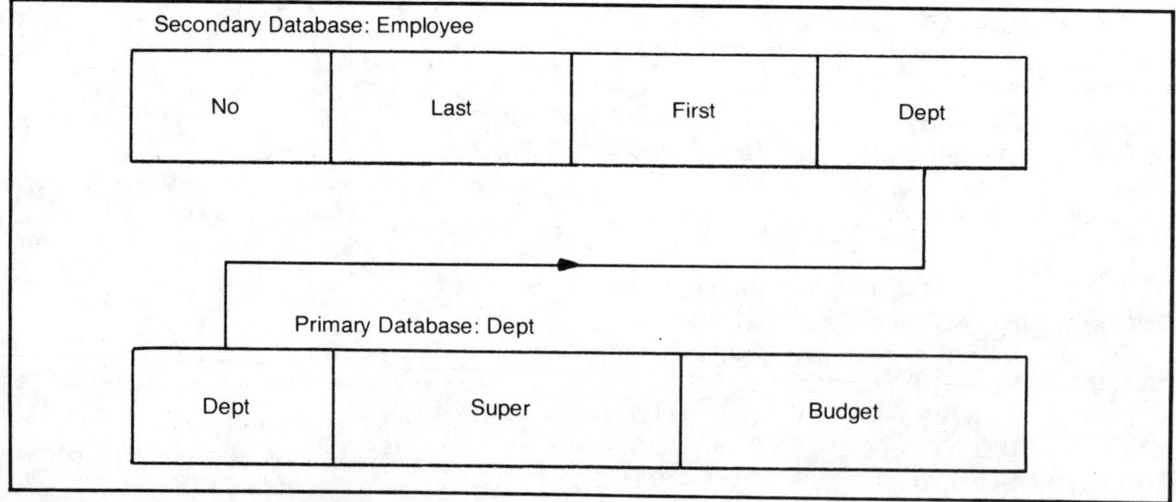

Fig. 2-4. Primary and secondary databases.

2) Fields which represent data only for the *single type of information* in each file.

3) A means to *link* more than one file by using values that each has in common.

This new structure has several advantages over our earlier attempts:

1) Our files are down to sizes that are easier to manage.
2) We face fewer limits on the number of items we can enter. The employee file still is limited to 32 people; for a larger staff we'd have to establish individual files, probably by department. Even here, though, each employee would be represented by a single record, not by a field in the database structure.
3) We don't waste valuable disk space with unused records or duplicate information.
4) We can make normal changes and corrections without disturbing unrelated items. We need not make the same change to several records.

A simple way to express the general idea is to modify an old adage:

A place for every fact, and every fact in its place.

Getting More Complex

The relationships in this set of files could be called one-on-one. Each employee works in only one department, for example, and draws only one weekly paycheck.

When you get into such subjects as inventories and billing, you'll find a more complex set of relationships. You might have a supply closet, for example, with a variety of items purchased from several vendors. In fact, a single type of item, like paper clips, could have come from several vendors, because you normally add these to larger orders for convenience or to qualify for discounts. What's more, there have been several orders from each vendor, for each type of item.

These relationships may sound complicated, but they actually are much the same as those for the employment files. You might set up your files as illustrated in Fig. 2-5. Again, we have established separate files for each type of information—and note that an order is a *separate kind* of information, not a characteristic of either the suppliers or the supplies.

Just as you did before, establish a unique index for each record in each file, and provide one data item to link each file with another.

DEVELOPING THE SYSTEM

The thought process that uses your desired output to direct the planned input skips almost completely over an inportant area in the middle: how you process the input to produce the output?

Now that we've defined the databases and are proceeding back toward the output side, it's time to take up that question. (Actually, it's known as "systems development." But anyone who uses "access" as a verb could never be accused of using perfect grammar.)

In the development phase you decide what processes you should put the data through to reach the expected result. The easiest way is an ad hoc approach: starting with the famous dBASE periods, use its query language to tell the program what you want to accomplish. This is the kind of process described in Chapter 1.

The major alternative is to write a dBASE command file—in other words, a program. dBASE programming isn't as difficult as most formal programming languages. At its essence, dBASE command

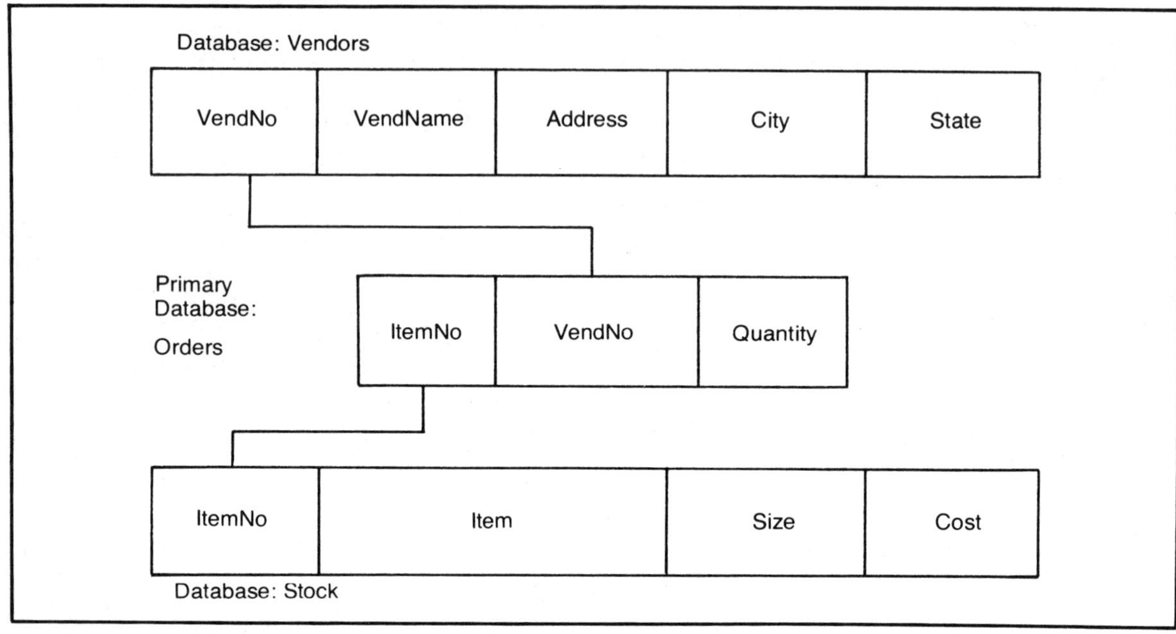

Fig. 2-5. Linking multiple files.

files string together an extended list of dBASE commands. The single command DO will take the process from beginning to end.

Choice Depends on Users

Whichever course you choose, *do everything with the user in mind.* This is particularly true if your system will be used by inexperienced employees. Don't make someone guess about what to do next. Don't unnecessarily confront an inexperienced user with the dBASE period—which one intimidated beginner aptly compared with a black hole. When you display a message, do so in clear, simple English.

When a user makes a mistake, as even you will do once in while, your procedure should make it clear exactly what the mistake was and how to correct it. Include error trapping routines that will stop the program and notify the user if, for example, you enter a date like February 31, or data that already is on file.

Make sure, too, that a user error cannot destroy valuable data. Close files as soon as you have finished using them.

If a searching or sorting operation will take more than a few seconds, the screen should indicate that the program is working and that the computer hasn't broken down.

And, finally, resist the temptation to confront the user with clever messages. The confounded user who encounters your message for the sixth time in a row will no longer be amused. The best error message explains as directly and specifically as possible what the user did wrong. It then should explain just as directly and specifically what to do about it.

Programs Are for Beginners

Most of these requirements, particularly those for the sake of inexperienced users, will require the use of command files. You can use these to set up menus, prompts, error traps, and other features that help the nervous beginner.

Ironically, while the query language may be the first thing a dBASE student learns, it really is best suited for use by more experienced hands. A host of prompts and menus with no hope for a bypass can change quickly from a convenience to an annoyance. Experienced hands will want to jump quickly to the command, or at least to a limited purpose command file, without the same series of choices and questions time after time.

Sometimes a program is so user-friendly you never can get it to stop talking and get to work.

I use dBASE for two purposes. One is to maintain a set of bibliographic records on various subjects; the other is to keep track of my business expenses and tax deductions. I've written exactly two command files.

One is an exercise in laziness. It cuts down the extended command I otherwise would need to find a particular key word within a biblographic file. This program asks me for the field and the word, then executes the rest of the process automatically.

I also wrote one to fill out an income tax form automatically. It would have been a lot easier, though, simply to let dBASE report the appropriate totals and subtotals with its report generator, and to copy the result onto the form myself. Besides, the IRS seems to redesign this form every year, limiting the ability to use the form-filling program again.

When Programs Are Useful

My own applications are fairly simple compared to the needs of even most small businesses. While helping and protecting inexperienced users, a well-written dBASE program can do such things as:

- Catch obviously incorrect entries before they get into your database.
- Check for duplicate entries.
- Keep confidential files confidential—vital for payroll records.
- Provide separate records for auditing purposes.
- Let you maintain a file of system constants.
- Give you a choice of immediate or delayed data entry.

Entry Type Important

This last choice can be an important one. Direct data entry, such as with the APPEND command or an equivalent process in a command file, has the advantage of placing the information immediately on file.

It also has some disadvantages. You can't check for errors or duplicates without waiting for dBASE to do some soul-searching. That cuts down on the speed. It also doesn't lend itself to recording things like routine retail sales. Instead of taking the time to do it at the point of sale, wait until the end of the day and update your inventory all at once.

A *batch* entry, on the other hand, checks and processes your entries and places them into a temporary data file. Once the process is through you can APPEND the new data to the permanent database.

The disadvantage, of course, is that your permanent file is seldom completely up to the minute. Often, that's not important, but there are times when it is.

Start the Instructions

This also is the time to start writing a user manual for the completed procedure. As you set up each element of the procedure, also take the time to write printed instructions for the proper procedure, what the error messages mean and how to retrace your steps when you've done something wrong. The problem with many software instructions is that their author didn't get started until the project itself was completed. At that point, no one is in a frame of mind to do the job properly.

If you jot down a rough draft or some notes as you go along, it will be much easier at the end to polish these into a completed set of instructions.

This is also the time to establish a standard format for any forms you will want to use, either on paper or the computer screen. A standard screen format makes menu selections data entry, and other operations much easier, and a matching output screen does the same for your completed reports.

GETTING TO WORK

Remember this: your completed procedure will *not* work right the first time. Again, thanks to dBASE's plain English structure, this probably won't happen as often as it might otherwise, but it will still happen.

The best way to handle a problem is, of course, to avoid it in the first place. Many dBASE users advocate writing your programs first in what they call *pseudocode*. Jot down notes in the order of what you want the program to do. List the instructions in your own words, as they make sense to you. Then, with the help of this book or the dBASE instruction manual, translate your language into words that make sense to dBASE. In that way, the procedure will follow a logical flow that is more likely to do what you want.

The building blocks or modules we'll develop later in this book will also help. Once you've established a procedure that works for setting up a menu, for example, or checking a date, save it as a separate command or format file. Then, whenever you need such a routine in your procedure, you can copy it and make any necessary modifications.

You'll also find that as you first run a program the results of searches, calculations, and other operations will be displayed on the screen. This can be a great diagnostic aid. Later, when your procedure is well polished, you can insert SET TALK OFF as an early line, and the program won't display the results unless you command it to SET TALK ON.

Other SET commands also can be useful. ECHO will display the commands as well as the responses, and STEP will stop the program at the problem area so you can try manual responses until you find the one that works correctly.

dBASE command files can be written with a word processor in its nondocument mode and corrected the same way. For short, quick corrections, you can use the dBASE MODIFY COMMAND function. With it you can write or edit a command file, again using the WordStar-like commands.

When dBASE encounters an improperly written command it will repeat the troublesome line on the screen and give you a chance to correct it. dBASE won't tell you what is wrong—you'll have to figure it out for yourself—but once you've decided what change to make it will walk you through a correction procedure.

One thing to remember, though: the corrections you enter through this procedure will not be saved as part of the permanent command files. You'll have to do that later, using the word processor or MODIFY COMMAND.

dBASE Procedures for More Flexibility

It's fear and trepidation time, for some of you at least. Here we go into that area of dBASE known as (shudder) *programming*.

Many personal computer users don't really want to get involved in the programming end of things. You've probably paid—or expect to pay—a significant amount of money for your copy of dBASE. For this, you're entitled to a program someone else has already written, debugged, and proven—not something you have to write yourself. All you really want to do it to *use* this program.

Even if you're willing to devote some effort to learning how to use dBASE, you may feel unsure of yourself when it comes to writing programmed procedures. After all, the programmers of your acquaintance probably speak a strange-sounding language in their ordinary conversation. Their programs can be even worse. And you've probably managed to become confused just by the direct dBASE commands you've already learned. If computerphobia is a disease, fear of programming must be one of its advanced stages.

MAKING IT EASIER

We'll try to make things as easy as we can, and in this vein here are a few points to consider:

☐ Those prewritten programs that require no great effort on your part also tend to be inflexible. If you need a function that's tailored to your particular business, they can't provide it.

☐ dBASE, you should recall, holds a midway position between a packaged program and a raw computer language. That means the authors of dBASE have done the hardest part. All you must really do is provide the commands that make dBASE do what you want.

☐ dBASE commands use reasonably straightforward English. Like any good English teacher, dBASE will insist that you use the language properly, but it won't go out of the way to confuse you.

☐ dBASE procedures can be written in small, compact modules. Once you have established a procedure that works well, or which sets up a standard form, you can use it again and again in a variety of operations.

☐ Many dBASE instructions, including the sample accounting program in the dBASE manual, have been criticized for requiring that you learn two things at once. You have to understand the accounting aspects before you can see what the program's author was trying to do. We'll try to avoid that problem by first applying fundamental dBASE procedures to some "generic" command modules that are written to work in all kinds of programs. First, we'll set up some of these modules. Later, we'll insert them into working procedures.

☐ If you're even mildly familiar with BASIC or with any other programming language, you soon should notice that the dBASE command language does many of the same things in much the same ways. (See Fig. 3-1 for a comparison of BASIC and dBASE commands.)

☐ dBASE programming really is a matter of simply writing down a list of commands, many of which are the direct commands we already have covered. Instead of typing in each command in order each time, you can just call up the procedure which executes these commands automatically.

☐ As with the earlier instructions, don't try to memorize everything right now. Instead, concentrate on learning what dBASE can do. Later, you always can refer back here or to the dBASE manual for the mechanics of how to do it.

☐ Last is a matter of terminology. Strictly speaking, a dBASE procedure isn't really a program. dBASE is the program; we'll be writing a string of commands that actually make a *procedure*. The procedure tells the dBASE program what to do. This is the kind of tricky terminology that's popular with politicians and advertising copywriters. If you're afraid to write a program, call it a procedure instead. (If it helps, don't knock it.)

THE SYSTEM PROFILE

Our first working file will primarily be an exercise in the mechanics of writing a command file. Every small business system has a certain amount of information that's common to nearly every procedure in its system. The company name is an obvious example. Its address and phone number are others.

If we STORE these items in a memory file, we then can RESTORE them as memory variables in any procedure we happen to be using at the time. Our first command file, called **Profile.Cmd**, will establish some basic pieces of information and store them in a file called **Profile.Mem**. (A reminder about the file suffixes. If you create the file through dBASE it will assign the proper suffix automatically. If you use a word processor to write a command file, *you* must assign the suffix. The **.CMD** suffix used here is the proper one for a typical 8-bit CP/M computer. You IBM PC people, and those with compatible 16-bit machines, will use a **.PRG** suffix on your command files. Refer back to Fig. 1-7 for a complete list of file suffixes.)

Put the dBASE disk in your A drive and a blank disk in B. If you have a word processing program, set it in the program or nondocument mode. This is a little easier and more flexible than dBASE's own file writer. If you don't have a word processor, call up the dBASE period and enter MODIFY COMMAND. In either case, the file you are about to write will be called **Profile.Cmd** (or **.Prg**). Type the **Profile** program listing, Fig. 3-2. I'll enter the data for my favorite newspaper. You may use the same information for your own company, if you'd like.

What's It Do?

Not much, actually. It simply establishes a central file of common information so we won't have to enter this data every time we need it; we can just call it up from the file. Another advantage of this file is

Many of the programming commands in dBASE II have counterparts in other languages. In particular, BASIC programmers should recognize some familiar commands in dBASE.

Here are some dBASE commands and functions with their BASIC counterparts— presented with one word of warning. The dBASE and BASIC commands do *approximately* the same things. You might not be able to make a direct translation from one to the other. However, the paired commands have the same *general* purposes.

dBASE	BASIC	Comment
WAIT	INKEY$	Both wait for a single keystroke from the operator.
INPUT	INPUT	These act much the same and are used primarily for numerical inputs.
ACCEPT	LINE INPUT	Specialized input commands for character entries.
?	PRINT	Identical
@, SAY	LOCATE	The dBASE command locates screen prompts and inputs at designated coordinates. BASIC's version is less sophisticated and must be used along with Print.
DO	RUN	Both initiate a program. In dBASE, DO also calls and executes separate program modules. In BASIC, you would do this with a Merge command or by calling a subroutine.
DO WHILE	FOR/NEXT	This is one version of the DO WHILE command. Combined with a Counter variable that increases with each loop, DO WHILE performs much like its BASIC counterpart.
IF/ELSE	IF/THEN/ELSE	Two close equivalents for issuing commands under stated conditions.
DO CASE	WHILE/WEND	Another matched pair, variations on the IF sequences.
STR	STR$	Convert a number to a character string.
VAL	VAL	Convert a string to a number
$(string)	MID$ (string)	Lift out specified characters from the interior of a string.
LEN	LEN	Measure the length of a string.
RENAME	NAME	Rename a program.

dBASE is a specialized program, and it shows up in these comparisons. dBASE is designed to make use of data files, and for this purpose it is much more versatile and flexible than BASIC. On the other hand, BASIC, as a general purpose language, has some features dBASE doesn't, particularly in the areas of graphics and mathematical fucntions.

Fig. 3-1. dBASE and BASIC compared.

```
* PROFILE.CMD
* Purpose:  Creates the file PROFILE.MEM, a file of commom
*  memory variables used in all system procedures.
* Used by:  All procedures
* Uses: ProfilUp.Cmd
*
SET DEFAULT TO B
SET TALK OFF
STORE 'Submetropolis Weekly Satellite' to Company
STORE 'All the News That Fits, We Print' to Slogan
STORE '1234 Gully Wash' to Street
STORE 'Yawning Gap, Wyoming 77776' to Address
STORE '(307) 555-4321' to Phone
STORE 16 to EmpMax
STORE 40 to WorkWk
STORE 2500 to Payflag
STORE 0.067 to FicaPct
STORE 35700 to FicaMax
STORE 0 to CheckNo
STORE 0 to Balance
STORE 0 to InvoiceNo
STORE 0 to OrderNo
STORE 84 to Year
SAVE to PROFILE.MEM
```

Fig. 3-2. Profile command file.

that should any of this information change (such as the Social Security data, for example), we can enter the change in this one place. We don't have to search our other files for every possible instance in which we might have used it.

Let's see how we've accomplished this:

```
* PROFILE.CMD
* Purpose:  Creates the file PROFILE.MEM, a file of common
*  memory variables used in all system procedures.
* Used by:  All procedures
* Uses: ProfilUp
```

The first five lines are some basic documentation. The "*" character indicates a comment line that won't be processed by the program—similar to the REM statement in BASIC. We've identified the procedure, its place in this book and its general purpose.

The "Used" and "Used by" lines will help us keep track of where this procedure fits in our overall system. The information in this file will be widely shared, by nearly every later procedure. In a little while, we will also be writing a procedure called **PROFILE.UP** which can be used to update the information in **Profile**.

SETting Up

The two lines below use SET commands to change dBASE's default settings, the ones you normally get when you don't specify anything else.

```
SET DEFAULT TO B
SET TALK OFF
```

SET DEFAULT TO B assumes that you'll be running dBASE in Drive A with your command and data files on Disk B. Using this command at the outset shifts the active drive to B, and it's one thing you won't have to worry about in the rest of the procedure.

Normally, as dBASE executes a command it will display the results of that activity on the screen. This is useful if you're debugging a procedure, but normally you don't need it. SET TALK OFF tells the program it need not "talk" to you as it works. If you want it to do so at any time, you can SET TALK ON.

Into STOREage

Next come the first "working" lines of this procedure:

```
STORE 'Submetropolis Weekly Satellite' to Company
STORE 'All the News That Fits, We Print' to Slogan
STORE '1234 Gully Wash' to Street
STORE 'Yawning Gap, Wyoming 77776' to Address
STORE '(307) 555-4321' to Phone
```

For each item in our company profile, we will STORE the appropriate information to a memory variable. For example, in the first STORE line we place the company's name in a variable called **Company**. Since the firm has a slogan it likes to print on its statements and other documents, we'll include that in the file. Then come a few basics like the address lines and phone number.

```
STORE 16 to EmpMax
STORE 40 to WorkWk
STORE 2500 to Payflag
STORE 0.067 to FicaPct
STORE 35700 to FicaMax
```

These lines are for payroll purposes. **EmpMax** holds the number of employees currently on the payroll; later programs will use that figure to make sure someone doesn't try to slip through a paycheck for a 17th employee. **Payflag** is a figure a little higher than the normal weekly payroll; if the total payroll for the week exceeds that figure, the payroll system will alert you to look for a problem. Next come the percentage to deduct for Social Security and the maximum wage on which this tax is deducted.

```
STORE 0 to CheckNo
STORE 0 to Balance
STORE 0 to InvoiceNo
```

The next four entries are for numbered checks and other forms. **CheckNo** is for a check number; enter the number of the last check you've used. When one of your check-writing procedures issues a check it will include the command:

```
STORE CheckNo+1 to CheckNo
```

That command increases the stored check number by one for each check written, and when you SAVE the new **Profile** entries they will include an updated check number. In similar fashion, the programs which issue invoices and orders will add the numbers as you go along. They also add deposits and subtract checks from the **Balance** variable.

```
STORE 84 to Year
```

You'll use this later when the program checks dates for errors such as the wrong year. Update it annually, and it's there when you need it.

```
SAVE to PROFILE.MEM
```

This final command SAVEs these values to the **Profile** memory file.

How It Works

To execute, shut down your word processor and load dBASE (or hit CTRL/W if you've been using MODIFY COMMAND). Then at the period, type the simple command:

```
. DO PROFILE
```

Since you set the TALK function off, you won't see much unless you made a mistake. In our first run-through of this program, dBASE found a couple of errors. The screen looked like this:

```
. DO B:PROFILE

*** SYNTAX ERROR ***
        ?
STORE 'Submetropolis Weekly Satellite" to Company

CORRECT AND RETRY (Y/N)?
```

If you answer "N" to this query, dBASE will try to run the program in spite of the error. Its success is questionable. If you think you must make major corrections, the ESC key will take you back to the dBASE dot. This was a simple error, though, and easy to correct. After we answered "Y" to this question, dBASE asked and we responded:

```
CHANGE FROM : "

CHANGE TO    : '

STORE 'Submetropolis Weekly Satellite' to Company

MORE CORRECTIONS (Y/N)? N
```

Did you see what we did wrong? You can use either single or double quotes around the contents of a character variable, but whatever your choice you must be consistent. You can't mix the two symbols as I accidentally did here.

The next error message reads (after corrections):

```
STORE 2,500 to Payflag

CORRECT AND RETRY (Y/N)? Y

CHANGE FROM :2,

CHANGE TO   :2

STORE 2500 to Payflag

MORE CORRECTIONS (Y/N)? N
```

dBASE doesn't like commas in its numeric variables.

Now, to see what we've done, order dBASE to:

. DISPLAY MEMORY

You then should see:

```
COMPANY       (C)    Submetropolis Weekly Satellite
SLOGAN        (C)    All the News That Fits, We Print
STREET        (C)    1234 Gully Wash
ADDRESS       (C)    Yawning Gap, Wyoming 77776
PHONE         (C)    (307) 555-4321
EMPMAX        (N)       16
WORKWK        (N)       40
PAYFLAG       (N)       2500
FICAPCT       (N)    0.067
FICAMAX       (N)       35700
CHECKNO       (N)     0
BALANCE       (N)     0
INVOICENO     (N)     0
ORDERNO       (N)     0
YEAR          (N)     84
** TOTAL **          15 VARIABLES USED   00171 BYTES USED
```

Notice how clever dBASE is. It knows that the name, slogan and similar entries are character variables, and the figures are numerical. How'd it figure that out?

dBASE, like any good computer program, is doing just what we told it to do. The quote marks that gave us trouble a few moments ago are the signal for a character string. A number without the quotes is taken as numerical. A T or F (without the quotes) would be taken as a logical entry.

Check the listing carefully; you'll be depending on it later. If you see any mistakes, MODIFY COMMAND will let you correct them. (Since you're already in dBASE it's probably a better choice for this purpose than returning to the word processor.) While you're at it, correct the two punctuation errors dBASE discovered while it ran the program. The correction messages you see on the screen *do not* correct the original listing. You'll have to do that yourself.

CONTROLLED ENTRY

One of the most important reasons to set up a **Profile** memory file is to update the information in it without having to search through every file that might do it. Items like the check number and bank balance will be updated automatically in the programs that use them. If you need to change one of the other items, it's a simple matter to call up **Profile.CMD** with your word processor or MODIFY COMMAND, make the necessary corrections and run the procedure again. For instance, should the government change the Social Security percentage or maximum pay base, you could easily make those corrections.

It's so simple, in fact, that what we're about to propose may be an example of unnecessary programming—of which dBASE experts are sometimes guilty. Our next exercise is s a formal procedure for updating the **Profile** data.

Why go through such an exercise when it's so easy to edit the command file? In your case it may not be worthwhile, particularly if you're the only person who normally would be expected to use your system. That's a rare case, though, and consider what would happen should you not be available at a crucial moment. More than one person ought to know what to do.

When you involve multiple users, you have to concern yourself with two serious questions:

☐ Ease of operation, commonly known as "user friendliness."
☐ Security: keeping unauthorized employees from messing with the files.

Later on, we'll create a password system you can use to govern access to the information in your files. We then can write procedures which force the user to go through the password procedure before dBASE will do anything else. That's something you can't do without a properly written procedure.

Right now, let's provide some help for the inexperienced user. A program that offers a menu of choices and plenty of on-screen prompts can make the details of dBASE almost invisible. All you need do is follow the instructions you're given. Figure 3-3 is a simple program which does that in a simple way. After you've typed that program you can run it with the command:

```
. DO UpdateA
```

The disk drive will moan and whir for a few moments, and then you should see:

```
COMPANY      (C)    Submetropolis Weekly Satellite
SLOGAN       (C)    All the News That Fits, We Print
STREET       (C)    1234 Gully Wash
ADDRESS      (C)    Yawning Gap, Wyoming 77776
PHONE        (C)    (307) 555-4321
EMPMAX       (N)      16
WORKWK       (N)      40
PAYFLAG      (N)      2500
FICAPCT      (N)    0.067
FICAMAX      (N)      35700
CHECKNO      (N)     0
BALANCE      (N)     0
INVOICENO    (N)     0
ORDERNO      (N)     0
```

```
* UPDATEA.CMD
* Purpose:  A preliminary version of ProfileUp, to update
*   the memory variables stored in Profile.Mem.
*
SET DEFAULT TO B
SET TALK OFF
* The next lines set up a loop which lets you enter as
*  many changes as necessary.
STORE T to Continue
DO While Continue=T
  ERASE
* The next two items recover and display the data stored
*   in Profile.Mem
  RESTORE from Profile.Mem
  DISPLAY Memory
* Prompts and Inputs
  ACCEPT 'Item to change' to Item
  INPUT 'Please Enter the New Value' to Value
  STORE Value to &Item
  RELEASE Item, Value
  SAVE to Profile.Mem
  INPUT 'Would you like to make more changes? (Y/N)' to Continue
ENDDO While Continue
RETURN
```

Fig. 3-3. UpdateA, the first update file.

```
DATE              (N)   84
** TOTAL **          15 VARIABLES USED   00171 BYTES
```

USED

There will be a few more moans, then dBASE will ask for

Item to change:

You've probably written some checks from your current account, so let's enter the last check number you've used. Enter the identification of that memory variable in response to the first prompt:

Item to change:CHECKNO

dBASE then will ask:

Please Enter the New Value:

Enter the number of the last check you used:

Please Enter the New Value:134

Now, your procedure will produce one more question

```
Would you like to make more changes? (Y/N):
```

The purpose of this is to let you make more than one change without having to reDO the program for each one. Let's see what happens when you answer "Y":

```
Would you like to make more changes? (Y/N):Y
```

The screen will go disconcertingly blank, again there will be some noises from the disks, and then you'll see:

```
COMPANY         (C)   Submetropolis Weekly Satellite
SLOGAN          (C)   All the News That Fits, We Print
STREET          (C)   1234 Gully Wash
ADDRESS         (C)   Yawning Gap, Wyoming 77776
PHONE           (C)   (307) 555-4321
EMPMAX          (N)    16
WORKWK          (N)    40
PAYFLAG         (N)    2500
FICAPCT         (N)   0.067
FICAMAX         (N)    35700
CHECKNO         (N)    134
BALANCE         (N)   0
INVOICENO       (N)   0
ORDERNO         (N)   0
DATE            (N)   84
** TOTAL **   15 VARIABLES USED   00171 BYTES USED
```

Look familiar? It's the same memory file the program displayed before—with one significant exception: **Checkno**, the item for the last check number, now reads 134.

Your procedure is again asking what item you'd like to change. Let's assume you noticed a mistake in the street address, so you enter:

```
Item to change:STREET

Please Enter the New Value:2134 Gully Wash

Would you like to make more changes? (Y/N):N
```

This time, the program returns you to the dBASE prompt. It might be a good idea, though, to check the memory file and make sure the last item was recorded correctly:

```
. LIST Memory

COMPANY         (C)   Submetropolis Weekly Satellite
SLOGAN          (C)   All the News That Fits, We Print
STREET          (N)    2134
ADDRESS         (C)   Yawning Gap, Wyoming 77776
PHONE           (C)   (307) 555-4321
EMPMAX          (N)    16
```

```
WORKWK          (N)      40
PAYFLAG         (N)      2500
FICAPCT         (N)      0.067
FICAMAX         (N)      35700
CHECKNO         (N)      134
BALANCE         (N)      O
INVOICENO       (N)      O
DATE            (N)      84
** TOTAL ** 15 VARIABLES USED   00142 BYTES USED
```

Aren't you glad you checked? Your street listing has somehow become a numerical entry, and the name of the street is gone. What happened?

Remember how the computer learned to distinguish between character and numerical items? It needs those quote marks again. Try this version:

```
Item to change:STREET

Please Enter the New Value:'2134 Gully Wash'

Would you like to make more changes? (Y/N):N


. LIST Memory

COMPANY         (C)     Submetropolis Weekly Satellite
SLOGAN          (C)     All the News That Fits, We Print
STREET          (C)     2134 Gully Wash
ADDRESS         (N)     Yawning Gap, Wyoming 77776
PHONE           (C)     (307) 555-4321
EMPMAX          (N)      16
WORKWK          (N)      40
PAYFLAG         (N)      2500
FICAPCT         (N)     0.067
FICAMAX         (N)      35700
CHECKNO         (N)      134
BALANCE         (N)      O
INVOICENO       (N)      O
ORDERNO         (N)      O
DATE            (N)      84
** TOTAL **  15 VARIABLES USED    00151 BYTES USED
```

That's more like it. But how did you do all this, anyway? The key operations in this procedure looked like this:

```
* The next lines set up a loop which lets you
*  enter as many changes as necessary.
STORE T to Continue
DO WHILE Continue=T
```

As the comment line points out, this pair of commands sets up a loop, which will keep repeating itself as long as a designated condition is in effect. If you're familiar with BASIC, this type of loop is similar to the WHILE/WEND routine.

In this case, we'll enter a change during each trip through the loop, on the condition that we still want to continue. To establish this condition, we set up a memory variable known as "Continue" and STORE in it the logical value of T, for True. (In its logical functions, dBASE treats T and Y as the same thing; it does the same with F and N. It also ignores the difference between upper and lowercase.)

Thus the program will continue to repeat the loop as long as we continue to say, "Yes, it is true we want to continue."

The program then clears the screen with the command:

```
ERASE
```

Then, as the comments explain:

```
* The next two items recover and display the data
*   in Profile.Mem
 RESTORE from Profile.Mem
 DISPLAY Memory
```

The RESTORE command picks up the values from the **Profile** memory file. The DISPLAY command puts them on the screen.

```
ACCEPT 'Item to change' to Item
INPUT 'Please Enter the New Value' to Value
```

Here is a pair of input commands that do the same thing—almost. The difference between the two helps to explain how we managed to get mixed up when we tried to change the address.

BASIC programmers will probably find the INPUT command the more familiar—it works much the same in either language. After the command (and in quote marks) you write the prompt that will appear on the screen. Then, with the TO command you name the memory variable in which you'll record the inputted information.

INPUT is intended primarily for numerical or logical items. If you INPUT a character variable, it must be in quotes.

ACCEPT, on the other hand, is designed specifically for character inputs. You don't need the quote marks, but if you enter a number through this command it will be recorded as a character item, not a numerical one. In this case, we use ACCEPT to specify the name of the variable that will be changed to the new value. Now follow carefully, because it gets a bit tricky.

```
STORE Value to &Item
```

The little "&" (ampersand) sign introduces what dBASE calls a *macro substitution*. When we created the variable called Item, we STORED in it the name of another character variable: the name of the variable to be changed. When we updated the check numbers, the variable item contained the character string **CheckNo.**

Then, using macro substitution, we stored the new value in the variable called **Checkno**, as represented by another variable called **Item**.

We could have taken a shortcut through this process. Instead of storing the new value in a separate variable of that name, we simply could have said:

```
INPUT 'Please Enter the New Value' to &Item
```

This time we took the longer route so we would only have to explain one thing at a time.

```
RELEASE Item, Value
SAVE to Profile.Mem
```

These are housekeeping commands. We RELEASE the two variables we used to transfer the new values so they don't clutter the memory file or count against our limit of 64. Then we save the updated values in **Profile.Mem**.

Now the operator must make a decision:

```
INPUT 'Would you like to make more changes? (Y/N)' to
Continue
```

You now hold the power of life or death over the variable called **Continue**. Notice that the prompt calls for the particular form in which it wants an answer. Since we have not included a way to correct or interpret a reply like "Yes" or "Shucks, no," we can try to keep out of trouble by directing the user to a response the program will accept.

Significantly, the reply to this question goes into the existing variable **Continue**. At the outset of the loop, we instructed the program to repeat itself if **Continue** was true. A "Y" in response to the prompt will keep the status in effect. The program will again display the variable list, including the latest update, and it again will ask what change you wish to make.

On the other hand, if you answer "N", **Continue** no longer holds a value of "true," and the loop will not repeat itself. Instead, you arrive at:

```
ENDDO While Continue
```

ENDDO signifies the end of the loop that began with DO. That would be enough as far as dBASE is concerned. The added phrase "While Continue" means nothing to the program, but there's a chance that it someday might mean something to you. In a program with several DO loops it can be useful to remind yourself of which DO you are ending.

```
RELEASE Continue
RETURN
```

Some final housekeeping: We're through with **Continue**, so we can RELEASE it. RETURN takes us back to the dBASE dot.

GETTING LOCATED

If you've never written a program before, playing around with something you've written, particularly an interactive program like this, can be fun. To tell the truth, though, this program isn't much of an improvement on the more rough-cut procedure, editing and rerunning **Profile.Cmd.** It certainly has one shortcoming where an inexperienced user is concerned: it simply flashes the memory data on the screen without bothering to tell anyone what it is.

We can cure that problem fairly easily by inserting this passage just before the order to display the memory:

```
?
?
```

```
* PROFILUP.CMD
* Purpose:  A preliminary version of ProfileUp, to update
*   the memory variables stored in Profile.Mem.
*
SET DEFAULT TO B
SET TALK OFF
* The next lines set up a loop which lets you enter as
*   many changes as necessary.
STORE T to Continue
DO While Continue=T
 ERASE
  ?
  ?
  ?'      Submetropolis Weekly Satellite'
  ?'      System Profile Update Program'
  ?'      ===============================' 
  ?
  ?'      Your current values are:'
  ?
* The next two items recover and display the data stored
*   in Profile.Mem
 RESTORE from Profile.Mem
 DISPLAY Memory
?
* Prompts and Inputs
 ACCEPT 'Item to change' to Item
 INPUT 'Please Enter the New Value' to Value
 STORE Value to &Item
 RELEASE Item, Value
 SAVE to Profile.Mem
 INPUT 'Would you like to make more changes? (Y/N)' to Continue
ENDDO While Continue
RETURN
```

Fig. 3-4. Profilup, the second update file.

```
?'      Submetropolis Weekly Satellite'
?'      System Profile Update Program'
?'      ==============================='
?
?'      Your current values are:'
?
```

With this addition, we'll save the file as **ProfileUp.Cmd**, listed in Fig. 3-4. DO that program, and your screen should look something like this:

```
Submetropolis Weekly Satellite
System Profile Update Program
===============================
```

```
     Your current values are:

COMPANY        (C)    Submetropolis Weekly Satellite
SLOGAN         (C)    All the News That Fits, We Print
STREET         (C)    1234 Gully Wash
ADDRESS        (C)    Yawning Gap, Wyoming 77776
PHONE          (C)    (307) 555-4321
EMPMAX         (N)       16
WORKWK         (N)       40
PAYFLAG        (N)     2500
FICAPCT        (N)    0.067
FICAMAX        (N)       35700
CHECKNO        (N)     0
BALANCE        (N)     0
INVOICENO      (N)     0
ORDERNO        (N)     0
DATE           (N)    84
** TOTAL **    15 VARIABLES USED    00171 BYTES USED
```

Item to change:

Now we have an appropriate title, a little more information and a small taste of graphic design. It saves some confusion and adds a little class. Your work looks—and is—more professional. Users will no longer get the impression they're working with something that's homemade.

Left to its own devices, dBASE will format its own screens. This is one way you can take command.

The question mark is dBASE's equivalent to the BASIC PRINT command. We used it in two ways here: by itself it produces a few blank lines to separate the elements of the display. Used with an expression in quote marks it will display that expression. If you want the display at some place other than the far left of the screen, note that you have to include the necessary number of spaces within the quotation.

There are better and more sophisticated ways to set up a screen display. This program should serve its purpose in its present form, but Fig. 3-5 applies a more advanced method to an all-purpose heading for our invoices, data screens and other purposes.

@ SAY WHAT?

This listing is a format file, a type of command file intended to be used within other programs. If you type this program, then issue the order:

```
. DO Heading.Fmt
```

the results should look like this:

```
        Submetropolis Weekly Satellite
        1234 Gully Wash
        Yawning Gap, Wyoming 77776
(307) 555-4321                                        00/00/00
        All the News That Fits, We Print
================================================================
```

```
*  HEADING.FMT
*  Purpose:   A standard heading for screens and reports
*
ERASE
RESTORE  from B:Profile
@  2,15 SAY Company
@  3,15 SAY Street
@  4,15 SAY Address
@  6,15 SAY Slogan
@  7, 0 SAY Phone
@  7,52 SAY Date()
@  8, 0 SAY "=================================================="
@  8,50 SAY "=========="
RETURN
```

Fig. 3-5. Screen heading.

The proper way to call this routine from a program is SET FORMAT to **Heading**. But in any event, how did we get from the odd-looking entries in the format file to the printed heading? Let's find out.

After the usual initial identification, the first "working command" is to:

```
RESTORE from B:Profile
```

This, you should remember, recalls the permanent memory variable stored in **Profile**. Next, the file puts them in their assigned places:

```
@  2,15 SAY Company
@  3,15 SAY Street
@  4,15 SAY Address
@  6,15 SAY Slogan
@  7, 0 SAY Phone
```

The @ stands for "at," and the two numbers are coordinates. @ 2,15 means "at line 2, column 15." At that point, dBASE will display the memory variable called **Company**. In similar fashion, this format file then spots the other items of information. There's also something else:

```
@  7,50 SAY Date()
```

The paired brackets at the end of this entry are a signal to display the date you entered when you first fired up dBASE. If you didn't do that, you could have accomplished the same thing later with the command SET DATE TO, followed of course by the date. If you had specified a date in either way, it would appear where the zeroes now are at the lower right of the heading.

The last two entries add a line to separate the heading from the material below it. Notice the quote marks. You'll also notice that this form is 60 spaces wide but there's room for only 50 dashes in the command file format we've chosen. Thus, it takes two command lines to dash from end to end:

```
@  8, 0 SAY "=================================================="
@  8,50 SAY "=========="
RETURN
```

RETURN is the standard way of ending a command file. It tells dBASE to return to whatever you were doing before you started this procedure.

CREATING A MENU

One of the most useful services you can give to the ordinary user of your system is a useful set of menus. At the earliest practical moment, the user should see a list of operations that can be performed and an invitation to make a choice. The program then should let the user enter a simple, easy-to-understand code entry for that choice and proceed to the task at hand.

This route should be as direct and as clearly marked as you can make it, and the user should not have to contend with difficult commands or tricky syntax. The purpose of a menu is to let the user deal with the computer on the user's terms, not the computer's. To do this, a good menu will have these qualities.

- ☐ It is simple, uncluttered and easy to read. If the screen presents too many options, the user will have trouble reading them all and making a choice. Instead, use a system of submenus, such as those in Fig. 3-6. Let the user choose the major function, such as payroll, accounts payable or inventory; that selection will lead to a second menu of specific jobs such as entering data or publishing a report.
- ☐ It always gives the user an escape route. There should always be a way back to the previous menu, to dBASE or to the operating system. The user who makes a bad choice from the menu should not be stuck with it. There should always be an easy way to go back and correct the error.
- ☐ The experienced user should not be required to use the menu. The same kind of escape routes that

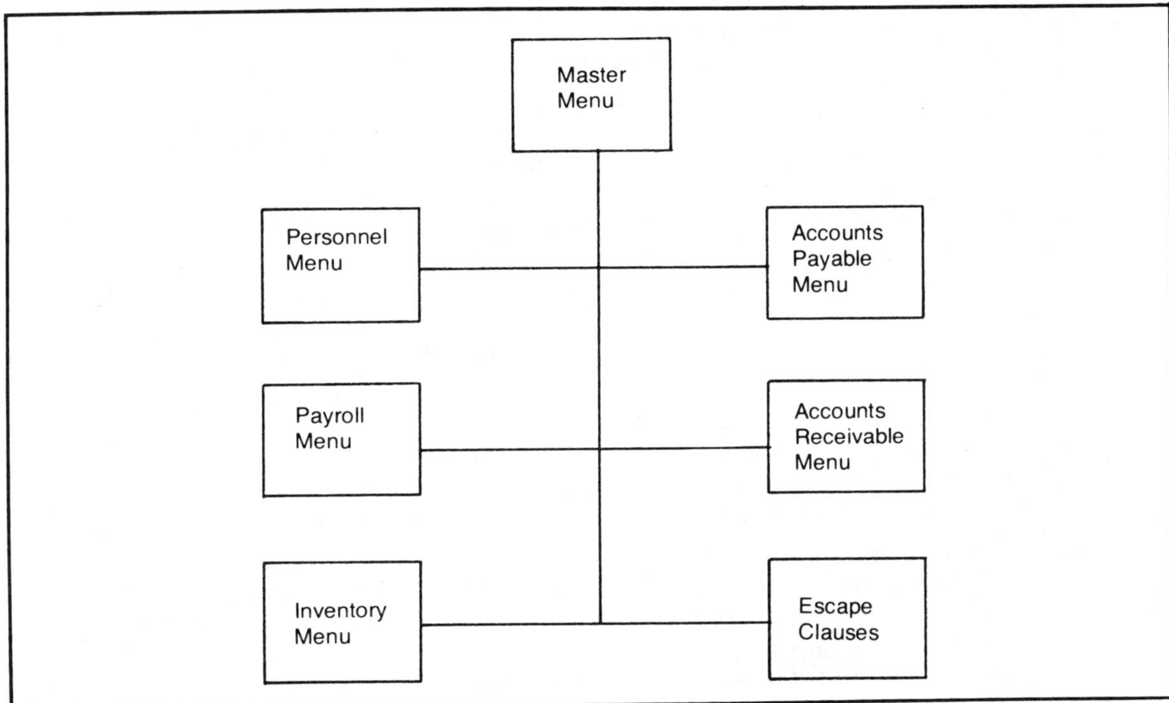

Fig. 3-6. The main menu structure.

```
* MASTER.CMD
* Purpose:  Master menu for business management system.
* Uses: Profile.Mem
* Variables: Choice (C).  Stores the selected option to
*                 direct the program to the proper file.
SET DEFAULT TO B
SET TALK OFF
ERASE
SET INTENSITY OFF
SET PRINT OFF
RESTORE from B:Profile
DO WHILE t
@  1,25 SAY Company
@  3, 0 SAY Slogan
@  3,72 SAY Date()
@  4, 0 SAY "========================================================="
@  4,50 SAY "================================================="
@  6,35 SAY "MASTER MENU"
@  7,21 SAY "You may select any of these activities:"
@  8,21 SAY "---------------------------------------------"
@  9,21 SAY "1    Human Resources"
@ 10,21 SAY "2    Payroll"
@ 11,21 SAY "3    Inventory"
@ 12,21 SAY "4    Accounts Payable"
@ 13,21 SAY "5    Accounts Receivable"
@ 14,21 SAY "---------------------------------------------"
@ 15,21 SAY "R    Return to Direct Command Level"
@ 16,21 SAY "X    Exit to the Operating System"
@ 18,21 SAY "PLEASE ENTER YOUR CHOICE:"
STORE ' ' to Choice
WAIT to Choice
STORE !(Choice) to Choice
DO CASE
 CASE Choice='1'
  * DO Employee
  ? 'When the program is completed, this'
  ? 'option will give you a choice of'
  ? 'personnel operations.'
 CASE Choice='2'
  * DO Paychek
  ? 'When the program is completed, this'
  ? 'option will give you a choice of'
  ? 'payroll operations.'
```

Fig. 3-7. Master menu command file. (Continued on page 67.)

```
CASE CHOICE='3'
  * DO Stock
  ? 'When the program is completed, this'
  ? 'option will give you a choice of'
  ? 'inventory operations.'
CASE CHOICE='4'
  * DO Payable
  ? 'When the program is completed, this'
  ? 'option will give you a choice of'
  ? 'accounts payable operations.'
CASE CHOICE='5'
  * DO Receive
  ? 'When the program is completed, this'
  ? 'option will give you a choice of'
  ? 'accounts receivable operations.'
CASE CHOICE='R'
  ERASE
  CANCEL
CASE CHOICE='X'
  ERASE
  QUIT
OTHERWISE
  @ 22,10 SAY 'The entry you have chosen is not available'
  @ 23,10 SAY 'Press any key to make another choice'
  WAIT
  ERASE
ENDCASE
ENDDO While t
RETURN
```

let you correct an error gracefully should also give you the means to enter a direct command in the dBASE query language.

The system outlined in Part II has six major functions: Personnel, Payroll, Inventory, Payables, Receivables and Budgeting. Figure 3-7 will set up the master menu with which you can choose among these activities. It creates a menu screen that should look like Fig. 3-8.

In Detail

We've added one more housekeeping item to this program. Take a look at the introductory remarks:

```
* MASTER.CMD
* Purpose:  Master menu for business management
* system
* Uses: Profile.Mem
```

```
* Variables: Choice (C).  Stores the selected
* option to direct the program to the proper
* file.
```

Consider this technique for your own files. It includes a description of the program's purpose and the memory variables the program will use. It gives future readers who may want to understand how the program works useful clues to its purpose and operation. Given the number of names you must assign to files, fields, variables and all the other elements of dBASE, it can be useful to include such a listing, just to help you keep things straight. This is a standard Pascal technique that's useful in dBASE as well.

```
SET DEFAULT TO B
SET TALK OFF
ERASE
SET INTENSITY OFF
SET FORMAT TO SCREEN
```

These SET commands establish the default settings for your program, altering them when appropriate from the dBASE defaults. This list sets the default drive to B, the TALK messages off, and the dual intensity off as well. It also sets up this file as a screen display rather than a printed report.

One reason to have such a list at the beginning is to wipe out any contrary instructions that still may be kicking around from a program you've previously run.

The intensity setting is optional. In its normal default setting, dBASE makes widespread use of bright and dim screen displays—too widespread for many tastes. In this case, at the normal setting the entire

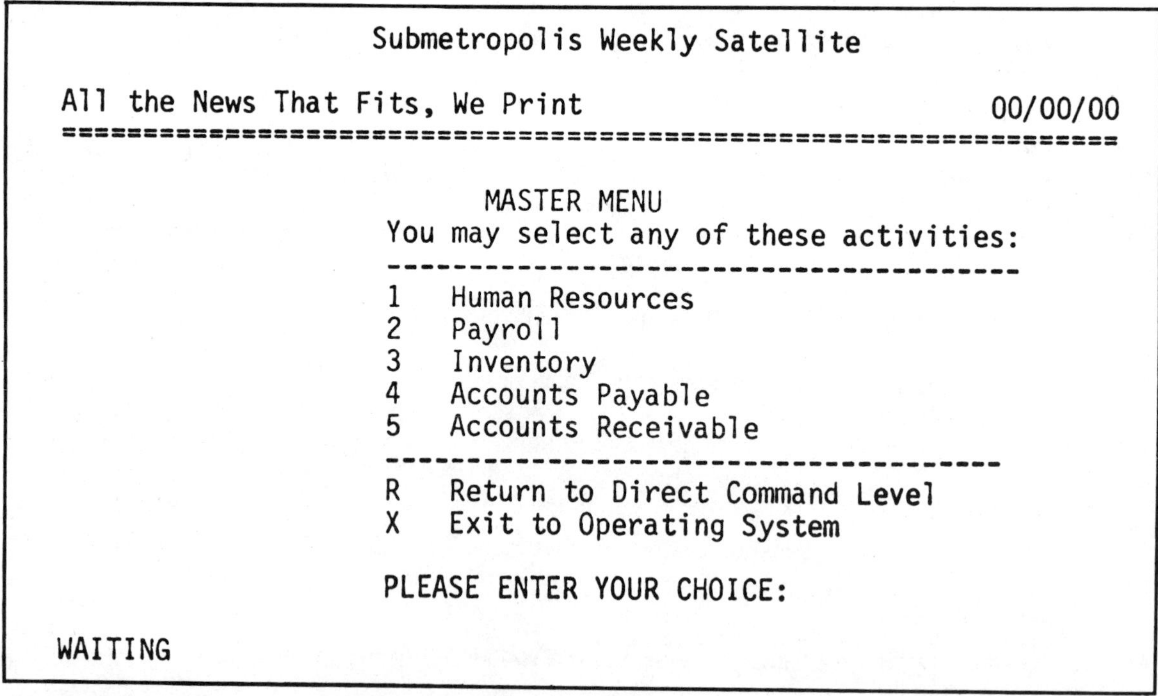

```
              Submetropolis Weekly Satellite

All the News That Fits, We Print                    00/00/00
=============================================================

                         MASTER MENU
              You may select any of these activities:
              ------------------------------------------
              1     Human Resources
              2     Payroll
              3     Inventory
              4     Accounts Payable
              5     Accounts Receivable
              ------------------------------------------
              R     Return to Direct Command Level
              X     Exit to Operating System

              PLEASE ENTER YOUR CHOICE:


WAITING
```

Fig. 3-8. Master menu on the screen.

menu would have been displayed in dimmer type. Setting the intensity off puts everything at normal brightness. If the dimmer displays don't bother you, you don't have to bother with this command.

RESTORE from B:Profile

Again, we're picking up the permanent memory variables stored in **Profile**. You must pick up all the variables in that file, even though you're only using a few of them. You also must issue any RESTORE commands before you establish any other memory variables. RESTORE wipes the memory slate clean, and anything already in storage will be wiped out. The recent dBASE upgrade, Version 2.4, has some ways around these restrictions; those who have earlier versions must live with them.

DO WHILE t

DO, as you know, is the standard command to execute a program. You also can impose conditions as in this statement, which translates, "DO WHILE true," or "DO until told to stop." This creates what is sometimes called an *infinite loop*. You will continue to have menu choices until you specifically indicate you are done. You'd do this by using the R or X commands at the bottom of the screen. Other variations on DO WHILE include:

DO WHILE .NOT. EOF

EOF means *end of file*. You'd use this instruction to sort through the records in the database, taking them up one by one until you reach the end.

```
STORE T to more
DO WHILE more
```

You'll use this version to enter data. Say, for example, you are adding new files to a database. After each entry, the program will present you with a choice: do you wish to add more? As long as you do, the variable **More** will be true, and the procedure will repeat itself. If you indicate you are through, More will be changed to false, and the program will move to its next step.

```
STORE 0 to Counter
DO WHILE Counter < 5
```

Here is dBASE's equivalent to BASIC's FOR/NEXT routine. After you issue this pair of commands, your program will do whatever, it's supposed to do on each swing through the loop. Then it will reach the command:

```
STORE Counter + 1 to Counter
```

This command increases the value of the variable **Counter** by one every time you pass through the loop. If you started with the counter at 0, the next time through it will read 1, and so on. Once the counter reaches 5, the program will move on to the next procedure.

```
@  1,25 SAY Company
@  3, 0 SAY Slogan
@  3,72 SAY Date()
@  4, 0 SAY "================================================================="
@  4,50 SAY "==============================="
@  6,35 SAY "MASTER MENU"
```

```
@  7,21 SAY "You may select any of these activities."
@  8,21 SAY "------------------------------------"
@  9,21 SAY "1    Human Resources"
@ 10,21 SAY "2    Payroll"
@ 11,21 SAY "3    Inventory"
@ 12,21 SAY "4    Accounts Payable"
@ 13,21 SAY "5    Accounts Receivable"
@ 14,21 SAY "------------------------------------"
@ 15,21 SAY "R    Return to Direct Command Level"
@ 16,21 SAY "X    Exit to the Operating System"
@ 18,21 SAY "PLEASE ENTER YOUR CHOICE:"
```

These instructions lay out the screen using @ theSAY sequence. Notice that, along with the listings for the six submenus we plan to write, there are two "escape valve" entries. The first will return the user to the dBASE dot. The second goes all the way back to the A) of the operating system.

```
STORE ' ' to Choice
WAIT to Choice
STORE !(Choice) to Choice
```

We'll use the memory variable **Choice** to store and execute the operator's selection. Unfortunately, it takes all three of these commands to do it properly. The first command uses the quote marks to define **Choice** as a character variable. At the moment it stores only a blank.

The second line instructs the program to WAIT for the user to make a selection. During this process dBASE will note (somewhat impatiently) that it's WAITing. The other input commands, ACCEPT and INPUT also could have been used here; WAIT is probably the best choice for a menu selection because it responds immediately to a single keystroke. Once the operator has hit any key, the value of that key is stored in the variable **Choice**.

The third line is one you'll need any time the user might enter a character. It automatically converts any letter stored in **Choice** to uppercase. The "!" indicates the dBASE function which makes such conversions. The mechanics of this command are to read the variable now stored as **Choice**, convert it to uppercase and store it back in the same place.

Why is this necessary? With only a few exceptions, such as T and t for "true," dBASE treats the capital and lowercase versions of the same letter as two *different* characters. Thus, should we wish to take the "R" option from this menu, an entry of "r" would bring an error message instead of the results we want. By using the uppercase conversion function, either entry is acceptable.

A Case of Options

dBASE recognizes an IF/ELSE set of options, but it also offers DO CASE/OTHERWISE as a useful alternative, particularly for applications like this menu. With this command you tell dBASE to DO something in CASE your specified conditions are met. You then can list the alternatives.

```
CASE Choice='1'
 * DO PersMenu
```

The long version of these instructions is this: in CASE the user entered a "1" into the variable **Choice**, dBASE should DO a command file called **Employee**. There will be a menu of choices within the human resources category.

Employee hasn't written yet, so the instruction to invoke it has been starred as a comment. We'll have to remove that star later, once there is an **Employee** file to DO.

```
? 'When the program is completed, this'
? 'option will give you a choice of'
? 'personnel operations.'
```

These three lines are known as a *stub*. Since the program can't perform its intended function yet, the stub gives the menu portion something to do: it will display that message. This will let you try out the menu without having to wait to complete the full program.

The listing continues:

```
CASE Choice='2'
 * DO PayMenu
 ? 'When the program is completed, this'
 ? 'option will give you a choice of'
 ? 'payroll operations.'
CASE CHOICE='3'
 * DO InvMenu
 ? 'When the program is completed, this'
 ? 'option will give you a choice of'
 ? 'inventory operations.'
CASE CHOICE='4'
 * DO PablMenu
 ? 'When the program is completed, this'
 ? 'option will give you a choice of'
 ? 'accounts payable operations.'
CASE CHOICE='5'
 * DO RecvMenu
 ? 'When the program is completed, this'
 ? 'option will give you a choice of'
 ? 'accounts receivable operations.'
```

The rest of the incomplete menu entries thus are handled the same way. Now we come to the two escape clauses:

```
CASE CHOICE='R'
 ERASE
 CANCEL
CASE CHOICE='X'
 ERASE
 QUIT
```

"R" is the user response that is supposed to return to the dBASE prompt, and within a dBASE procedure, CANCEL is the command to do that; QUIT is the command to shut down dBASE itself.

First, though, it's important to clear the screen with the command ERASE. Otherwise you may find your next commands overlaying each other—while the menu scrolls into oblivion somewhere over the top of the console. Even the most experienced and tolerant user will not willingly put up with this. ERASE is an easy way to get a fresh start after you retreat.

Otherwise . . .

This is the final option in a DO CASE sequence; it's dBASE's way of saying, "None of the above." If none of the CASEs fit the current condition—in other words, if the user hit the wrong key by mistake—this is the command dBASE will execute. We'll use it to tell the user of the error and offer another chance:

```
@ 22,10 SAY 'The entry you have chosen is not available'
@ 23,10 SAY 'Press any key to make another choice'
```

Of all the sad words of computer and word processor, the saddest are *syntax error*. No phrase does more to tell you you're in trouble or less to tell you what to do about it.

It's impossible to diagnose every possible mistake a user might make, but you should try, at least, to suggest a starting place in the search for a solution. In the case of a simple menu entry like this, the easiest solution is to let the user go back and try again.

That may sound obvious to you, but it might not be obvious to the user. Be a good person. Include a line that tells the user what to do next.

```
WAIT
ERASE
```

WAIT, you'll remember, responds to the first keystroke it receives. This time the program needs wait only until the user has read and responded to the message; there's no need to store or process the entry. As the instructions suggest, any key will do. Again, we ERASE the screen before it has a chance to produce more confusion.

```
ENDCASE
ENDDO While t
RETURN
```

These three commands take care of the loose ends. ENDCASE is the signal to end the DO CASE routine, and ENDDO ends the DO WHILE sequence. The note after the command is optional but useful. Some procedures have more than one DO WHILE command; it can be helpful to know which of these you are ending.

This program also is an example of nested commands—one working inside another. The DO WHILE command was in effect for most of the program; while it was operating you also used the DO CASE sequence. Along with identifying the commands you are starting and ending, it is helpful to indent the listings to show which sequences are working inside which others.

It's also important to make sure that you end these commands exactly in the *reverse order* you started them. For example, in this program the DO WHILE command came ahead of DO CASE. You could not issue an ENDDO before you first provided an ENDCASE—at least you couldn't do it successfully.

RETURN closes out the operation and returns you to your starting point.

Type up this program and try it out. See what happens when you make an entry. More important, see what happens when you hit the wrong key.

THE ART OF GETTING A DATE

When dBASE first comes online it asks you for the date. You don't have to enter it at that time, but it's a good idea for at least two reasons:

□ The date then stays on record until you issue the QUIT command at the end of the run. Any time you want the date you can recall it with the internal function DATE( ).

□ dBASE checks the date for you. If you make an obvious mistake like calling for a 13th month or a 32nd day, dBASE will simply ignore your request and ask for the date again. This process can't screen out every error, but it can correct dates that obviously are incorrect.

There are times, though, when you'll want to bypass the dBASE date function and enter the date yourself during the course of a program. The **DateChek** procedure, Fig. 3-10 can run the same kind of check on these entries. It does so by screening out months with a number larger than 12, days with a number larger than 31, and years that don't match the current one. It also will remind you if no date has been entered.

This is not a self-contained program. It is a module to be used within a larger program, either by writing it in or by calling it up with a DO command. In its present form it's written so you can enter a date and test your work. A minor change—deleting the first line—may be needed to make it a usable module for other programs:

```
* DATECHEK.CMD
* Purpose:  Checks for date entries and for obvious errors.
* Variables: Date (C)  A memory variable for the current
  date.
* NoDate (L)  Memory variable used in processing.
*   If true, the date has not been confirmed.
```

```
* DATECHEK.CMD
* Purpose:  Checks for date entries and for obvious errors.
* Variables: Date (C)  A memory variable for the current date.
* NoDate (L)  Memory variable used in processing.
*   If true, the date has not been confirmed.
*
STORE DATE() to Date
STORE T to NoDate
DO WHILE NoDate
  IF VAL($(Date,1,2)) > 12;
    .OR. VAL($(Date,1,2)) < 1;
    .OR. VAL($(Date,4,2)) > 31;
    .OR. VAL($(Date,4,2)) < 1;
    .OR. VAL($(Date,7,2)) <> 84
    STORE "          " to Date
    @ 23, 5 SAY "Date Incorrect or Not on Record"
    ACCEPT "     Please Enter Correct Date (MM/DD/YY)" to Date
    STORE T TO NoDate
  ELSE
    STORE F to NoDate
  ENDIF
SET DATE TO &DATE
ENDDO
RETURN
```

Fig. 3-9. Datecheck command file.

Before you can use this procedure, the date to be tested must be saved in a memory variable called, naturally enough, **Date**. The **NoDate** variable indicates whether an acceptable date is on record; the program will continue to run until that is done.

```
STORE DATE() to Date
```

To test this procedure, first use the SET DATE TO command to enter the date of your choice. This line then will STORE your selected date to the variable **Date**. In actual use, this line should appear only if you have previously set the dBASE Date() function. If the program has STORED the date in a memory variable, delete this line.

```
STORE T to NoDate
DO WHILE NoDate
```

You declare that **Nodate** is true—that you do not have a confirmed date on record. You then use the DO WHILE command to order the program to run as long as that is the case. (The full, official version of this command would be DO WHILE NoDate=T, but the version in this program is acceptable shorthand.)

Now we come to one long line (the semicolons mean the line continues) that will make you wonder about all those statements that dBASE uses plain English:

```
IF VAL($(Date,1,2)) > 12;
 .OR. VAL($(Date,1,2)) < 1;
 .OR. VAL($(Date,4,2)) > 31;
 .OR. VAL($(Date,4,2)) < 1;
 .OR. VAL($(Date,7,2)) <> 84
```

Here, you folks who know other programming languages, particularly BASIC, should not jump to conclusions. There's a good chance this passage does almost, but not quite, what you think it does.

This is the heart of the procedure, and it does several things. Let's take them one at a time.

First, this sequence uses dBASE's IF command. Much like DO CASE, it sets up a certain list of conditions. If the program meets these conditions it will do one thing; if not, it will do another.

In this instance there are several conditions, separated by the Boolean .OR. This means that if *any* of these items is true, the conditions have been met. Using .AND. in this situation would have meant that *all* the items must be true.

But what conditions are we setting up? A look at the end of each command might give you a clue.

The first line will do whatever it does if it encounters a value that is greater than 12. That sounds suspiciously like the number of months in a year. The next entry suggests that the same thing will happen if the value is less than 1.

In similar fashion, the next pair of entries screens out values that are more than 31 or less than 1. Sounds like the maximum number of days in a month. The last entry rejects anything that isn't equal to 84. You can change that figure, of course, to represent the current year. It's stored in the **Profile** for just that purpose.

Notice the way this sequence is structured. It looks for exceptions—entries that are *outside* the ranges of a normally correct date.

Figuring the Date

It is clear, then, that this sequence checks out your entries for the month, day and year. But how does it obtain the entries to check? A "zoom lens" approach can help find the answer. First, let's focus on just one line:

```
IF VAL($(Date,1,2)) > 12;
```

This is the segment that checks for month entries larger than 12. Let's zoom in a little closer on the part that expresses that entry:

```
VAL($(Date,1,2))
```

As it stands now in this procedure, **Date** is a character variable. That's necessary for the string search operation we'll be doing in a few moments. To check the entries against the appropriate numbers, though, we must convert it to a numeric version. VAL is the dBASE function which does that.

In its simplest form, we could convert the date from character to numerical simply by saying VAL(Date). The VAL command converts everything within the brackets to a numerical entry. In this case it would convert the entire date.

But we don't want the whole date all at once. At this point in the proceedings we want only the part that indicates the month. That's indicated in the program by this part of the listing:

```
$(Date,1,2)
```

The "$" calls up dBASE's substring function. It searches for a particular sequence of characters within a full string variable. Earlier, we used a version of it to search for a key word within the titles of a list of articles. Here, we use it to search for a pair of digits within the date we are testing.

Which digits? Within this pair of brackets we specify, in order, that we will look in the variable **Date**, start with the first character and pull out the first two. Those happen to be the two digits that represent the month. Then we apply the test of whether they're more than 12. The next portion of this sequence calls up the same two digits for the less-than-one test.

When we get to the month portion, we specify:

```
VAL($(Date,4,2))
```

This means we want the value of the substring within **Date** that begins with the fourth character and contains two characters. (Remember, the slash in the standard date format makes the first digit of the month the fourth, not the third). Having extracted the value, we can test it against the range of legitimate possibilities. Then we can do the same with the seventh and eighth digits, which represent the year.

A word, too, about the punctuation: the expression to be converted by VAL is within the outer set of brackets; the location of the substring is within the inner set.

Making the Correction

Remember, we're still within a loop that continues to operate if we do not have a valid date. If the results of the tests we've run indicate that that still is the case, the program sets up a way to correct the error:

```
STORE "         " to Date
@ 23, 5 SAY "Date Incorrect or Not on Record"
ACCEPT "     Please Enter Correct Date (MM/DD/YY)" to Date
STORE T TO NoDate
```

Here, the program blanks out the incorrect date and at the bottom of the screen displays an error message: either the date is incorrect or you have not yet entered one. Just below that, the ACCEPT command will display a prompt, including the correct form for the entry, and will store your new entry in the variable **Date**.

But is the new date correct? We haven't verified that, so again we'll signal dBASE that **NoDate** is true and there is a date to be verified. The procedure then will run the test again.

If the date passes the test this time, ELSE will take us to the alternative of the IF command:

```
   STORE F to NoDate
  ENDIF
SET DATE TO &Date
ENDDO
RETURN
```

Pardon the double negative, but we now can tell the program that **NoDate** is false—that the date has been checked out successfully. Then we can close out the IF and DO WHILE commands, remembering that they're nested and must be closed in the proper order. To complete the job, we set the dBASE date function to reflect our newly verified date and RETURN to the program that will use it.

Other Possibilities

It is possible to make this program more sophisticated. For example, an extended IF sequence could be set up to SAY, for example, that if the month is 06, the maximum number of days is 30. If you want to go deeper, you could allow for the added day in a leap year. A real programming challenge awaits us at the turn of the century. We may use some of these techniques in later programs.

Remember, though, that **DateChek** is designed to catch only certain types of errors. Its limited scope doesn't justify an intensive programming effort—although as you become more comfortable with dBASE it might be fun to try.

Part 2

Putting dBASE to Work

At this point the emphasis is going to change. The purpose of Part I was to help you understand what dBASE can do and to give you some idea, at least, of how to go about it. It was not a complete tutorial by any means. In particular, we passed over some commands that do *almost* the same things as those we did mention, but in slightly different ways. You can pick these up as you encounter them in this part or by checking in the dBASE manual.

By now, though, you should have some fundamental understanding of what dBASE is and how it works, and now our object is to start putting dBASE to useful work in your business.

The shift in emphasis also means some changes in the dBASE procedures you will encounter. The procedures listed in Part I were designed primarily to help you understand what dBASE can do. In this part, the procedures will be written for the sake of getting your work done. At times that may mean a slightly different approach. The procedures you encounter here may have counterparts in Part I, but they might not be the same.

Since no prewritten program is exactly right in every detail for every business, these procedures are written and explained so you can follow them easily and, if you wish, modify them to better suit your own purposes.

Another point of emphasis in this section will be on some of the things that other widely available programs *don't* do.

For example, you'll find some accounting and inventory routines here; you'll find them many other places, too. Chances are, though, that few if any will exactly meet your needs. In fact, there are consulting firms that do nothing but match up small businesses with the appropriate microcomputer accounting programs for their particular needs. The emphasis here, then, will not be on building a system that easily might not work for you but on starting with the kind of results you desire, then providing model routines that can provide those results.

In other areas, you won't readily find counterparts for these routines. The personnel management system in Chapter 4, for example, is adapted from established mainframe practices, but it adapts these techniques specifically to the needs of a small business. Take a look, too, at the ratio analysis techniques in the inventory section. This can be a valuable technique for balancing your inventory and cash needs—something that's often vital to a small company's survival. There are also many other routines that you might not readily find somewhere else, particularly in a form tailored for small businesses.

Throughout this section, too, there is an emphasis on *keeping it simple*. As a small business manager, you probably don't have time to struggle with the details of a sophisticated program designed primarily for larger operations. We'll try to keep things to your level, offering practical programs that you can put to immediate, productive use.

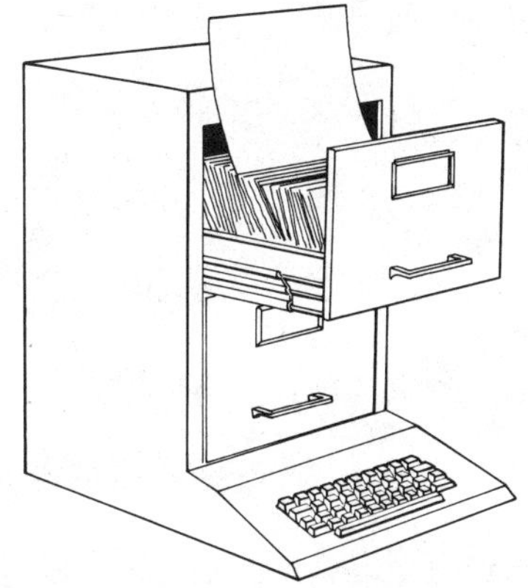

Chapter 4

Managing
Human Resources

Many people see the computer as an impersonal kind of device, turning thinkers into typists and technicians into robots. These things have happened but, as it's often been said before, the computer is a totally neutral piece of equipment. It behaves *exactly* the way you tell it to behave.

This seemingly inhumane piece of hardware actually can be a tool to improve the all-important "human factors" in your company. Applied to the job of managing your personnel, the computer can go farther: it can help you make best use of the human resources in your organization. You can identify the skills and talents you have available, it can help make sure people are assigned to useful, productive work and are paid according to their contributions. You can help people develop their career potential and show that there is room to grow even within the confines of a small business. The result is better use of your human resources, accompanied by better morale and stronger loyalty.

HOW DO WE DO ALL THAT?

The basic technique, as suggested earlier, is to begin at the end—to decide what you want to accomplish. This is essentially a goal-setting process. A typical small business manager might set goals like this:

- ☐ Reducing the clerical workload of maintaining personnel records.
- ☐ Keeping track of who is eligible for what benefits, and of which employees have chosen things like optional group insurance coverage.
- ☐ Making sure you pay your people fairly, offering neither too little to compensate for their time and talent nor paying a great deal more than the local labor market demands.

☐ Identifying people who are ready for higher responsibilities, and providing the training or other necessary background.

☐ Having the information on hand to meet regulatory requirements, back up tax deductions and so on.

☐ Making sure you maintain only information that is essential. Unneeded information only takes up disk space and risks an invasion of the employees' privacy.

WHAT'S IT TAKE?

Computers have yet to do very much about the tedium of entering data into the system in the first place. A system like dBASE can keep you from having to enter the same information more than once. It can use the same files for multiple purposes.

Where dBASE really shines, however, is in getting the information back out again. Under a manual system it could take hours to check each individual's record to determine, for example, how many people are old enough to qualify for vested pension benefits. With dBASE you can get the information in seconds, just by making the right request.

The next step in setting up the personnel system, then, is to decide what kinds of information and reports the system must provide to meet the goals you have set.

The goal of reducing clerical work can be met in general by dBASE's capacity to extract and report information. That feature alone will save hours of manual labor. The basic *personnel module* is set up so you can use it in combination with the other modules, retrieving things like names and addresses so you need record them only once.

The second goal can be met by a *benefits report*. One module in this section will set up a report that asks such things as who has chosen optional benefits or is contributing to a simplified pension plan.

A *career module* will help you keep track of employee assignments and evaluations. It will include a simple method to evaluate the demands of each job in your organization and the ability of each employee. This is a simplified system to help you judge a proper rate of pay for the person and position.

This module also will let you record each employee's individual evaluations, raises, and promotions, and to identify future potential. The reports you generate from this module can do two things: keep track of each employee's promise and potential, and help you identify the people who might meet future needs in the organization.

The basic personnel module will include room for information on sex, race, handicaps, and other special conditions you might need to satisfy an equal opportunity requirement.

Avoid the temptation to call for unnecessary information. At best it wastes storage space in your system; at worst you could find yourself with a data file full of sensitive personal information, and with the increasing interest in employee rights and privacy, unnecessary personal data is only an invitation to trouble. Make sure the reports you specify contain only useful and necessary information, and make sure that only this type of data goes into your dBASE files.

To begin the process, the command DO EMPLOYEE will produce the menu shown in Fig. 4-1. It is generated by the command file **Employee.Cmd,** Fig. 4-2.

SETTING UP THE MASTER FILE

The first file to create is the one around which the rest of the employee system will revolve—the employee master file. We'll call it **Employee.Dbf,** but with the warning that it's not the faulty file of the same name we used in Part I. Our new **Employee** file will look like this:

```
================================================================
                  PERSONNEL SYSTEM MENU
                  ---------------------
           1:  Maintain Employee Files
           2:  Maintain Career Development Files
           3:  Maintain Applicant Files
           4:  Monitor Equal Opportunity
           5:  Produce Reports
           6:  Index Databases
           -----------------------------------
           R:  Work Directly in dBASE
           X:  Return to Operating System

           Please Enter Your Choice ==>
```

Fig. 4-1. Personnel menu.

```
STRUCTURE FOR FILE:   EMPLOYEE.DBF
NUMBER OF RECORDS:    00000
DATE OF LAST UPDATE:  00/00/00
PRIMARY USE DATABASE
FLD        NAME        TYPE WIDTH    DEC
001     SSNO            C     011
002     LAST            C     010
003     FIRST           C     010
004     INITIAL         C     001
005     STREET          C     015
006     CITY            C     010
007     STATE           C     002
008     ZIP             C     005
009     PHONE           C     012
010     BORN            C     008
011     SEX             C     001
012     MINORITY        L     001
013     HIRED           C     012
014     MARRIED         L     001
015     DEPEND          N     002
016     HEALTH          L     001
017     MMED            L     001
018     DENTAL          L     001
019     LIFE            L     001
020     PENSION         L     001
** TOTAL **                   00118

. INDEX ON SSNO TO EMPNO

. INDEX ON LAST TO EMPNAME
```

```
* EMPLOYEE.CMD
SET TALK OFF
SET CONSOLE ON
SET FORMAT TO SCREEN
SET COLON OFF
SET BELL OFF
SET INTENSITY OFF
USE EMPLOYEE INDEX EMPNO, EMPNAME
STORE T TO more
DO WHILE more
ERASE
@  3, 0 SAY "========================================================="
@  3,50 SAY "==============================="
@  5,29 SAY "PERSONNEL SYSTEM MENU"
@  6,29 SAY "---------------------"
@  7,24 SAY "1:  Maintain Employee Files"
@  8,24 SAY "2:  Maintain Career Development Files"
@  9,24 SAY "3:  Maintain Applicant Files"
@ 10,24 SAY "4:  Monitor Equal Opportunity"
@ 11,24 SAY "5:  Produce Reports"
@ 12,24 SAY "6:  Index Databases"
@ 13,24 SAY "-------------------------------"
@ 14,24 SAY "R:  Work Directly in dBASE"
@ 15,24 SAY "X:  Return to Operating System"
@ 18,24 SAY "Please Enter Your Choice ==>"
SET CONSOLE OFF
WAIT TO choice
SET CONSOLE ON
DO CASE
        CASE CHOICE = '1'
                DO EMPLOYEE.CMD
        CASE CHOICE = '2'
                DO CAREER.CMD
        CASE CHOICE = '3'
                DO APPLY.CMD
        CASE CHOICE = '4'
                DO EQUAL.CMD
        CASE CHOICE = '5'
                DO EMPLOYEE.RPT
        CASE CHOICE = '6'
                DO REINDEX.CMD
        CASE CHOICE = 'R'
                CANCEL
        CASE CHOICE = 'X'
                QUIT
ENDCASE
ENDDO
RELEASE more, choice
RETURN
```

Fig. 4-2. Personnel command file.

The employee's Social Security number will be the key to linking this file with the others in the system. It's a useful identifier which uniquely identifies the employee to whom it has been assigned. The file should be indexed on that number. Since we also probably will want to extract names in alphabetical order, index the file on the last name as well.

Many companies use separate employee numbers for this purpose, and for some that may be a good idea. An employee number can be tailored, for example, to indicate such things as the department to which the employee is assigned. If you have a good reason to assign your own employee number, by all means do so. Otherwise, the Social Security number can adequately serve the purpose in most small firms, so we'll use it here.

The last name, first name, and middle initial are stated separately—it helps in sorting and alphabetizing, particularly when more than one employee has the same last name.

Then come some standard address and phone number entries. The way this file is set up, it has room only for a local number (for example, 555-1234). If your employees live in more than one area code, you'll have to expand the number of spaces in this field to take in the three added digits, the two brackets and another space.

The minority field will identify members of recognized minority groups. You can retrieve information based on this entry to examine how your minority group members have fared in such areas as pay and promotions. The sex field lets you do the same for women. Not all small businesses have equal opportunity problems, but monitoring these figures can help avoid the troubles that could come should there be a serious imbalance.

The Data Entry Screen

This new database needs some data, of course. One way is directly, with the APPEND command, but that can be clumsy for inexperienced users. Most good working programs let the operators enter data by setting up a form on the screen and letting the user fill in the blanks. For the **Employee** module, the data entry screen looks like Fig. 4-3.

When the operator calls up the routine for adding data to the personnel file, this should appear on the screen. The cursor is in position to make the first entry, the last name. As you enter each item and press

```
                  EMPLOYEE MASTER DATA FORM
    ================================================================
          LAST NAME ==>
          FIRST ==>
          INITIAL ==>
          SOCIAL SECURITY NUMBER (999-99-9999) ==>
          HOME PHONE ==>
          STREET ADDRESS ==>
          CITY ==>
          STATE ==>
          ZIP ==>
          DATE OF BIRTH (MM/DD/YY) ==>
          SEX (M or F) ==>
          MINORITY GROUP MEMBER? ==>
          ================================================
```

Fig. 4-3. Employee screen display.

```
*  EMPLOYEE.FMT
*  Data entry form for EMPLOYEE.DBF
@  1,19 SAY "EMPLOYEE MASTER DATA FORM"
@  2, 0 SAY "==========================================================="
@  2,50 SAY "========="
@  3, 8 SAY "LAST NAME ==>"
@  3,22 GET mlast
@  4, 8 SAY "FIRST ==>"
@  4,18 GET mfirst
@  5, 8 SAY "INITIAL ==>"
@  5,20 GET minitial
@  6, 8 SAY "SOCIAL SECURITY NO. (999-99-9999) ==>"
@  6,46 GET mssno
@  7, 8 SAY "HOME PHONE (999-9999) ==>"
@  7,34 GET mphone
@  8, 8 SAY "STREET ADDRESS ==>"
@  8,27 GET mstreet
@  9, 8 SAY "CITY ==>"
@  9,17 GET mcity
@ 10, 8 SAY "STATE ==>"
@ 10,18 GET mstate
@ 11, 8 SAY "ZIP (99999) ==>"
@ 11,24 GET mzip
@ 12, 8 SAY "DATE OF BIRTH (MM/DD/YY) ==>"
@ 12,37 GET mborn
@ 13, 8 SAY "SEX (M or F) ==>"
@ 13,25 GET msex
@ 14, 8 SAY "MINORITY GROUP MEMBER? ==>"
@ 14,31 GET mminority
@ 16,12 SAY "=============================================="
```

Fig. 4-4. Employee format file.

RETURN, the cursor will move to the next line. This file also is set up such that if you try to use more space than is allocated in the database field, the cursor will automatically move on. You can come back and condense the affected entry either now or later. After the operator has proceeded through the entries, a prompt in the lower part of the screen will ask whether all the entries are correct. A negative answer will let you go through them again and make any necessary changes.

Programs Within Programs

The commands to lay out the screen are in the format file **Employee.Fmt,** Fig. 4-4. This file is called, in turn, by the data entry program, **Employee.Add,** Fig. 4-5. The combined procedure works like this:

```
SET DEFAULT TO B
SET INTENSITY OFF
SET TALK OFF
SET CONSOLE ON
SET COLON OFF
SET BELL OFF
```

These commands establish the initial settings of the system. You might remember some of them. They put you on Disk B, present everything on the screen at the same intensity, and cut out the screen display that repeats the results of your command. We then set the console to the "on" status, just in case the previous program had left it in some other state. This command is necessary to see the screen.

If the colon setting was left on, the screen would appear with those punctuation marks to note the beginning and end of each entry. The bell—actually a beeper in most computers—alerts you to such things as the end of the allocated space for an entry. I find these more irritating than useful, so I set them off. You're entitled to your own opinion, so specify your settings accordingly.

```
STORE T to more
DO WHILE more
```

This sets up the outermost of two loops in this program. The initial T setting leaves the system ready to accept more entries. At the end of the file, a prompt will ask whether you want to make more entries. A positive answer will leave the setting a T, and the loop will repeat itself. A negative answer changes the setting to F, and the procedure will go on to its end.

```
ERASE
STORE '                ' to mlast
STORE '                ' to mfirst
STORE ' ' to minitial
STORE '                  ' to mstreet
STORE '             ' to mcity
STORE '   ' to mstate
STORE '      ' to mzip
STORE '         ' to mphone
STORE '           ' to mssno
STORE '         ' to mborn
STORE ' ' to msex
STORE F to mminority
STORE '               ' to mhired
STORE Y to mmarried
STORE O to mdepend
```

The format file uses a series of GET commands to retrieve memory variables and display them on the screen. Before it can do that, it obviously must have the variables to GET. These commands store rows of blanks to the series of character variables—but make sure the length of each row matches the space allocated in the database.

```
STORE Y to mhealth
STORE Y to mmmed
```

```
* EMPLOYEE.ADD
* Purpose:  Enter basic data on employees into the database
*           Employee.Dbf.
*
* Set up initial format
SET DEFAULT TO B
SET INTENSITY OFF
SET TALK OFF
SET CONSOLE ON
SET COLON OFF
SET BELL OFF
*
* Set up outer loop to repeat when operator orders
*           further entries
STORE T to more
DO WHILE more
*
* Clear screen and set initial values for variables to be
* added to the file.  The "m" prefix indicates memory
* variables, to distinguish them from their corresponding
* data base fields.
ERASE
STORE '            ' to mlast
STORE '            ' to mfirst
STORE ' ' to minitial
STORE '              ' to mstreet
STORE '            ' to mcity
STORE '   ' to mstate
STORE '      ' to mzip
STORE '          ' to mphone
STORE '            ' to mssno
STORE '        ' to mborn
STORE ' ' to msex
STORE N to mminority
STORE '          ' to mhired
STORE Y to mmarried
STORE 0 to mdepend
STORE Y to mhealth
STORE Y TO mmmed
STORE Y to mdental
STORE Y to mlife
STORE Y to mpension
*
```

Fig. 4-5. Add new employees. (Continued on page 87.)

```
*   Set up inner loop which gives operator a chance to
    correct
* entries before they are added to the file.
STORE T TO continue
DO WHILE continue
*
*   Use format file to produce screen display
SET FORMAT TO EMPLOYEE.FMT
READ
*
*   Select a location near bottom of screen and prompt for
* corrections.
@ 19,0 SAY ' '
INPUT 'DO YOU WISH TO MAKE CORRECTIONS? (Y or N) ==>' to continue
ENDDO WHILE continue
ERASE
*
*   If entries are correct, add them to database.
USE EMPLOYEE INDEX empname, empno
APPEND BLANK
REPLACE LAST with mlast, FIRST with mfirst, INITIAL with minitial
REPLACE STREET with mstreet, CITY with mcity, STATE with mstate
REPLACE ZIP with mzip, PHONE with mphone, BORN with mborn
REPLACE SEX with msex, MINORITY with mminority
REPLACE HIRED with mhired, MARRIED with mmarried, DEPEND with mdepend
REPLACE HEALTH with mhealth, MMED with mmmed, DENTAL with mdental
REPLACE LIFE with mlife, PENSION with mpension
*
* Prompt for further entries.
@ 19,0 SAY ' '
INPUT 'MORE ENTRIES? (Y or N) ==>' to more
ERASE
ENDDO while more
RETURN
```

```
STORE Y to mdental
STORE Y to mlife
STORE Y to mpension
```

This group sets initial variables to indicate which benefits the employee is receiving. The program will assume they are receiving all unless you indicate otherwise when entering the personal data.

```
STORE T TO continue
DO WHILE continue
```

As you might suspect, here's the beginning of the inner loop. It will use **continue** instead of **more** as its variable; otherwise, it works the same.

```
SET FORMAT TO EMPLOYEE.FMT
```

We now call in the separate format file that sets up the screen format. It includes matched pairs of commands like this:

```
@  1,19 SAY "EMPLOYEE MASTER DATA FORM"
@  2, 0 SAY "=================================================
   ==="
@  2,50 SAY "========="
@  3, 8 SAY "LAST NAME ==>"
@  3,22 GET mlast
@  4, 8 SAY "FIRST ==>"
@  4,18 GET mfirst
@  5, 8 SAY "INITIAL ==>"
@  5,20 GET minitial
```

And so on. At the designated line and column coordinates, the commands will SAY the screen heading, the decorative line and the list of entries starting with the last name. After each entry, the program will GET the indicated variable. At this point, it will GET a row of blanks or whatever other initial variable we set earlier. The operator can change these from the keyboard.

Notice that when we get to an entry that requires a particular format, we remind the operator how the entry should look:

```
@  6, 8 SAY "SOCIAL SECURITY NO. (999-99-9999) ==>"
@  6,46 GET mssno
@  7, 8 SAY "HOME PHONE (999-9999) ==>"
@  7,34 GET mphone
```

At the end of the format commands, RETURN does just that, taking us back to the main program, where the next command is:

```
READ
```

Again, this is a command which dBASE will take literally. It will READ the entries you have placed in the GET locations, and these become the new memory variables. Remember that at the next step:

```
@ 19,0 SAY ' '
INPUT 'DO YOU WISH TO MAKE CORRECTIONS? (Y or N) ==>' to
   continue
ENDDO WHILE continue
ERASE
```

The blank on line 19 simply gets the cursor down to that location so the next prompt will appear where we want it, on line 20. There probably are more sophisticated ways to do this, but this is quick and simple—and it works.

The answer to this prompt will determine whether you want to continue or abandon the inner loop. If you reset the continue variable to F (a reply of N will do this, you recall), the program will proceed to its next step. Otherwise, it will go back to the beginning of the inner loop and execute the format program again. The purpose of this is to provide a chance to make any final corrections.

The GET commands again will display the memory variables—but this time they contain the values you just entered. Use the RETURN key to work your way down to any incorrect entries, and make whatever changes are in order.

The loop returns us to the correction prompt again, where a N answer takes us on to:

```
USE EMPLOYEE INDEX empname, empno
```

In setting up the **Employee** database, we called for an index on the employee's last name, calling it **Empname,** and on the Social Security number, calling it **Empno.** This entry opens the database for additions and makes sure the new entries will be properly acknowledged in both indexes.

```
APPEND BLANK
REPLACE LAST with mlast, FIRST with mfirst, INITIAL with
    minitial
REPLACE STREET with mstreet, CITY with mcity, STATE with
    mstate
```

And so on through the list. APPEND BLANK gives you a blank record to work with. The contents of the memory variables then are inserted into the corresponding fields in that record.

```
@ 19,0 SAY ' '
INPUT 'MORE ENTRIES? (Y or N) ==>' to more
ERASE
ENDDO while more
RETURN
```

This sequence closes the outer loop much in the same manner as the inner one. The difference is this: if we repeat this loop it will take us back near the beginning, where the program will again enter blanks into the variables. Thus, the entry screen will be ready to take new entries instead of correcting or replacing old ones.

THE SPECIALIZED FILES

The basic personnel record is the foundation for your main personnel records. It includes basic personal information on each employee, plus the data you need to keep track of employees' fringe benefits, payroll deductions, and pension status. The separate **Career** file will track each employee's personal development and future potential.

Why not include this information with the master file? It could be done, but there are a couple of good reasons to keep them separate.

The **Career** module contains information that treads on at least the edges of your employees' personal privacy. Such personal information should be available only on a need-to-know basis. It shouldn't be widely available to those who need only the type of information that's in the basic file. Setting up the career information in a separate file also lets you share this data with Payroll without sending that department a batch of information not relevant to its needs. If you'd like, you can also use the password procedure we'll describe in the Payroll section to control access to one or more modules.

There's an additional reason for making the **Career** module a separate file. It's a matter of good database design. This will be a running file with a new record added every time the employee gets a raise, promotion or annual review. If we tried to force these into the structure of the basic record, we would find ourselves with limits on the number of entries and an awkward search procedure. Here, the **Career** file is structured to accept these entries as they occur, up to the capacity limits of dBASE and your computer.

Both files will use the employee's Social Security number as links to the general information in the basic file, and for that purpose both will be indexed on that number.

File Structure

The structure of the **Career** file is:

```
STRUCTURE FOR FILE:    CAREER.DBF
NUMBER OF RECORDS:     00000
DATE OF LAST UPDATE:   00/00/00
PRIMARY USE DATABASE
FLD        NAME        TYPE WIDTH      DEC
001        SSNO        C     011
002        REVDATE     C     008
003        DEPT        C     005
004        POSITION    C     010
005        JOBRATE     N     002
006        LEADER      N     001
007        KNOWLEDGE   N     001
008        DECISION    N     001
009        PLANNING    N     001
010        PHYSICAL    N     001
011        PERFORM     N     002
012        PAY         N     007
013        PROMOTED    L     001
014        NEXTEVAL    C     008
015        QUALIFIED   C     020
016        TRAINING    C     020

** TOTAL **                  00122
```

Entering Data

The command file for entering information into this database makes use of the same general system and the same type of screen form as the entry command for the basic file. One reason: an operator's life is much simpler and more pleasant if all the data entry forms follow the same general style and format. The screen display, Fig. 4-6, differs mainly in the number of items to be entered. The data entry and format files, Figs. 4-7 and 4-8, also should look familiar.

The operator will fill in these screens just like the first one. You can leave the job and performance ratings blank for now. Filling them in is the next step.

Right Pay for the Right Job

As you probably can see, the **Career** file is the beginning of a system through which you can evaluate both the challenges of the jobs in your organization and the abilities of your people to fill them.

```
            CAREER DEVELOPMENT DATA FORM
=========================================================
          SOCIAL SECURITY NO. (999-99-9999) ==>
          REVIEW DATE (MM/DD/YY) ==>
          DEPARTMENT ==>
          POSITION ==>
          JOB RATING ==>
                        ----------
PERFORMANCE RATING  from 1 (poor) to 5 (exceptional) ==>
          Knowledge:              Decision-making
          Planning                Leadership
          Physical                OVERALL RATING
                        ----------
          PAY RATE ==>
          PROMOTED THIS PERIOD? ==>
          NEXT REVIEW DATE (MM/DD/YY) ==>
          QUALIFIED FOR ==>
          TRAINING NEEDS ==>
                 =================================
```

Fig. 4-6. Career screen display.

As any student of job and employee evaluation will quickly see, it's possible to set up a much more sophisticated system than the one you're about to encounter. This system, though, is tailored to the small business manager who doesn't have time to operate all the bells and whistles of a typical corporate program. It is useful as long as you realize that any evaluation system, no matter how sophisticated or how thoroughly computerized, can give you an absolute bottom-line answer. This system, like all others of its kind, is intended to help guide your decisions, not to make them for you.

The job evaluation program is based on the guideline method of establishing job ratings and pay grades. It uses one of the simplest possible databases:

```
STRUCTURE FOR FILE:    JOBEVAL.DBF
NUMBER OF RECORDS:     00005
DATE OF LAST UPDATE:   00/00/00
PRIMARY USE DATABASE
FLD          NAME       TYPE WIDTH    DEC
001     CLASS          C      010
002     SALARY         N      007
** TOTAL **                   00018
```

Determine a set of classes for the jobs in your organization. For this purpose, we've chosen five: Unskilled, Low Skill, High Skill, Technical, and Managerial. Pick a number and a range that fairly reflect the span of jobs in your own company. Don't bother with a "technician" scale, for example, if you have no technicians. On the other hand, if you have more than one level of technical skill in your firm, you might want to establish two levels.

Then pick a typical job from each group, one that has counterparts in other companies in your

```
* CAREER.CMD
* Purpose:  Enter data on employee evaluation and career
*           potential into the database Career.Dbf.
*
* Set up initial format
SET DEFAULT TO B
SET INTENSITY OFF
SET TALK OFF
SET CONSOLE ON
SET COLON OFF
SET BELL OFF
*
* Set up outer loop to repeat when operator orders
*           further entries
STORE T to more
DO WHILE more
*
* Clear screen and set initial values for variables to be
* added to the file.  The "m" prefix indicates memory
* variables, to distinguish them from their corresponding
* data base fields.
ERASE
STORE '              ' to mssno
STORE '       ' to mdept
STORE '              ' to mposition
STORE 00 to mjobrate
STORE 00 to mperform
STORE 0.00 to mpay
STORE '          ' to mhired
STORE '          ' to mpromoted
STORE '          ' to mrevdate
STORE '          ' to mnexteval
STORE '              ' to mqualified
STORE '              ' to mtraining
STORE '              ' to mremarks
*
*  Set up inner loop which gives operator a chance to correct
* entries before they are added to the file.
STORE T TO continue
DO WHILE continue
*
** Use format file to produce screen display
SET FORMAT TO CAREER.FMT
READ
```

Fig. 4-7. Career command file. (Continued on page 93.)

```
*
*   Select a location near bottom of screen and prompt for
* corrections.
@ 19,0 SAY ' '
INPUT 'DO YOU WISH TO MAKE CORRECTIONS? (Y or N) ==>' to continue
ENDDO WHILE continue
ERASE
*
*   If entries are correct, add them to database.
USE CAREER INDEX career, position
APPEND BLANK
REPLACE SSNO with mssno
REPLACE DEPT with mdept
REPLACE POSITION with mposition
REPLACE JOBRATE with mjobrate
REPLACE PERFORM with mperform
REPLACE PAY with mpay
REPLACE HIRED with mhired
REPLACE PROMOTED with mpromoted
REPLACE REVDATE with mrevdate
REPLACE NEXTEVAL with mnexteval
REPLACE QUALIFIED with mqualified
REPLACE TRAINING with mtraining
REPLACE REMARKS with mremarks
*
* Prompt for further entries.
@ 19,0 SAY ' '
INPUT 'MORE ENTRIES? (Y or N) ==>' to more
ERASE
ENDDO while more
RETURN
```

community. Find out the typical starting salary for such a job. Balance it against your own needs. You may have some reason to pay less or more than your fellow employers. Pick a starting figure, and enter it into the database. Plan to update these figures at least once a year.

A filled-in database (with some thin-air figures entered for the sake of illustration) might look like this:

```
00001    UNSKILLED        383
00002    LOW SKILL        512
00003    SKILLED          733
00004    TECHNICAL        900
00005    MANAGERIAL      1066
```

Nothing much there but some jobs and some starting salaries. This time, we'll make the dBASE report generator do some work for a change. Start to set up the report form like this:

```
*    Data entry form for EMPLOYEE.DBF
@  1,16 SAY "CAREER DEVELOPMENT DATA FORM"
@  2, 0 SAY "================================================================"
@  2,50 SAY "=========="
@  3, 8 SAY "SOCIAL SECURITY NO. (999-99-9999) ==>"
@  3,46 GET mssno
@  4, 8 SAY "DEPARTMENT ==>"
@  4,23 GET mdept
@  5, 8 SAY "POSITION ==>"
@  5,21 GET mposition
@  6, 8 SAY "JOB RATING ==>"
@  6,23 GET mjobrate
@  7, 8 SAY "PERFORMANCE RATING ==>"
@  7,31 GET mperform
@  8, 8 SAY "PAY RATE ==>"
@  8,21 GET mpay
@  9, 8 SAY "DATE HIRED =="
@  9,23 SAY mhired
@ 10, 8 SAY "DATE OF LAST PROMOTION ==>"
@ 10,36 GET mpromoted
@ 11,8 SAY "LAST REVIEW DATE (MM/DD/YY) ==>"
@ 11,40 GET mrevdate
@ 12,10 SAY "Enter hiring or promotion date if later"
@ 13, 8 SAY "NEXT REVIEW DATE (MM/DD/YY) ==>"
@ 13,40 GET mnexteval
@ 14, 8 SAY "QUALIFIED FOR ==>"
@ 14,26 GET mqualified
@ 15, 8 SAY "TRAINING NEEDS ==>"
@ 15,27 GET mtraining
@ 16, 8 SAY "REMARKS ==>"
@ 16,20 GET mremarks
@ 18,12 SAY "==============================================="
```

Fig. 4-8. Career format file.

. REPORT FORM JOBEVAL

The sequence for drawing the form is:

```
ENTER OPTIONS, M=LEFT MARGIN, L=LINES/PAGE, W=PAGE WIDTH
PAGE HEADING? (Y/N) JOB EVALUATION AND PAY SCALE REPORT
DOUBLE SPACE REPORT? (Y/N) N
ARE TOTALS REQUIRED? (Y/N) N
COL       WIDTH,CONTENTS
001        10,CLASS
ENTER HEADING: CLASS
```

```
002       8,SALARY
ENTER HEADING: BASE PAY
003       8,SALARY*1.25
ENTER HEADING: MIDPOINT
004       8,SALARY*1.5
ENTER HEADING: MAXIMUM
```

Let's take a closer look at this. The first two columns of the report will repeat the class and base pay fields of the database. In the third column, though, we make the report generator perform a little mathematics, adding 25 percent to the base salary for each job class. In the fourth column we add 50 percent. The two salaries give us the midpoint and a maximum salary for each type of job. As you update the base figures each year, this report form will recalculate the rest.

```
CLASS         BASE     MIDPOINT MAXIMUM
              PAY


UNSKILLED      383     478.75     574.50
LOW SKILL      512     640.00     768.00
SKILLED        733     916.25    1099.50
TECHNICAL      900    1125.00    1350.00
MANAGERIAL    1066    1332.50    1599.00
```

Actually, a table like this should use a varied range of percentages. The range of 50 percent between the top and bottom salaries is appropriate for the top-ranked jobs on the scale. At the unskilled level, 30 percent would be more like it, and the other levels would be scaled in between. You can use this procedure, though, and can keep the proper spread in mind when you assign employees to particular points on the pay scale.

EVALUATING EMPLOYEES

A basic principle that's easy to state and hard to observe is this:

Jobs should be evaluated separately from the people who happen to hold them at the moment.

Even when you know and understand this idea it's easy to get mixed up. Try to remember, though, that you analyze a job for what it *requires*—the jobholder for what he or she has to *offer*. The trick is to match the two.

The career data entry screen is designed to guide you through the process of evaluating an employee *after* you've evaluated the job. The details go like this:

```
        CAREER DEVELOPMENT DATA FORM
==================================================================
        SOCIAL SECURITY NO. (999-99-9999) ==>
        REVIEW DATE (MM/DD/YY) ==>
        DEPARTMENT ==>
        POSITION ==>
        JOB RATING ==>

                  -----------
```

You'll fill out this form, creating another entry in the database, every time an employee is given a periodic evaluation—every year is normal. Fill in the Social Security number, the data of the review, the department, and the position. For the job rating, use a scale of 1 to 5 (or any other numbers you'd like) to match the scale of job types you used in the evaluation. In advance, obtain the current salary scale for this type of position.

```
PERFORMANCE RATING    from 1 (poor) to 5 (exceptional) ==>
      Knowledge:                Decision-making
      Planning                  Leadership
      Physical                  OVERALL RATING
                        ----------
```

Rate the employee on a similar scale of 1 to 5 for each of the characteristics you wish to evaluate; it doesn't necessarily have to be the ones listed here. (If you add something, set up a corresponding memory variable in two places in the data entry command file: once when it initializes the values and again when it places them in the database.) Give the employee an overall rating, based on the sum of these factors, and emphasizing those that are particularly important to the job.

On the basis of the employee's rating, determine what spot the employee should have within the pay scale for the job. Only superior employees should progress very far or very rapidly past the midpoint. Determine the salary, and enter it in the remaining portion of the form:

```
PAY RATE ==>
PROMOTED THIS PERIOD? ==>
NEXT REVIEW DATE (MM/DD/YY) ==>
QUALIFIED FOR ==>
TRAINING NEEDS ==>
      =========================================
```

If the employee has moved up to a better job as a result of this review, or during the preceding year, enter a Y at the promotion prompt. Pick a date a year away for the next review date.

The final two items are for general career development possibilities. Note any other jobs the employee is now qualified to take on; you can check this entry later should you need to fill a vacancy. If the employee could use further training, experience, or some similar benefit to qualify for future advancement, the last line is the place to note that. It's something you can check through dBASE when you plan a training program.

KEEPING TRACK OF APPLICANTS

Your camel washer has suddenly resigned to accept a minor league contract with the New York Mets, and you must fill the vacancy immediately. You have a file of job applications in the drawer. Does anyone in there possess the particular skill you need?

One advantage to dBASE is that it can search your files in a matter of minutes. If you have a basic data file of recent job applicants, and if any of them has experience or training in dealing with camels, dBASE can tell you right away. This sort of searching is one of the things dBASE does best.

First, of course, it must have a file to be searched. You can set up a file of job applicants similar to the one you maintain on your active employees. Include room to list the applicants' training and skills so you can look for these key words later.

This file can serve another purpose, too. If it includes information on sex and minority group membership, you can check your records regularly to monitor your equal opportunity status.

```
                      JOB APPLICATION DATA FORM
==================================================================
           LAST NAME ==> #MLast
           FIRST ==> #MFirst
           INITIAL ==> #MMi
           SOCIAL SECURITY NO. (999-99-9999) ==> #MSSno
           HOME PHONE (999-9999) ==> #MPhone
           STREET ADDRESS ==> #MStreet
           CITY ==> #MCity
           STATE ==> #MState
           ZIP (99999) ==> #MZip
           DATE OF BIRTH (MM/YY/DD) ==> #MBorn
           SEX (M or F) ==> #MSex
           MINORITY GROUP MEMBER? ==> #MMinority
           MARRIED? (Y of N) ==> #MMarried
           EXPERIENCE ==> #MLastjob
           EDUCATION AND SKILLS ==> #MSkills
           JOBS CREDIT? (Y/N) ==> #Mcredit
           HIRED? (Y/N) ==> #Mhired
==================================================================
```

Fig. 4-9. Job application screen display.

Figure 4-9 shows the screen, while Figs. 4-10 and 4-11 give the commands. Here's the file:

```
STRUCTURE FOR FILE:    APPLY.DBF
NUMBER OF RECORDS:     00003
DATE OF LAST UPDATE:   00/00/00
PRIMARY USE DATABASE
FLD         NAME      TYPE WIDTH    DEC
001      SSNO          C    011
002      LAST          C    010
003      FIRST         C    010
004      INITIAL       C    001
005      STREET        C    015
006      CITY          C    010
007      STATE         C    002
008      ZIP           C    005
009      PHONE         C    012
010      BORN          C    008
011      SEX           C    001
012      MARRIED       L    001
013      MINORITY      L    001
014      LASTJOB       C    020
015      SKILLS        C    020
016      CREDIT        L    001
017      HIRED         L    001
** TOTAL **                 00130
```

```
* APPLY.CMD
* Purpose:  Enter basic data on job applicants into the
*         database Employee.Dbf.
*
* Set up initial format
SET DEFAULT TO B
SET INTENSITY OFF
SET TALK OFF
SET CONSOLE ON
SET COLON OFF
SET BELL OFF
*
* Set up outer loop to repeat when operator orders
*         further entries
STORE T to more
DO WHILE more
*
* Clear screen and set initial values for variables to be
* added to the file.  The "m" prefix indicates memory
* variables, to distinguish them from their corresponding
* data base fields.
ERASE
STORE '            ' to mssno
STORE '           ' to mlast
STORE '          ' to mfirst
STORE ' ' to minitial
STORE '             ' to mstreet
STORE '         ' to mcity
STORE '  ' to mstate
STORE '     ' to mzip
STORE '        ' to mphone
STORE '       ' to mborn
STORE ' ' to msex
STORE Y to mmarried
STORE N to mminority
STORE '                    ' to mlastjob
STORE '        ' to mskills
STORE N to mcredit
STORE N to mhired
*
*  Set up inner loop which gives operator a chance to correct
* entries before they are added to the file.
STORE T TO continue
```

Fig. 4-10. Application command file. (Continued on page 99.)

```
DO WHILE continue
*
*   Use format file to produce screen display
SET FORMAT TO APPLY.FMT
READ
*
*   Select a location near bottom of screen and prompt for
*   corrections.
@ 22,0 SAY ' '
INPUT 'DO YOU WISH TO MAKE CORRECTIONS? (Y or N) ==>' to continue
ENDDO WHILE continue
ERASE
*
*   If entries are correct, add them to database.
USE APPLY INDEX appname, appno
APPEND BLANK
REPLACE LAST with mlast, FIRST with mfirst, MI with minitial
REPLACE STREET with mstreet, CITY with mcity, STATE with mstate
REPLACE ZIP with mzip, PHONE with mphone, BORN with mborn
REPLACE SEX with msex, MINORITY with mminority
REPLACE LASTJOB with mlastjob, SKILLS with mskills
REPLACE HIRED with mhired
*
* Prompt for further entries.
@ 22,0 SAY ' '
INPUT 'MORE ENTRIES? (Y or N) ==>' to more
ERASE
ENDDO while more
RETURN
```

The first 13 fields should be familiar. They were copied directly from the **Employee** file. The next two provide some room to enter information about the applicant's previous jobs, skills, and training.

The final two fields are special-purpose items. If you hire a young summer employee, a disadvantaged Vietnam veteran, or anyone from several other "targeted" groups, you could be eligible for a substantial income tax credit. Check with your tax advisor for the details.

If the prospect would qualify, enter a Y for this item. At tax time, you can scan the list for qualified people who were hired.

The final item is a place to indicate whether the applicant was hired. Your scan for the tax credit, then, could be:

```
. LIST SSNO, LAST FOR CREDIT .AND. HIRED
```

It's that simple, and there's no programming involved. You then could find the salaries of these people and figure the appropriate percentage as your tax credit.

A checkup on your minority hiring rate could be just as simple:

```
X Format for applicant data entry
@  1,19 SAY "JOB APPLICATION DATA FORM"
@  2, 0 SAY "========================================================="
@  2,50 SAY "========="
@  3, 8 SAY "LAST NAME ==>" GET MLast
@  4, 8 SAY "FIRST ==>" GET MFirst
@  5, 8 SAY "INITIAL ==>" GET MMi
@  6, 8 SAY "SOCIAL SECURITY NO. (999-99-9999) ==>" GET MSSno
@  7, 8 SAY "HOME PHONE (999-9999) ==>" GET MPhone
@  8, 8 SAY "STREET ADDRESS ==>" GET MStreet
@  9, 8 SAY "CITY ==>" GET MCity
@ 10, 8 SAY "STATE ==>" GET MState
@ 11, 8 SAY "ZIP (99999) ==>" GET MZip
@ 12, 8 SAY "DATE OF BIRTH (MM/YY/DD) ==>" GET MBorn
@ 13, 8 SAY "SEX (M or F) ==>" GET MSex
@ 14, 8 SAY "MINORITY GROUP MEMBER? ==>" GET MMinority
@ 15, 8 SAY "MARRIED? (Y of N) ==>" GET MMarried
@ 16, 8 SAY "EXPERIENCE ==>" GET MLastjob
@ 17, 8 SAY "EDUCATION AND SKILLS ==>" GET MSkills
@ 18, 8 SAY "JOBS CREDIT? (Y/N) ==>" GET Mcredit
@ 19, 8 SAY "HIRED? (Y/N) ==>" GET Mhired
@ 20, 8 SAY "========================================================="
```

Fig. 4-11. Application format file, APPLY.FMT.

```
. COUNT FOR MINORITY .AND. HIRED
```

Another version:

```
. COUNT FOR SEX = 'F' .AND. HIRED
```

You then could compare either figure with the results of:

```
. COUNT FOR HIRED
```

The command and format files for entering data on the applicants are adapted from the entry format for the **Employee** database, and they will work about the same.

The purpose of entering this data, of course, is to get something useful out of it. To check for qualified applicants, we'll use dBASE substring search capability, the ability to find a particular character string wherever it may appear within an indicated field. The results of the search can be reported on form **Apply.Frm.**

```
ENTER OPTIONS, M=LEFT MARGIN, L=LINES/PAGE, W=PAGE WIDTH
PAGE HEADING? (Y/N) N
DOUBLE SPACE REPORT? (Y/N) n
ARE TOTALS REQUIRED? (Y/N) n
```

```
COL        WIDTH,CONTENTS
001        11,SSNO
ENTER HEADING: SS NO.
002        20,TRIM(LAST)+' '+TRIM(FIRST)+' '+INITIAL
ENTER HEADING: NAME
003        25,TRIM(LASTJOB)+' '+SKILLS
ENTER HEADING: EXPERIENCE AND SKILLS
```

If we let it, this report could string itself clear across the page before it came to anything more significant than the applicant's middle initial. So, we've used the TRIM function to cut the unused blanks out of the fields we report and the "+" sign to put several of these trimmed fields together. The "+" is a symbol for what is called concatenation, a forbidding word which simply means you are joining two pieces end to end.

Thus, at Line 2 we string together the last name, trimmed of the remaining blanks in the field, a space, the trimmed first name and the middle initial, all into one column of the report. At Line 3 we do the same, stringing together the entries in the job and skill fields.

Then, to search for someone who has any skill at handling camels, we could:

```
. USE APPLY

. REPORT FORM APPLY FOR 'CAMEL' $(SKILLS)
```

This command searches the **Skills** field for the word CAMEL. (Warning: it won't find Camel or camel, so it pays to make all entries in a consistent style.) If it finds something, it will list the information on that person as called for by the report form. You might get lucky and turn up:

```
123-45-6789 FRAMMIS STAN     ACTOR
                             CAMEL WASHER
```

A skilled camel washer has indeed applied. (You also have the answer to a trivia question: name an early screen credit for actor Jamie Farr.)

You say you want an experienced camel washer? Search the **Lastjob** field instead of **Skills.** Or, perhaps there's someone on your present payroll with camel washing skills. Use the same commands and report form to search the **Qualified** field of your **Career** database.

It would be possible to program this operation with a short, quick command file:

```
ACCEPT 'Skill Needed' to mskill
ACCEPT 'Database to search' to mfile
ACCEPT 'Field to search' to mfield
USE &mfile
REPORT FORM APPLY FOR &mfield $(&mskill)
```

This short sequence saves a little typing and, probably, a few typographical errors. It lets you enter only the key phrases for your search, then uses the "&" or macro substitution function, to plug these phrases into the proper commands.

It would be possible to write an even more elaborate procedure for this function, but this is a case where you probably should make primary use of direct, ad hoc queries to dBASE. A written program asks dBASE the questions that are written into the program in advance. Sometimes you only need to ask what's on your mind at the moment. This can be just such a case; the program would be nice, but the query

```
* EQUAL.CMD
* Reports pay, hiring and promotion of women and
* minority group members
* Variables:  mstart and mstop represent the beginning
* and ending dates of the reporting period.
* Variables used in the reporting form represent
* total numbers, percentages of the whole, average
* salaries and numbers hired and promoted for women,
*  minority group members and the work force as a whole.
SET DEFAULT TO B
SET FORMAT TO SCREEN
SET TALK OFF
SET INTENSITY OFF
SET BELL OFF
SET COLON OFF
SET EJECT OFF
ERASE
* Preliminary setup screen
?
?
?
?
?'        PREPARING EQUAL OPPORTUNITY REPORT'
ACCEPT 'For evaluations from (MM/DD/YY) ==>' to mstart
ACCEPT 'And ending (MM?DD/YY)               ==>' to mstop
@ 20, 5 say 'ONE MOMENT, PLEASE ...'
* Establishes a combined data base of employees whose last
* review dates fell within the reporting period.
USE EMPLOYEE INDEX EMPNO
SELECT SECONDARY
USE CAREER INDEX CARRNO
SELECT PRIMARY
JOIN TO EQUAL FOR p.ssno = s.ssno FIELDS ssno, sex,;
 minority, pay, hired, promoted, revdate
USE EQUAL
* Initialize variables for report
STORE 0 to noall
STORE 0 to payall
STORE 0 to proall
STORE 0 to nowom
STORE 0 to paywom
STORE 0 to prowom
STORE 0 to nomin
```

Fig. 4-12. Equal opportunity program command file. (Continued on page 103.)

```
STORE 0 to paymin
STORE 0 to promin
STORE 0 to hirall
STORE 0 to hirwom
STORE 0 to hirmin
* Locate women and minority group members; extract promotion
* and pay information
GO TOP
DO WHILE .NOT. EOF
DO CASE
CASE REVDATE >= mstart .and. revdate <= mstop
  STORE noall + 1 to noall
  STORE PAY + payall to payall
  IF PROMOTED
      STORE proall + 1 to proall
  ENDIF
  IF HIRED >= mstart .and hired <= mstop
      STORE hirall + 1 to hirall
  ENDIF
 IF SEX = 'F'
    STORE nowom + 1 to nowom
    STORE PAY + paywom to paywom
    IF PROMOTED
        STORE prowom + 1 to prowom
    ENDIF
    IF HIRED >= mstart .and hired <= mstop
        STORE hirwom + 1 to hirwom
    ENDIF
 ENDIF
 IF MINORITY
    STORE nomin + 1 to nomin
    STORE PAY + paymin to paymin
    IF PROMOTED
        STORE promin + 1 to promin
    ENDIF
    IF HIRED >= mstart .and hired <= mstop
        STORE hirmin + 1 to hirmin
    ENDIF
 ENDIF
ENDCASE
SKIP
ENDDO
* Compute figures for report
```

```
STORE paywom/nowom to avewom
STORE paymin/nomin to avemin
STORE payall/noall to aveall
@ 20, 5 SAY '                              '
?
INPUT'      Print this report?' to mprint
IF mprint = Y
 ?'      Prepare printer'
 ?'      Then press any key to continue'
 SET FORMAT TO PRINT
 WAIT
ENDIF
ERASE
DO EQUAL.FMT
?
USE
DELETE FILE EQUAL
RETURN
```

Fig. 4-12. Equal opportunity program command file. Continued from page 103.

language lets you search for the skills you want in the places you want. What you lose in "user-friendliness" you gain in flexibility.

PROMOTING EQUAL OPPORTUNITY

Equal opportunity is a well-known principle backed up by a mixture of rules and requirements. As a small business, you might not be subject to every requirement the state and federal governments have seen fit to impose. Then again, you might.

For example, if you're in broadcasting you must meet an affirmative action requirement if you have as few as five employees—that's a special requirement of the Federal Communications Commission (FCC).

Government contractors also are subject to special requirements. The Labor Department started in 1980 to define a proper affirmative action program for contractors; four years later it still had not finished the job. Then there are state and local requirements to worry about. Beyond that is the amount and type of guidance you accept from your conscience.

No single computer program could possibly account for all these variations. In that light, the exercise that follows might be an example of gratuitous programming. It asks a certain number of questions the answers to which will probably be useful. That is not to say it asks all the questions, or the right questions, to produce exactly the information you need to meet your particular requirements. Neither does it provide an automatic formula that determines with a few whirs of the disk drives whether you're complying with the rules.

This procedure does give you a way, though, to extract hiring, promotion, and salary information from your files. You can alter it to call for other kinds of information. Or, you can follow its example in direct queries to dBASE. Figures 4-12 and 4-13 provide the commands.

The program starts with a modest data entry screen:

```
@  3,10 SAY "EQUAL OPPORTUNITY REPORT, Period"
@  3,43 SAY mstart
@  3,52 SAY "through"
@  3,60 SAY mstop
@  4, 0 SAY "========================================================"
@  4,50 SAY "==============================="
@  6, 0 SAY "CLASS           NUMBER          AVE. SALARY      PR"
@  6,50 SAY "OMOTED      HIRED"
@  7, 0 SAY "------          ------          ------------      --"
@  7,50 SAY "------      -----"
@  8, 0 SAY "Women"
@  8,16 SAY NOWOM
@  8,32 SAY AVEWOM
@  8,48 SAY PROWOM
@  8,64 SAY HIRWOM
@ 10, 0 SAY "Minorities"
@ 10,16 SAY NOMIN
@ 10,32 SAY AVEMIN
@ 10,48 SAY PROMIN
@ 10,64 SAY HIRMIN
@ 12, 0 SAY "Full Staff"
@ 12,16 SAY NOALL
@ 12,32 SAY AVEALL
@ 12,48 SAY PROALL
@ 12,64 SAY HIRALL
@ 14, 0 SAY "========================================================"
@ 14,50 SAY "==============================="
```

Fig. 4-13. Equal opportunity format file, EQUAL.FMT.

```
PREPARING EQUAL OPPORTUNITY REPORT
    For evaluations from (MM/DD/YY)  ==>
    And ending (MM/DD/YY)            ==>
```

Your report will cover your activities over a particular period. Enter the starting and ending dates; later, the program will isolate employee appraisals and other actions completed during that time.

After the dates have been entered, the succeeding steps will take several moments of varied disk drive motion. While this is in progress, a message assures the user that all this really is supposed to be happening:

```
ONE MOMENT, PLEASE ...
```

In the meantime, a lot is happening:

```
USE EMPLOYEE INDEX EMPNO
SELECT SECONDARY
USE CAREER INDEX CARRNO
SELECT PRIMARY
```

In this sequence, we call the **Employee** database as the primary file, select **Career** as the secondary, and index both on the Social Security numbers. The program then goes back to **Employee**.

```
JOIN TO EQUAL FOR p.ssno = s.ssno FIELDS ssno, sex,;
     minority, pay, hired, promoted, revdate
```

This sequence creates a new database from the original two. Individual records will be joined on the basis of the same Social Security number—when the number in the primary file (**p.ssno**) matches its counterpart in the secondary file (**s.ssno**). Since we won't be working with every field in both original files, we specify only the fields we want in the new one, called **Equal.**

You might get the same results with joining the databases by using the **p.** and **s.** prefixes throughout the program to designate the source of each item. With the number of variables we'll soon be dealing with, though, it would be easy to lose track. If we create and use a new database for the purpose, we eliminate one good chance for programming errors. Also, if you plan to use the report function you must use a single database.

```
STORE 0 to noall
STORE 0 to payall
STORE 0 to proall
STORE 0 to nowom
STORE 0 to paywom
STORE 0 to prowom
STORE 0 to nomin
STORE 0 to paymin
STORE 0 to promin
STORE 0 to hirall
STORE 0 to hirwom
STORE 0 to hirmin
```

We have a group of numerical variables this time. There are three groups to be considered: women, minorities, and the staff as a whole: for each we will examine their numbers, pay, and whether they were hired or promoted during the review period.

```
USE EQUAL
GO TOP
DO WHILE .NOT. EOF
DO CASE
CASE REVDATE >= mstart .and. revdate <= mstop
```

We call the **Equal** file, make sure the record pointer is at the top and instruct it to start looping through the file, record by record. It is to stop at the record of every employee whose performance was reviewed during the period the report is to cover. DO CASE sets up an outer loop to establish this condition.

```
STORE noall + 1 to noall
STORE PAY + payall to payall
IF PROMOTED
     STORE proall + 1 to proall
```

```
ENDIF
IF HIRED >= mstart .and hired <= mstop
     STORE hirall + 1 to hirall
ENDIF
```

Within the DO CASE loop is a sequence that stores statistics for every employee who was reviewed during the period. We use **noall** to count them and **payall** to add up their combined salaries.

A pair of inner loops asks, first, if the employee was promoted during the reporting period, advancing the counter **proall** if that was true. A slightly more complicated version, again checking dates, advances the counter **hirall** if the employee was hired during the period. (This is made necessary by the structure of the **Employee** database. It records not just whether an employee is on the payroll but when that employee was hired. You'll often need that information.)

The program then repeats the same sequence, but only for female employees.

```
IF SEX = 'F'
   STORE nowom + 1 to nowom
   STORE PAY + paywom to paywom
   IF PROMOTED
       STORE prowom + 1 to prowom
   ENDIF
   IF HIRED >= mstart .and hired <= mstop
        STORE hirwom + 1 to hirwom
   ENDIF
ENDIF
```

Then again for minority group members.

```
IF MINORITY
   STORE nomin + 1 to nomin
   STORE PAY + paymin to paymin
   IF PROMOTED
             STORE promin + 1 to promin
   ENDIF
   IF HIRED >= mstart .and hired <= mstop
      STORE hirmin + 1 to hirmin
   ENDIF
ENDIF
```

The program then declares an end to the DO CASE routine, skips to the next record and repeats the loop:

```
ENDCASE
SKIP
ENDDO
```

Now, the program calculates the average pay for the women, minorities, and the group as a whole.

```
STORE paywom/nowom to avewom
STORE paymin/nomin to avemin
STORE payall/noall to aveall
```

The "one moment" message has been on the screen all this time, but now the waiting user is entitled to see something else:

```
ERASE
?
?
?
?
INPUT'     Print this report?' to mprint
IF mprint = Y
     ?'       Prepare printer'
     ?'       Then press any key to continue'
     SET FORMAT TO PRINT
     WAIT
ENDIF
```

We clear the screen and give the user a choice: displaying the report on the screen or having it printed. If the answer is Yes, the program waits until the printer has been set up and the user enters a signal to continue.

```
ERASE
DO EQUAL.FMT
?
USE
DELETE FILE EQUAL
RETURN
```

The screen is cleared, and the report itself, using the **Equal** format file, is called either to the screen or the printer. The unadorned USE command then turns off the **Equal** file, and we can delete it since it is no longer needed.

You have a question about the question mark? That's a trick for the printer. It seems dBASE sends its carriage returns and line feeds in the opposite order to the sequence many printers expect. The printer, still waiting for a final carriage return, never prints the last line of the form. The "?" character sends a dummy new line, including one more carriage return, so the printer can finish its business.

Getting the News

Whether the final report is on the screen or printed, for each of the three groups you'll get the total number, their average salary, and the numbers promoted or hired during the reporting period. This chart may not answer every equal opportunity question, but if there's a problem in your organization it should show up as a visible discrepancy in these figures.

Making Changes

No database is set for all time. About the time you settle back for a lull in the hiring, evaluation, or equal opportunity process someone gets married or decides to take out more group insurance. The **Edit** program shown here lets you identify the file to be changed and the affected employee, and activates the dBASE EDIT command. The entire record will then be displayed for your changes and corrections.

MORE-AND-SIMPLER REPORTS

There are many useful reports for which prewritten programs are unnecessary, or at least optional. You can call up the dBASE period and type the few commands to generate these useful personnel reports. If you prefer, you also can list these in sequence in simple command files; you might want to do this when the sequences include longer commands where errors are easy to make.

Here's how to generate a simple roster of your current employees:

```
. USE EMPLOYEE INDEX EMPNAME
. REPORT FORM ROSTER
```

This will activate the dBASE form generator and its series of queries, which you can answer like this:

```
ENTER OPTIONS, M=LEFT MARGAIN, L=LINES/PAGE, W=PAGE WIDTH
PAGE HEADING? (Y/N) Y
ENTER PAGE HEADING: Submetropolis Weekly Satellite; EMPLOYEE
   ROSTER
```

The semicolon in that line will give you a two-line heading.

```
DOUBLE SPACE REPORT? (Y/N) N
ARE TOTALS REQUIRED? (Y/N) N
COL        WIDTH,CONTENTS
001        20,TRIM(LAST)+' ', '+TRIM(FIRST)+' '+INITIAL+'.'
```

Here's yet another refinement of the TRIM command. This time we've included some punctuation marks.

```
ENTER HEADING: NAME
002      11,SSNO
ENTER HEADING: SOCIAL SECURITY NO.
003      15,STREET
ENTER HEADING: STREET ADDRESS
004      10,CITY
ENTER HEADING: CITY
005      2,STATE
ENTER HEADING: ST
006      5,ZIP
ENTER HEADING: ZIP
007      8,PHONE
ENTER HEADING: PHONE
```

With a few odd names in the **Employee** file, the resulting report looks like this:

```
NAME                  SOCIAL          STREET ADDRESS    CITY      ST ZIP    PHONE
                      SECURITY
                      NO.


DIAMOND, MINNIE H.    333-33-3333 222 EAGER LA      NASHVILLE   TN 22222 333-3333
JEMIMA, AUNT E.       222-22-2222 MAGNOLIA WAY      JACKSON     MS 44444 222-2222
```

```
PAGE NO. 00001


            Submetropolis Weekly Satellite
            JOB EVALUATION SCHEDULE


  POSITION    RATE    SOCIAL      LAST NAME    NEXT
                     SECURITY                  REVIEW
                      NUMBER                    DATE


  X DEPARTMENT: SECUR
  GUARD          3 111-11-1111 VILLA      01/10/84


  X DEPARTMENT: KITCH
  COOK           3 222-22-2222 JEMIMA     01/10/85


  X DEPARTMENT: FIN
  MGR            5 028-34-5678 JONES      03/10/84


  X DEPARTMENT: EDIT
  CHIEF          5 355-28-4495 SMITH      03/15/84


  X DEPARTMENT: STAGE
  COMEDY         4 333-33-3333 DIAMOND    07/07/84
```

Fig. 4-14. Job evaluation screen display.

```
JONES, RICHARD H.    355-28-4495 2107 CAMELBACK   DRINKWATER CT 03546 555-9219
SMITH, BEVERLY M.    028-34-5678 1270 PINETREE    GRASSROOTS FL 33456 555-5555
VILLA, PANCHO X.     111-11-1111 111 MAIN ST      S. ANTONIO TX 98765 111-1111
```

Study of Payroll Costs

Which departments account for what parts of your payroll costs? This report takes data from two files to give you the breakdown:

```
. SET ALTERNATE ON
. USE EMPLOYEE INDEX EMPNO
. SELECT SECONDARY
. USE CAREER INDEX CARRNO, CARRDEPT
. SELECT PRIMARY
. JOIN to deptpay for P.ssno=S.ssno FIELD S.dept,
      S.position, S.jobrate, P.ssno, P.last, S.salary
```

```
. USE DEPTPAY
. INDEX ON DEPT TO DEPTPAY
. REPORT FORM DEPTPAY
```

When specifying the fields in the JOIN command, dBASE requires that you use the **P.** or **S.** prefix to identify fields from the file you have *not* selected at the moment. If you identify all of them in this way it can save some confusion and possible errors. The report form:

```
ENTER OPTIONS, M=LEFT MARGAIN, L=LINES/PAGE, W=PAGE WIDTH W=60
PAGE HEADING (Y/N) Y
ENTER PAGE HEADING: Submetropolis Weekly Satellite; DEPARTMENTAL PAY
REPORT
DOUBLE SPACE REPORT? (Y/N) N
ARE TOTALS REQUIRED? (Y/N) Y
SUBTOTALS IN REPORT? (Y/N) Y
ENTER SUBTOTALS FIELD: DEPT
SUMMARY REPORT ONLY? (Y/N) N
EJECT PAGE AFTER SUBTOTALS? (Y/N) N
ENTER SUBTOTAL HEADING: DEPARTMENT:
COL        WIDTH, CONTENTS
001        10, position
ENTER HEADING: POSITION
002         4, JOBRATE
ENTER HEADING: rate
ARE TOTALS REQUIRED? (Y/N) N
```

Jobrate, you might remember, is a numerical field, so dBASE will ask about the totals. You have no reason, though, to add this field.

```
003        11,ssno
ENTER HEADING:  SOCIAL SECURITY NUMBER
004        10, last
ENTER HEADING:  LAST NAME
005         7, pay
ENTER HEADING: PAY RATE
ARE TOTALS REQUIRED? (Y/N)  Y
```

This report will list individual salaries, with subtotals for each department. One major requirement: be sure you index the file on the department field before you try to organize subtotals on that field.

Scheduling Review Dates

You can use nearly the same format to produce a schedule of coming employee review dates. Each department head can be given a copy of the scheduled reviews, listed in order of the date. The sequence:

```
. USE CAREER INDEX NEXTEVAL'
. SELECT SECONDARY
. USE EMPLOYEE INDEX EMPNO
```

```
*       EMPLOYEE.RPT
*   A command driven routine for producing payroll reports.
*   List existing report formats
ERASE
?
?
LIST FILES LIKE *.FRM
?
?'================================================================
    ============'
* Choose printer or disk file for report
STORE   ' '    TO Rlpt
DO WHILE !(Rlpt) <>  'Y'   .AND. !(Rlpt) <>  'N'
STORE   'Y'   TO Rlpt
@ 19,10 SAY  ' WANT REPORT SENT TO THE PRINTER? '   GET Rlpt
READ
ENDDO
  STORE   ' '    TO Rdsk
  DO WHILE !(Rdsk) <>  'Y'   .AND. !(Rdsk) <>  'N'
  STORE   'N'   TO Rdsk
@ 19,10 SAY  ' WANT REPORT SENT TO A FILE ?        '   GET Rdsk
READ
ENDDO
IF !(Rdsk)= 'Y'
STORE '              '  TO Rfile
DO WHILE Rfile = '              '
@ 20,10 SAY  ' ENTER FILE NAME '  GET Rfile
READ
ENDDO
STORE TRIM(Rfile) TO Rfile
ENDIF  RDSK
STORE '          '  TO report
  DO WHILE report = '      '
@ 21,10 SAY  ' ENTER REPORT NAME '   GET report
@ 22,10 SAY  ' SPECIFY CONDITIONS'   GET cond
READ
ENDDO
IF !(Rlpt) =   'Y'
@ 23,10 SAY  ' PLEASE SET UP PRINTER            '
SET CONSOLE OFF
WAIT
SET CONSOLE ON
SET PRINT ON
```

Fig. 4-15. Personnel report form. (Continued on page 113.)

```
ENDIF Rlpt
X  Open the disk file named earlier
IF !(Rdsk) =  'Y'
SET ALTERNATE TO &Rfile
SET ALTERNATE ON
ENDIF RDSK
ERASE


   X Call for report form.  If it does not already exist,
   X         dBASE will go through the report creation sequence.
   REPORT FORM &report FOR &cond
   SET PRINT OFF
   SET ALTERNATE OFF
   IF !(Rdsk) = 'Y'
     RELEASE Rdsk,Rfile
   ENDIF
   RELEASE Rlpt, report
```

```
. SELECT PRIMARY
. JOIN TO EVALDATE FOR P.SSNO=S.SSNO FIELD S.LAST, DEPT
     POSITION, JOBRATE, SSON, NEXTEVAL
. USE EVALDATE
. INDEX ON DEPT TO EVALDEPT
. INDEX ON NEXTEVAL TO EVALDATE
. REPORT FORM EVALDATE
```

```
ENTER OPTIONS, M=LEFT MARGAIN, L=LINES/PAGE, W=PAGE WIDTH W=60
PAGE HEADING? (Y/N) Y
ENTER PAGE HEADING:  Submetropolis Weekly Satellite; JOB EVALUATION
SCHEDULE
DOUBLE SPACE REPORT? (Y/N) N
ARE TOTALS REQUIRED (Y/N) Y
SUBTOTALS IN REPORT? (Y/N) Y
ENTER SUBTOTALS FIELD: dept
```

This is a little trick we're playing on the report generator. We ask it to set up again for subtotals by department, but in this report it won't find any totals to be added. It still will arrange the listing by department, however, which is what we want it to do.

```
SUMMARY REPORT ONLY? (Y/N) N
EJECT PAGE AFTER SUBTOTALS? (Y/N) N
ENTER SUBTOTAL HEADING: DEPARTMENT:
```

```
COL        WIDTH,CONTENTS
001        10, POSITION
ENTER HEADING: POSITION
002        4, JOBRATE
ENTER HEADING: RATE
ARE TOTALS REQUIRED? (Y/N) N
003        11, SSNO
ENTER HEADING: SOCIAL SECURITY NUMBER
004        10, LAST
ENTER HEADING: LAST NAME
005        7, PAY
ENTER HEADING: PAY RATE
```

Figure 4-14. shows the layout of this report.

There probably are many other ways you can massage the data in the personnel system to produce useful information. If you need to know something, put the question in a form dBASE will understand and simply ask. If you'd like, the command file **Employee. Rpt,** Fig. 4-15, will guide you through the process.

In particular, don't let yourself be limited to the reports produced by prewritten programs. dBASE procedures can make the computer easier and more attractive to the users, they can help avoid mistakes, and they can get you through things like those long, tricky JOIN statements. The object of many programmers is to make dBASE "transparent" to the user.

There are both advantages and drawbacks to letting dBASE take control of your field of vision. If you rely only on prewritten program routines, dBASE will let you see only what the program lets you see. If you allow yourself to look beyond the prewritten obvious—including the procedures in this book—it will be you, not the computer, who takes command.

SOME NECESSARY MAINTENANCE

One last item is a short **Reindex** file, Fig. 4-16, that can reset all the proper indexes called for in the

```
* REINDEX.CMD
* Reinstates index files when needed
*
USE EMPLOYEE
INDEX ON SSNO TO EMPNO
INDEX ON LAST TO EMPNAME
USE CAREER
INDEX ON DEPT TO CARRDEPT
INDEX ON SSNO TO CARRNO
INDEX ON REVDATE TO CARRDATE
USE APPLY
INDEX ON SSNO TO APPNO
RETURN
```

Fig. 4-16. Reindex command file.

main programs of this file. Various additions and modifications of the files sometimes can throw off the indexing. You'll normally learn of this when you unexpectedly get a message that dBASE has unexpectedly reached the end of the file. A record out of range is a popular alternative.

Either message could mean your indexing has gone out of whack. This file will put it back into whack.

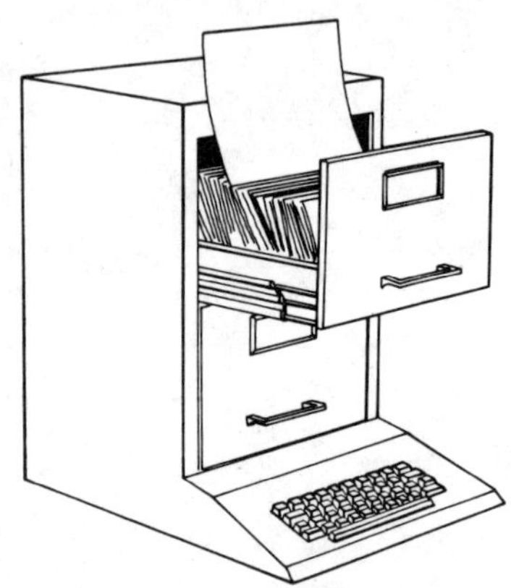

Chapter 5

Meeting the Payroll

The person who makes out the payroll is like a championship poker player surrounded by a crowd of kibitzers. The employees are looking over one shoulder to make sure there are no mistakes in bestowing the rewards for their work. Officials at several levels of government look over the other shoulder to make sure there are no mistakes in bestowing the rewards on which *they* insist. As the manager, you find it hard to elbow through this crowd just to exercise some minimal supervision of your own.

dBASE can help. In this chapter, we'll show how a **Payroll** database, spun off from the personnel database of the previous chapter, can store the vital records of your payroll system. From these records, dBASE can retrieve the information and make accurate calculations of everyone's paycheck. There's no need to repeat the process manually every payday, and there is less room for mistakes.

At the same time, in a small business it is possible, and desirable, to keep a necessary amount of human control over the process. Larger firms may make use of highly automated payroll systems that spit out paychecks—or even electronic fund transfers—untouched by human hands. For small business use, this chapter will present a system designed for a smaller payroll that relies a little more on human intervention. This isn't a fully automated system. Instead, it is designed to do the major work of keeping the records and making the calculations while a human operator oversees the process to verify the information, correct errors, and make any last minute changes.

The advantage is that your human operator can monitor the entire operation. You need not risk a computer that grinds out mistakes of which you learn only when someone complains.

Another advantage is that it is set up to generate custom-tailored reports. You can specify your own format, particularly for the ad hoc reports you need only on request. This system includes formats for a pair of common reports, a payroll register, and a list of tax deposits due—but there's also room to specify what *you* want to see. Remember, the best database in the world is no good unless you make use of its flexibility to generate the information you need to know.

A PAIR OF UTILITIES

When you're working with a payroll, security and accuracy are vital concerns. Let's start, then, with a couple of utility programs to help you meet those needs. The first is a password system you can install at any point in your system merely by inserting the command:

```
. DO PASSWORD
```

The second checks dates for obvious inaccuracies. Call it anywhere you'd like with:

```
. DO DATECHEK
```

Neither of these commands appears right now in the other files of the payroll system. You can insert them yourself wherever you feel a need: at the outset there's a good reason to leave them out. You'll be modifying, testing, and correcting these programs several times as you put them into service. The third time you have to get past your password to correct a simple typing error is the time you'd take that command out of the file until you get it into shape. Why not leave it out in the first place and insert it when you're ready?

Joe Sent Me

The command file for the password utility is called, naturally, **Password.** It's Fig. 5-1. Let's read the good parts:

```
SET BELL OFF
SET COLON OFF
ERASE
```

This trio of preliminaries is more important than usual. Previous files have set the bell off because I find it irritating. This time we'll set it off because it has some other work to do. We'll be hearing from it in a moment. The colons should go, because otherwise they'd sit there telling an unauthorized user the exact length of your password. Why tell such a person anything? The third command creates an empty theater for the effects of any violations.

Choose any term to be used as your password and use it in this command file. Select it carefully, remembering that the user—who might be you—must match it exactly, including capitalization:

```
STORE "JoeSentMe" to password
```

The next command will ask anyone who uses the file to type this simple phrase—if they know it:

```
@ 20, 5 SAY 'Please Enter the Password ==>'
```

Now we get a little tricky

```
STORE 0 to char
STORE '36' to col
```

This is a pair of counters. The 0 starts counting the number of characters in the password; the 36 indicates the starting position for typing it (as set up here, the entry prompt will end in column 34). It's a character variable because it will be used in a macro substitution later.

```
* PASSWORD.CMD
*
* Called from operating programs by command DO PASSWORD
*        Hides password entry; sounds alarm when unauthorized
*        access attempted.  Reset is the only escape.
*
* Variables:  Password contains the authorized password.
*        Char is a counter to check each letter individually.
*        Counter repeats loop for each letter.  It is used
*        as a character variable for the sake of macro
*        substitution.
*        Test will collect each entry and compare it with the
*                 actual password.
SET BELL OFF
SET COLON OFF
ERASE
* Choose any term to be used as your password.  The user
*        must match it exactly, including capitalization.
STORE "JoeSentMe" to password
@ 20, 5 SAY 'Please Enter the Password ==>'
* Initial values.  The counter value will place the first
*        password entery after the prompt.
STORE 0 to char
STORE '36' to X
DO WHILE char < len(password)
        STORE char + 1 to char
        STORE ' ' to test
        SET CONSOLE OFF
        @ 20, &X GET test
        READ
        CLEAR GETS
        SET CONSOLE ON
        @ 20, &X SAY '#'
* Signal of inaccurate entry
        IF test <> $(password,char,1)
                DO WHILE t
                        ERASE
                        @ 12,10 SAY 'NOT AUTHORIZED TO USE THIS FILE'
                        ? chr(7)
                        @ 12,10 SAY '
                ENDDO
        ELSE
        STORE STR((val(X)+1),2) to X
        ENDIF
ENDDO
SET ESCAPE ON
RELEASE Password, Char, Counter, Test
RETURN
```

Fig. 5-1. Password command file.

```
DO WHILE char < len(password)
     STORE char + 1 to char
```

Char, you'll remember, is a counter that will proceed letter by letter through the password. With that in mind, set up the DO WHILE loop to progress through the length of your chosen term, increasing by one the character count each time. We're also setting up a blank variable for the operator's first character entry:

```
STORE ' ' to test
SET CONSOLE OFF
@ 20, &col GET test
```

In the position just after the end of the prompt (line 20 and the column indicated by the contents of "col") the computer will record that first letter. With the console off, though, it won't show on the screen (or will flash so briefly a casual passerby probably won't be able to read it).

```
READ
CLEAR GETS
SET CONSOLE ON
@ 20, &col SAY '#'
```

After reading the entry, doing some housecleaning and turning the screen back on, we will indeed see a new entry. It will not, however, be the first letter of the password. Instead, dBASE will put a "#" character in that spot.

If the operator has correctly entered the first letter of the password, the program will loop back and repeat itself for the succeeding letters. If the entry isn't right, this will happen:

```
IF test <> $(password,char,1)
     DO WHILE t
          ERASE
          @ 12,10 SAY 'NOT AUTHORIZED TO USE THIS FILE'
          ? chr(7)
          @ 12,10 SAY '
     ENDDO
```

If the entry does not match the first character of your password, the screen will clear and the warning message will appear. Not only that, but **chr(7)** will ring the bell (or beeper) we turned off earlier. Then a blank line will cover the warning and an endless loop will begin, flashing the message and sounding the beeper. Unless your unauthorized user is a dBASE expert—in which case this entire program would be easy to evade—there will be very few ways to shut off the noise and the flashing. If you have any knowledge of computer graphics, you might have even more fun with a brighter and more visible message.

```
     ELSE
     STORE STR((val(col)+1),2) to col
     ENDIF
ENDDO
SET ESCAPE ON
RELEASE Password, Char, Counter, Test, Col
RETURN
```

These final commands reset the loop after a correct entry and do the usual housekeeping.

As stated, anyone who's even moderately familiar with dBASE could evade or disable this program just by rewriting the command file. It is aimed at the casual user who strays into unauthorized material, either deliberately or by accident. It is designed to embarrass, not to block access, as an aid to a more thorough security system.

Actually, the best way for a microcomputer user to protect sensitive data is to keep the disk in a locked storage place. No password or any other security measure is nearly as effective. This program can help, though, to stop the merely curious and to head off accidental security violations.

What Day Is It?

The best way to get a date into a working program is to enter it at the prompt when dBASE is fired up. The programs here assume you've done that, calling for the special form Date() whenever they must retrieve something from the calendar. If you enter the date at the prompt, dBASE will ignore any month with too many days or year with too many months.

Sometimes, though, it isn't practical to enter the date in advance. In that case, you should have your own date checking utility. Again, it is a routine you can call from anywhere in any program. Since it is a working tool instead of a learning tool, it is a bit more sophisticated than the date check program in Chapter 3, particularly where February is concerned.

Like virtually all date checkers, this routine compares the date being tested against a range of permissible entries. This doesn't guarantee that the date you have entered is correct, but it will assure you that the date is on the calendar. As it does this, it will screen out many obvious errors.

The datecheck routine is Fig. 5-2. Its operative portions work like this:

```
STORE DATE() to date
STORE T to nodate
DO WHILE nodate
```

This version uses the Date() notation that indicates the internal dBASE function. If it was entered at the beginning or through the command SET DATE TO . . . , your date will be in this form. If you are testing a date entered in any other way, replace the first line with:

```
STORE '        ' to date
```

Leave eight spaces, initializing a character variable with room for the standard date notation. After setting up a loop based on **nodate**, a variable indicating you do not yet have a verified date, the routine launches into this confusing-looking mess:

```
DO CASE
  CASE VAL($(date,1,2)) > 12
```

It's simpler than it looks. Starting with the date in the center, as a character variable, we pick out the two characters beginning at the first one. We then use the VAL function to convert these two digits to a number. Finally, we ask if it is larger than 12. As you might expect, we've asked whether the date being tested tries to put too many months in the year. The next line checks against the unlikely but possible event that we've created a month 00:

```
CASE VAL($(date,1,2)) < 1
CASE VAL($(date,4,2)) > 31
```

```
* DATECHEK.CMD
* Purpose:  Checks for date entries and for obvious errors.
* Variables: Date (C)  A memory variable for the current date.
* Nodate (L)  Memory variable used in processing.
*    If true, the date has not been confirmed.
*
STORE DATE() to date
STORE T to nodate
DO WHILE nodate
DO CASE
  CASE VAL($(date,1,2)) > 12
  CASE VAL($(date,1,2)) < 1
  CASE VAL($(date,4,2)) > 31
  CASE VAL($(date,4,2)) < 1
  CASE VAL($(date,7,2)) < 01
  CASE VAL($(date,7,2)) > 99
  CASE VAL($(date,1,2))=04 .AND. VAL($(date,4,2)) > 30
  CASE VAL($(date,1,2))=06 .AND. VAL($(date,4,2)) > 30
  CASE VAL($(date,1,2))=09 .AND. VAL($(date,4,2)) > 30
  CASE VAL($(date,1,2))=11 .AND. VAL($(date,4,2)) > 30
  CASE VAL($(date,1,2)) = 02 .AND. VAL($(date,4,2)) > 29
  CASE  VAL($(date,1,2)) = 02;
  .AND. INT(VAL($(date,7,2))/4.0) <> VAL($(date,7,2))/4.0;
  .AND. VAL($(date,4,2)) > 28
  OTHERWISE
        STORE F to nodate
        SET date to &date
ENDCASE
 IF nodate
        @ 22, 5 SAY "Date Incorrect or Not on Record"
        ACCEPT "     Please Enter Correct Date (MM/DD/YY)" to date
ENDDO
SET date TO &date
RETURN
```

Fig. 5-2. Date check command file.

```
CASE VAL($(date,4,2)) < 1
CASE VAL($(date,7,2)) < 01
CASE VAL($(date,7,2)) > 99
```

The succeeding lines apply the same kind of tests to the month (which begins at position 4) and the year (starting at position 7). If everything's okay so far, we move into some coding that makes this version a little more sophisticated than some others. Follow closely:

```
CASE VAL($(date,1,2))=04 .AND. VAL($(date,4,2)) > 30
```

In English: if the indicated month is April, we should not show more than 30 days. We can continue in the same vein through the other 30-day months:

```
CASE VAL($(date,1,2))=06 .AND. VAL($(date,4,2)) > 30
CASE VAL($(date,1,2))=09 .AND. VAL($(date,4,2)) > 30
CASE VAL($(date,1,2))=11 .AND. VAL($(date,4,2)) > 30
```

People in most northern hemisphere climates would rather do without February, but it's as inevitable in a date check procedure as it is in the year. Here's how to handle it:

```
CASE VAL($(date,1,2)) = 02 .AND. VAL($(date,4,2)) > 29
```

At this point it is important to note that as this program moves along it searches for *bad* dates, not good ones. That means we have to take February more or less in reverse, first screening out the dates past the 29th. If we first kicked out everything over the 28th, we'd have nothing left for the really fancy part of this routine:

```
CASE  VAL($(date,1,2)) = 02;
.AND. INT(VAL($(date,7,2))/4.0) <> VAL($(date,7,2))/4.0;
.AND. VAL($(date,4,2)) > 28
```

Translation: using the traditional leap year test, divide the year by 4. How can the program tell if it comes out even? By comparing the result with the *integer*—the whole number result—of the same calculation. Only in a leap year will the two be the same. In other years, the noninteger version will have a decimal remainder. Then, since we've already tested for Februaries of more than 29 days we can check for other Februaries of more than 28.

```
OTHERWISE
        STORE F to nodate
        SET date to &date
ENDCASE
 IF nodate
        @ 22, 5 SAY "Date Incorrect or Not on Record"
        ACCEPT "     Please Enter Correct Date (MM/DD/YY)"
                        to date
ENDDO
SET date TO &date
RETURN
```

If the date has passed this gauntlet without being declared incorrect, the date is set to the proper figure. Otherwise, the program prompts you to try again.

There is one problem lurking in this procedure, and in fact it exists in most computer programs using dates: it is only good for the twentieth century. Programmers are only now realizing they're in for some trouble in 2001, when the twenty-first century *really* begins.

OUTLINE OF THE SYSTEM

The basic outline of the payroll system is reflected in the menu, Fig. 5-3. Let's take the items one by one.

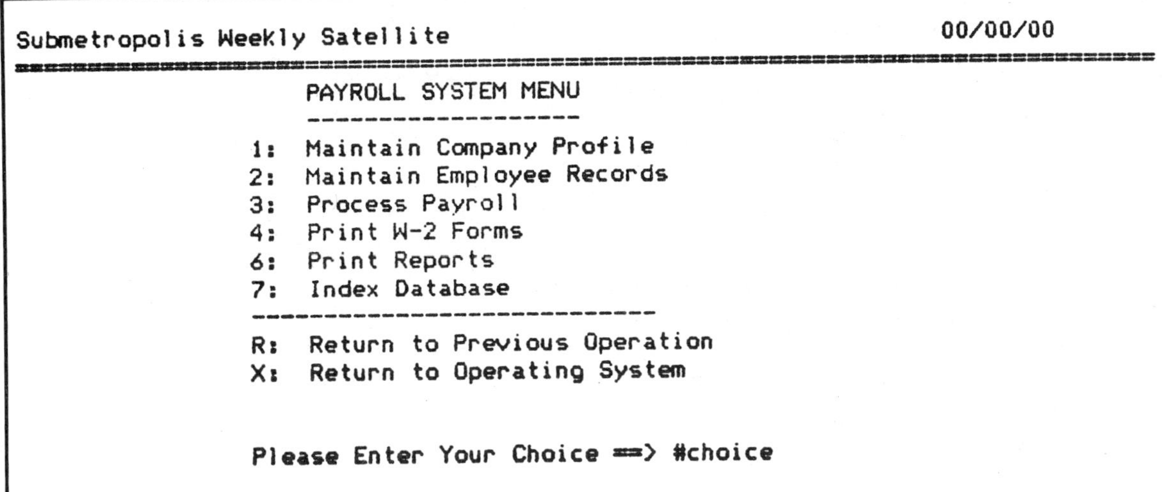

Fig. 5-3. Payroll system menu display.

Maintain Company Profile. A **Profile** memory file was illustrated in an earlier chapter; this section has a similar file. It contains continuing, basic data such as the company name and the formula for computing Social Security tax deductions. The command file that sets up the payroll menu also calls up these variables and saves any new versions of them.

Often, though, you'll find that the data in the file must be changed. The first menu listing calls up a file maintenance program for the purpose.

Maintain Employee Records. This item calls another file maintenance function, this one to add to the basic **Payroll** file when new employees join the company.

Process Payroll. Here is the main file, the one that processes the payroll, and prints the checks. In the process, your operator also has a chance to update the information, adding overtime pay for example, and to recalculate the pay and deductions.

Print W-2 Forms. At the end of the year, this function will use a transaction file, a record of all the checks issued during the previous period, and use them to print the employees' income tax records.

Print Reports. The information you put into a database is only as useful as the information you can get back out of it. This function lets you choose from a series of payroll reports of the types many companies use. Included are the report formats for a weekly payroll register and to compute quarterly deposits of withholding and Social Security deductions. You also have the means to design custom reports of your own.

Index Database. Anything that's heavily used tends to suffer wear and tear, and a database is no exception. The programs in this section are designed to call and properly index the two databases used in the payroll system. Even so, the indexing sometimes tends to fall out of whack—a RECORD OUT OF RANGE warning is the usual symptom. When you encounter it, simply run this program; it's the proven cure for most database problems.

```
R:   Return to Previous Operation
X:   Return to Operating System
```

Never leave your operator (or yourself) without a way out of a system. The R command will take you back to the dBASE dot. X will go one step further and give you an A>.

```
* PAYROLL.CMD
* A command file to set up main payroll menu.
SET TALK OFF
SET FORMAT TO SCREEN
SET CONSOLE ON
SET COLON OFF
SET BELL OFF
SET INTENSITY OFF
USE PAYCHEK INDEX PAYCHEK
SELECT SECONDARY
USE TRANSFIL INDEX TRANSFIL
SELECT PRIMARY
RESTORE FROM PAYMAINT.MEM
STORE T TO more
DO WHILE more
ERASE
@  1, 0 SAY company
@  1,64 SAY Date()
@  2, 0 SAY "==========================================================="
@  2,50 SAY "============================================"
@  3,20 SAY "PAYROLL SYSTEM MENU"
@  4,20 SAY "--------------------"
@  5,16 SAY "1:   Maintain System Profile"
@  6,16 SAY "2:   Maintain Employee Records"
@  7,16 SAY "3:   Process Payroll"
@  8,16 SAY "4:   Print W-2 Forms"
@  9,16 SAY "5:   Print Reports"
@ 10,16 SAY "6:   Index Database"
@ 11,16 SAY "-------------------------------"
@ 12,16 SAY "R:   Return to Previous Operation"
@ 13,16 SAY "X:   Return to Operating System"
@ 15,16 SAY "Please Enter Your Choice ==>"
READ
SET CONSOLE OFF
WAIT TO choice
SET CONSOLE ON
DO CASE
  CASE choice = '1'
  DO PAYMAINT
  CASE choice = '2'
  DO PAYCHEK.ADD
  CASE choice = '3'
  DO PAYCHEK.GET
```

Fig. 5-4. Payroll system command file. (Continued on page 125.)

```
        CASE choice = '4'
        DO WTWO.CMD
        CASE choice = '5'
        DO PAYCHEK.RPT
        CASE choice = '6'
        DO PAYCHEK.GO
        CASE choice = 'R'
        CANCEL
        CASE choice= 'X'
        QUIT
     ENDCASE
     ENDDO
     RELEASE more, choice
     SAVE TO Paymaint.Mem
```

The command to start all this off is:

. DO PAYROLL

It activates a command file that sets up the menu, using a DO CASE routine to process the options. The full file is shown in Fig. 5-4.

This file does some other things, too, to get your system ready to use and to close it down again at the end of the session:

```
SET TALK OFF
SET FORMAT TO SCREEN
SET CONSOLE ON
SET COLON OFF
SET BELL OFF
SET INTENSITY OFF
```

Take a look at the extensive list of SET commands in the dBASE manual. This group is used to set up the working parameters of the program. Talk puts the results of each command on the screen—invaluable when you're using query language, impossible when you're working with a dBASE procedure through a formatted screen. The screen and console commands put you in the normal screen oriented mode.

The bell, colon, and intensity settings reflect personal preferences. The colons and varied screen intensities that dBASE sets up make for a busy and distracting screen. If the "bell" sets up its beeping noise, it had better be a genuine emergency. You may feel otherwise. If so, it's your program. Use the available SET commands to tailor the system to your needs and preferences.

```
USE PAYCHEK INDEX PAYCHEK
SELECT SECONDARY
USE TRANSFIL INDEX TRANSFIL
SELECT PRIMARY
RESTORE FROM PAYMAINT.MEM
```

We introduce you now to the data files that will accompany you on your trip through payroll land. There are three:

☐ **Paychek** is a database file of personal information about each employee on the payroll. Its structure:

```
STRUCTURE FOR FILE:   PAYCHEK.DBF
NUMBER OF RECORDS:    00003
DATE OF LAST UPDATE:  00/00/00
PRIMARY USE DATABASE
FLD        NAME      TYPE WIDTH    DEC
001     LAST          C    010
002     FIRST         C    010
003     INITIAL       C    001
004     SSNO          C    011
005     VAC           C    001
006     TERM          C    001
007     REGPAY        N    007     002
008     OTPAY         N    007     002
009     SICK          N    007     002
010     GROSS         N    007     002
011     TAXABLE       N    007     002
012     WHHOLD        N    007     002
013     CHKFICA       N    007     002
014     INS           N    007     002
015     PENSION       N    007     002
016     NET           N    007     002
** TOTAL **                00105
```

This file is indexed on the Social Security number to, naturally enough, **Paychek.Ndx.** The number also is its link to the secondary file, **Transfil.** It looks like:

```
STRUCTURE FOR FILE:   TRANSFIL.DBF
NUMBER OF RECORDS:    00002
DATE OF LAST UPDATE:  00/00/00
PRIMARY USE DATABASE
FLD        NAME      TYPE WIDTH    DEC
001     LAST          C    010
002     FIRST         C    010
003     INITIAL       C    001
004     SSNO          C    011
005     VAC           C    001
006     TERM          C    001
007     REGPAY        N    007     002
008     OTPAY         N    007     002
009     SICK          N    007     002
010     GROSS         N    007     002
```

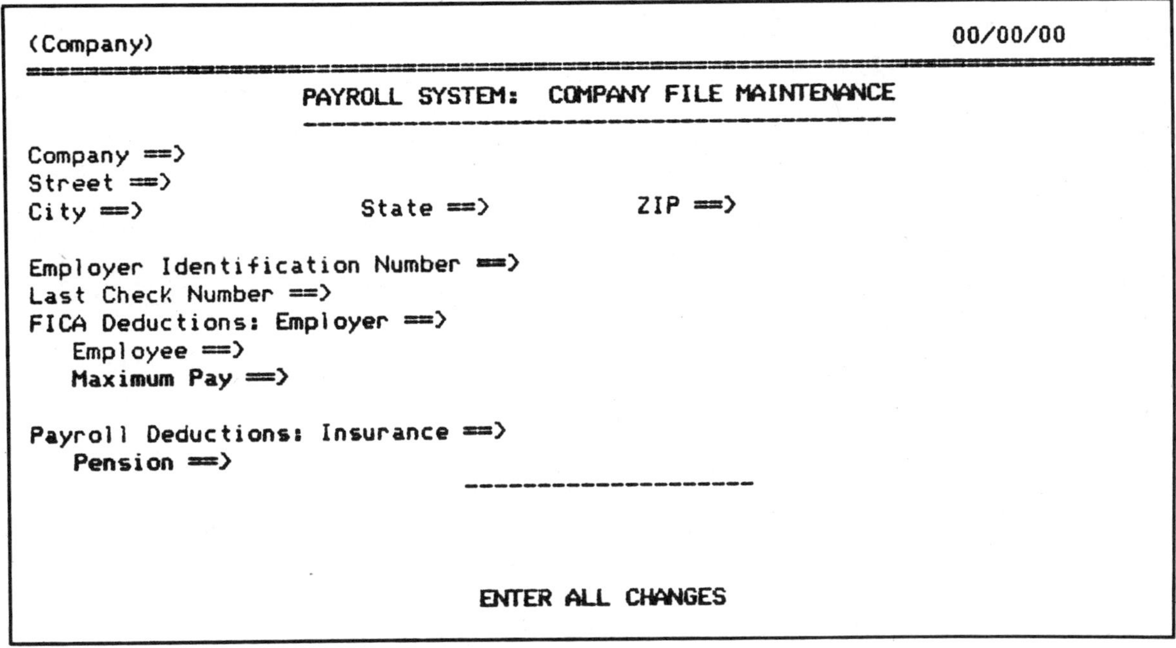

Fig. 5-5. Payroll file maintenance screen display.

011	TAXABLE	N	007	002
012	WHHOLD	N	007	002
013	INS	N	007	002
014	PENSION	N	007	002
015	NET	N	007	002
016	DATE	C	008	
017	CHECK	N	004	
** TOTAL **			00110	

Look almost the same, don't they. Actually, they store similar information for different purposes. **Paychek** is a list of employees. **Transfil** is a list of payroll transactions. **Paychek** will add or drop a record only when someone joins or leaves the payroll. **Transfil** will create a new file every time a check is issued. **Paychek** is the source of information for the payroll process. **Transfil** is a transaction file that records its results. You'll be able to see the difference when we begin printing checks.

The third source of information isn't a database. It's the profile list mentioned earlier—specifically, it's known as **Paymaint.Mem.** It's full of odd stuff like this:

CHECKNO	(N)	0
MORE	(L)	.T.
COMMAND	(C)	N
COMPANY	(C)	SUBMETROPOLIS WEEKLY SATELLITE
CSTREET	(C)	1234 MAIN ST
CCITY	(C)	SUBMETROPOLIS
CSTATE	(C)	NM
CZIP	(C)	99999

```
COFICA          (N)    0.07
DEDFICA         (N)    0.067
FICAMAX         (N)     37500
PENSION         (N)    2.50
EMPID           (N)    99-9999999
INS             (N)    2.50
```

We have here the company's name and address, the Social Security taxes and maximum pay (as of late 1983), the company's employer identification number, and a couple of normal payroll deductions. We've stuck with two kinds of deductions in this system to simplify the illustrations; you can add the number and variety you want.

To set up the file in the first place, STORE the information to dBASE's memory, then SAVE it in the standing memory file. Once you've established the file, you can call up a screen, Fig. 5-5, to enter and alter new data. In the likely event that you'd like to maintain different types of data, the easy way to create the screen is to use the dBASE ZIP program, its 16-bit equivalent, or one of the add-on screen programs listed in the chapter on dBASE accessories.

Paymaint.Cmd, Fig. 5-6, guides the screen manipulation. It uses a separate format file,

```
* PAYMAINT.CMD
*   Edits constant data in Paymaint.Mem
* OBTAIN EXISTING DATA
SET TALK OFF
SET CONSOLE ON
SET COLON OFF
SET BELL OFF
SET INTENSITY OFF
RESTORE FROM PAYMAINT.MEM
STORE T TO more
DO WHILE more
ERASE
* GET SCREEN INPUT
 DO  PAYMAINT.IO
 @ 21,10 SAY  ' ENTER ALL CHANGES '
 READ
 STORE  'N'  TO command
 @ 21,10 SAY  ' ANY MORE CHANGES (Y/N)? '   GET command
 READ
* PUT NEW ENTRIES INTO FILE
 SAVE TO PAYMAINT.MEM
 IF  !(command)<> 'Y'
  STORE F TO more
 ENDIF
ENDDO
RETURN
```

Fig. 5-6. Payroll file maintenance command file.

```
* PAYMAINT.IO
* Input/output screen for company file maintenance
@ 01,000 GET Company
@ 01,065 SAY Date()
@ 02,000 SAY '===================='
@ 02,020 SAY '===================='
@ 02,040 SAY '===================='
@ 02,060 SAY '===================='
@ 03,000 SAY '        PAYROLL SYSTEM:'
@ 03,022 SAY 'COMPANY FILE MAINTENANCE'
@ 04,000 SAY '      ----------------'
@ 04,020 SAY '--------------------'
@ 04,040 SAY '-------'
@ 05,000 SAY 'Company ==>'
@ 05,013 GET Company
@ 06,000 SAY 'Street ==>'
@ 06,012 GET cstreet
@ 07,000 SAY 'City ==>'
@ 07,009 GET ccity
@ 07,022 SAY ' State ==>'
@ 07,033 GET cstate
@ 07,041 SAY ' ZIP ==>'
@ 07,050 GET czip
@ 09,000 SAY 'Employer Identification Number ==>'
@ 09,035 GET empid
@ 10,000 SAY 'Last Check Number ==>'
@ 10,022 GET Checkno
@ 11,000 SAY 'FICA Deductions: Employer ==>'
@ 11,030 GET Cofica PICTURE '9.999'
@ 12,000 SAY '     Employee ==>'
@ 12,016 GET Dedfica PICTURE '9.999'
@ 13,000 SAY '     Maximum Pay ==>'
@ 13,019 GET ficamax
@ 15,000 SAY 'Payroll Deductions: '
@ 15,020 SAY 'Insurance ==>'
@ 15,034 GET ins PICTURE '9999.99'
@ 16,000 SAY '     Pension ==>'
@ 16,015 GET pension PICTURE '9999.99'
@ 17,000 SAY '          ---------------------'
RETURN
```

Fig. 5-7. Payroll file maintenance input screen format.

Paymaint.IO, Fig. 5-7, to lay out the screen. (Anyone who's familiar with Fox & Geller's QUICKCODE may recognize that program generator as the source of the last title. For the record, both ZIP and QUICKCODE were used to create the screen layouts and generate the basic dBASE code for many

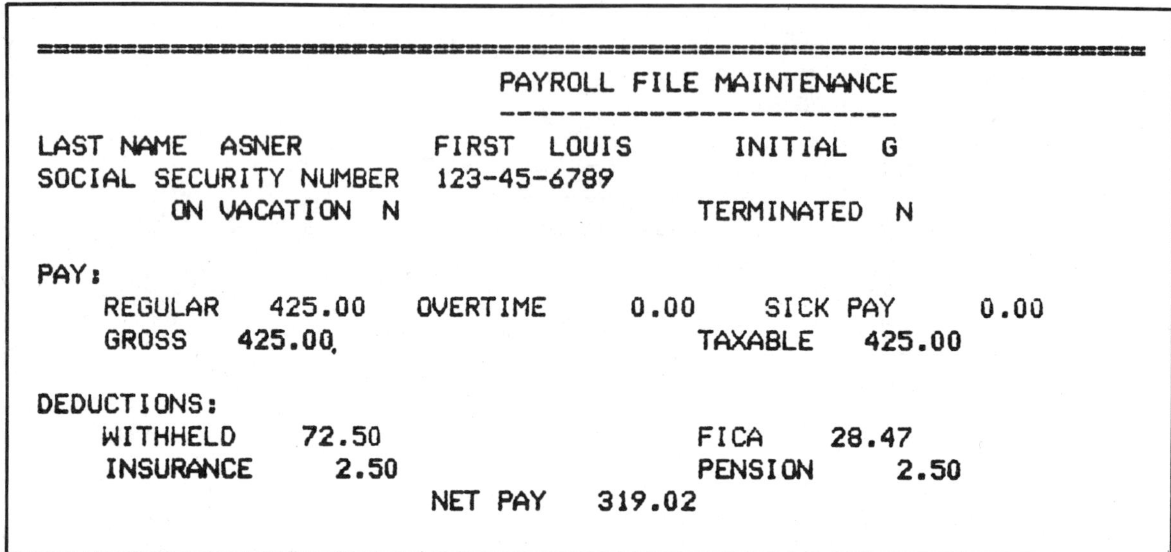

Fig. 5-8. Payroll screen display.

programs in this book. Usually, though, the generated programs have been enhanced and modified to improve their performance and usefulness.)

ADDING NEW RECORDS

The second menu listing presents a different screen, as seen in Fig. 5-8. It is a screen for entering information on new employees, and we see listed some of the confidential salary information for an old friend from some previous chapters. The operator enters the information on Asner's name, Social Security information, base pay, and deductions. Some items, such as taxable pay and the Social Security deduction, are calculated fields, and the system will not let you enter figures here.

Some of this data could be appended from the **Employee** database in the personnel system, or the operator could work from a printed employee record prepared from that system.

Notice that in this system the payroll deduction is a manual calculation which the operator enters. This can be a complicated procedure involving many factors, including the employee's pay rate, family status and number of withholding exemptions—plus your choice among the several options the Internal Revenue Service (IRS) offers for computing the deduction.

A routine could be written to calculate all these factors, but with a small payroll it's probably just as easy to use the standard tables in IRS Circular E, the basic *Employer's Tax Guide*.

If you're interested in automating the process, call or visit an IRS office and get a copy of Circular E. Once you obtain it, the most important information for payroll automation is on page 7 (of the July, 1983, edition). It tells you that the booklet you should *really* have is Publication 493, which outlines several calculation methods for automated payroll systems.

Paychek.Add, Fig. 5-9, is the program for adding new employees to the file; it uses **Paychek.OUT**, Fig. 5-10, to set up the screen format.

The Add program also calls a default values program, **Paychek.Fau**, (Fig. 5-11) which is included here mainly to show you what it might be good for. Its main function here is to initialize the variables with their proper size and type. It also includes a pair of values for the payroll deductions.

These values also appear in the profile listing **Paymaint.Mem,** suggesting that a procedure like

Payroll.Fau could be set up with the same values to achieve the same purpose. In other words, you could put the company name, the Social Security percentage and similar information into either the profile listing or the default file. You would use the dBASE EDIT command to update the default file. In any event, both options are available, and the choice is yours.

THE PAYDAY PROCESS

It stands to reason that the most complex operation in this system will be to issue the paychecks. The central command file is **Paychek.Get**, Fig. 5-12, which calls up information from the **Paychek** database and offers several options for processing and printing. In the process it uses a separate editing procedure, **Paychek.Ed**, Fig. 5-13; a format file for the paycheck, **Paychek.Fmt**, Fig. 5-14 and another screen file program, **Paychek.Out**, Fig. 5-15.

Let's go through the normal process first. For each employee on the list, **Paychek.Get** will present the data record and offer these options:

```
ENTER N FOR NEXT, P FOR PREVIOUS '
     S FOR SEARCH, M TO PROCESS CHECKS '
' PRESS RETURN WHEN DONE '   GET Gcmd
```

The N and P commands allow you to move forward and backward through the file, while S lets you search for a particular record. The normal procedure is to start with the first record in the file and press M to begin processing the check. It will redisplay the current record with this new set of options:

```
ENTER F TO FIGURE PAY, D TO DELETE,
     P TO PRINT CHECKS, C TO dSCAL
PRESS RETURN WHEN DONE
```

At this point, it's important that the operator remember this: the record you see displayed was retrieved from the database as it was entered—on the basis of last week's paycheck. If there have been no changes in the employee's pay, hours, or other information, you can go ahead and print the check.

If the employee has been terminated, the D option takes you through the normal dBASE procedure of deleting the item and then, after confirming your action, packing the file. Before you do that, though, make sure you process the final paycheck.

The C option is your main vehicle for entering new information and recomputing the pay. If the employee receives a raise, changes withholding exemptions, goes on vacation, or has some other change in status, this is the place to record it. Again you'll see the employee's record, this time displayed by the **Paychek.Ed** command (Fig. 5-13), a procedure that gives you the power to edit any noncalculated entry in the file. You'll see the file again and will be prompted to:

```
ENTER ALL CHANGES
```

Do so. When you're done you'll get a new set of prompts. Be careful here. Take notice that the calculated fields have not yet been recalculated on the basis of your new entries. Pressing "Y" at this point will do so and give you yet another chance. Answering "N" will close out the process taking you back to the *last recalculated record.* This is the one that will be used to print the paycheck.

This is where human surveillance can help head off a computerized error. Only when the operator is satisfied that *every* entry is correct should the process proceed. This is a point to make clear in your instructions and training. The program gives the operator a chance to verify the information on the screen.

```
*       PAYCHEK.ADD
* Adds new employees to payroll file Paychek.Dbf
* Uses format file Paychek.IO for screen display
* Uses Paychek.Fau to set up default values
STORE T TO Amore
DO WHILE Amore
* SET UP DEFAULT VALUES
 DO  PAYCHEK.FAU
ERASE
* GET DATA TO ADD
DO  PAYCHEK.IO
@ 21,10 SAY  '  ADD NEW EMPLOYEES TO THE PAYROLL '
@ 22,10 SAY  ' WHEN DONE ENTER A BLANK FORM'
READ
* ARE WE DONE?
IF Mssno  <>  '000-00-0000'
 APPEND BLANK
* PUT SCREEN DATA INTO FILE
 REPLACE   last   WITH  Mlast
 REPLACE   first  WITH  Mfirst
 REPLACE   initial  WITH  Minitial
 REPLACE   ssno  WITH  Mssno
 REPLACE   vac  WITH  Mvac
 REPLACE   term  WITH  Mterm
 REPLACE   regpay  WITH  Mregpay
 REPLACE   otpay  WITH  Motpay
 REPLACE   sick  WITH  Msick
 REPLACE   gross  WITH  Mgross
 REPLACE   taxable  WITH  Mtaxable
 REPLACE   whhold  WITH  Mwhhold
 REPLACE   chkfica WITH  Mchkfica
 REPLACE   ins  WITH  Mins
 REPLACE   pension  WITH  Mpension
 REPLACE   net  WITH  Mnet
ELSE
    STORE F TO Amore
ENDIF
ENDDO
RELEASE Amore
* RELEASE INPUT FIELDS
RELEASE Mlast
RELEASE Mfirst
RELEASE Minitial
```

Fig. 5-9. Command file for adding new employees to payroll. (Continued on page 133.)

```
RELEASE Mssno
RELEASE Mvac
RELEASE Mterm
RELEASE Mregpay
RELEASE Motpay
RELEASE Msick
RELEASE Mgross
RELEASE Mtaxable
RELEASE Mwhhold
RELEASE Mchkfica
RELEASE Mins
RELEASE Mpension
RELEASE Mnet
```

That's done on purpose. It should never be blindly accepted. The computer will do all the formatting, calculating, and other routine work, but verifying the correct amount of a paycheck should be a human function, particularly in a small business with a short payroll.

Once the operator is satisfied, the P command will begin the printing process detailed in Fig. 5-14. You'll have to hit the RETURN key a couple of times as the program computes and configures the check, but at the end the result should look like Fig. 5-15.

By the way, the standard forms shown here are from Uarco Business Forms (121 North 9th Street, DeKalb, Illinois 60115). The check form shown here is No. C699-2. If you use a different form, measure the horizontal and vertical locations of each entry and convert them to format file coordinates at the normal printer settings of 6 lines and 10 spaces per inch.

Search Options

This procedure gives you two ways to locate a record. Normally you would use the N and P commands to page your way through the file.

There's also a way to look up a particular employee's record. Enter S, and you'll be given a blank version of the payroll entry form. Type in the name and Social Security number of the employee you want. The program will call that record and display the rest of it. Now you can go on to edit and recalculate it with the C command. This might be useful if you want to enter payroll changes as they are received, instead of waiting for the next paycheck cycle.

You might notice that the computer does considerable bumping and grinding and requires a couple of stabs at the RETURN key before it will print each check. This happens because it's busy adding to the secondary database, **Transfil.Dbf.**

You should create a new **Transfil** each year. During the year it stores a running account of every paycheck issued. You'll use **Transfil** to create most of your reports, including a weekly payroll register, the annual W-2 forms, and the figures you'll need for your withholding tax deposits. It can generate other forms, too—all you need do is tell dBASE what you want. Most often, you'll find yourself adding up the payments or deductions for a particular purpose, such as the annual totals on the W-2 forms. **Transfil.Cmd,** Fig. 5.16, is called upon as the mechanism to transfer the data.

The W-2 forms in this system are generated by a dBASE staple: a looping program that runs from the beginning to the end of the file, printing a form for each entry. For each employee it adds the year's pay,

```
*       PAYCHEK.OUT
* Format file for output of payroll screen
@ 01,000 SAY '=================='
@ 01,020 SAY '=================='
@ 01,040 SAY '=================='
@ 01,060 SAY '=================='
@ 02,028 SAY 'PAYROLL FILE MAINTEN'
@ 02,048 SAY 'ANCE'
@ 03,028 SAY '--------------------'
@ 03,048 SAY '----'
@ 04,000 SAY 'LAST NAME'
@ 04,011 SAY last
@ 04,024 SAY 'FIRST'
@ 04,031 SAY first
@ 04,042 SAY 'INITIAL'
@ 04,051 SAY initial
@ 05,000 SAY 'SOCIAL SECURITY NUMB'
@ 05,020 SAY 'ER'
@ 05,024 SAY ssno
@ 06,008 SAY 'ON VACATION'
@ 06,021 SAY vac
@ 06,040 SAY 'TERMINATED'
@ 06,052 SAY term
@ 08,000 SAY 'PAY:'
@ 09,004 SAY 'REGULAR'
@ 09,013 SAY regpay
@ 09,023 SAY 'OVERTIME'
@ 09,033 SAY otpay
@ 09,044 SAY 'SICK PAY'
@ 09,054 SAY sick
@ 10,004 SAY 'GROSS'
STORE regpay+otpay+sick to gross
@ 10,011 SAY gross
@ 10,040 SAY 'TAXABLE'
STORE regpay+otpay to taxable
@ 10,049 SAY taxable
@ 12,000 SAY 'DEDUCTIONS:'
@ 13,004 SAY 'WITHHELD'
@ 13,014 SAY whhold
@ 13,040 SAY 'FICA'
STORE taxable*dedfica to chkfica
@ 13,046 SAY chkfica
@ 14,004 SAY 'INSURANCE'
```

Fig. 5-10. Output format for payroll reports. (Continued on page 135.)

```
@ 14,015 SAY ins
@ 14,040 SAY 'PENSION'
@ 14,049 SAY pension
@ 15,024 SAY 'NET PAY'
STORE whhold+chkfica+ins+pension to deduct
STORE gross-deduct to net
@ 15,033 SAY net
```

withholding, and other statistics and formats them to fit one version, at least, of the familiar form. If you have a different version, you'll have to find the coordinates. The listing is Fig. 5-17. Note that it gives you the option of issuing a separate form for a single employee. That can be handy in case a form is lost or there is an error in the original. You might also want to prepare W-2 forms for departing employees so you need not keep them on record the rest of the year.

Other Reports

Paychek.Rpt, Fig. 5-18, is the vehicle that gives you the option of producing self-defined reports and making ad hoc queries through the payroll system.

First, the program displays the names of any report formats you've already created. It then offers you the options of a printed or disk file report and calls for the name of the report you wish to produce and any conditions you want to impose.

For example, reporting on form **Taxlist** for:

```
*       PAYCHEK.FAU       -DEFAULT VALUES PROGRAM
STORE   '            '  TO  Mlast
STORE   '            '  TO  Mfirst
STORE   ' '  TO  Minitial
STORE   '000-00-0000'  TO  Mssno
STORE   ' '  TO  Mvac
STORE   ' '  TO  Mterm
STORE   0.00  TO  Mregpay
STORE   0.00  TO  Motpay
STORE   0.00  TO  Msick
STORE   0.00  TO  Mgross
STORE   0.00  TO  Mtaxable
STORE   0.00  TO  Mwhhold
STORE   0.00  TO  Mchkfica
STORE   2.50  TO  Mins
STORE   2.50  TO  Mpension
STORE   0.00  TO  Mnet
```

Fig. 5-11. Default file for payroll system.

```
*       PAYCHEK.GET
*  Calls data from file for payroll processing
*  Offers searching and update options
*  Uses Paychek.Ed to update files, Paychek.Fmt to print
*          checks and Paychek.Out for screen display.
SELECT SECONDARY
USE TRANSFIL INDEX TRANSFIL
SELECT PRIMARY
STORE  ' T '  TO Gselect
STORE T TO Gmore
STORE  'N'  TO Gdel
DO WHILE Gmore
ERASE
* DISPLAY CURRENT RECORD
IF &Gselect
 DO  PAYCHEK.OUT
ENDIF
STORE  ' '  TO Gcmd
@ 21,10 SAY  ' ENTER N FOR NEXT, P FOR PREVIOUS '
@ 22,10 SAY  '     S FOR SEARCH, M TO PROCESS CHECKS '
IF Gselect <>  ' T '
 @ 23,4 SAY 'XX'
ENDIF
@ 23,10 SAY  ' PRESS RETURN WHEN DONE '   GET Gcmd
READ
IF !(Gcmd)= 'S'
STORE T TO Smore
DO WHILE Smore
 ERASE
* GET FIELDS TO SEARCH FOR
@ 01,000 SAY '===================='
@ 01,020 SAY '===================='
@ 01,040 SAY '===================='
@ 01,066 SAY '===================='
@ 02,028 SAY 'PAYROLL RECORD SEARCH'
@ 03,028 SAY '---------------------'
@ 04,000 SAY 'LAST NAME'
 STORE  '              '  TO  Mlast
@ 04,010 GET Mlast
@ 04,024 SAY 'FIRST'
@ 04,042 SAY 'INITIAL'
@ 05,000 SAY 'SOCIAL SECURITY NUMBER'
 STORE  '000-00-0000'  TO  Mssno
```

Fig. 5-12. Search file for payroll system. (Continued on page 137.)

```
@ 05,023 GET Mssno PICTURE '999-99-9999'
@ 06,008 SAY 'ON VACATION'
@ 06,040 SAY 'TERMINATED'
@ 08,000 SAY 'PAY:'
@ 09,004 SAY 'REGULAR'
@ 09,023 SAY 'OVERTIME'
@ 09,044 SAY 'SICK PAY'
@ 10,004 SAY 'GROSS'
@ 10,040 SAY 'TAXABLE'
@ 12,000 SAY 'DEDUCTIONS:'
@ 13,004 SAY 'WITHHELD'
@ 13,040 SAY 'FICA'
@ 14,004 SAY 'INSURANCE'
@ 14,040 SAY 'PENSION'
@ 15,024 SAY 'NET PAY'
 @ 21,10 SAY  '   PLEASE ENTER VALUES TO SEARCH FOR  '
 IF Gselect <>  ' T '
  @ 23,4 SAY 'XX'
 ENDIF
 READ
X EXIT FROM LOOP IF FOUND
 GOTO TOP
 STORE TRIM(Mssno+Mlast) TO Gkey
 IF Gselect=  ' T '
  FIND &Gkey
  IF # <> 0
     STORE F TO Smore
 ELSE
  @ 22,10 SAY  '   NOT FOUND  '
  @ 23,10 SAY  ' TRY AGAIN(Y/N)? '
  SET CONSOLE OFF
  WAIT TO Gagain
  SET CONSOLE ON
  IF !(Gagain) <>  'Y'
  STORE F TO Smore
 ENDIF  Y
 RELEASE Gagain
  ENDIF  # <> 0
 ELSE
  LOCATE FOR  ssno+Mlast  = Mssno+Mlast .AND. &Gselect
  IF .NOT. EOF
    STORE F TO Smore
 ELSE
```

```
     @ 22,10 SAY  '   NOT FOUND  '
     @ 23,10 SAY  ' TRY AGAIN(Y/N)? '
     SET CONSOLE OFF
     WAIT TO Gagain
     SET CONSOLE ON
     IF !(Gagain) <>  'Y'
     STORE F TO Smore
   ENDIF  Y
   RELEASE Gagain
    ENDIF EOF
   ENDIF  Gselect=T
ENDDO  Smore
RELEASE Smore
RELEASE Gkey
ELSE
IF !(Gcmd) =   'N'
  STORE T TO Gno
  DO WHILE Gno
     SKIP
     IF &Gselect
       STORE F TO Gno
     ENDIF
     IF EOF
       STORE F TO Gno
       STORE  ' T '  TO Gselect
       @ 23,4 SAY ' '
     ENDIF
  ENDDO
  RELEASE Gno
ELSE
IF !(Gcmd)= 'P'
     STORE  ' T '  TO Gselect
     @ 23,4 SAY '  '
     SKIP -1
ELSE
  IF !(Gcmd)= 'M'
  STORE T TO Mmore
  DO WHILE Mmore
  STORE  ' '  TO Mmd
  @ 21,10 SAY  ' ENTER C TO FIGURE PAY, D TO DELETE,
  @ 22,10 SAY  '         P TO PRINT CHECKS'
  IF Gselect <>  ' T '
   @ 23,4 SAY '**'
```

Fig. 5-12. Search file for payroll system. (Continued on page 139.)

```
    ENDIF
    @ 23,10 SAY  ' PRESS RETURN WHEN DONE ' ' GET Mmd
    READ
    IF !(Mmd) = 'C'
        ERASE
IF Gselect <>  ' T '
 @ 23,4 SAY 'XX'
ENDIF
X EDIT RECORD
        DO  PAYCHEK.ED
ELSE
IF !(Mmd)= 'D'
        STORE  'N'  TO Gans
  IF Gselect <>  ' T '
   @ 23,4 SAY 'XX'
  ENDIF
@ 23,10 SAY  ' ARE YOU SURE(Y/N)?
@ 23,28 GET Gans
        READ
IF !(Gans)= 'Y'
        DELETE
        STORE  'Y'  TO Gdel
ENDIF
RELEASE Gans
ELSE
IF !(Mmd)= 'P'
 @ 23,10 SAY  ' PLEASE SET UP PRINTER
 SET CONSOLE OFF
 WAIT
 STORE checkno+1 to checkno
 DO TRANSFILE
 SET CONSOLE ON
 SET FORMAT TO PRINT
 DO  PAYCHEK.FMT
 SET FORMAT TO SCREEN
ELSE
 STORE F TO Mmore
ENDIF  F
ENDIF  P
ENDIF  D
ENDIF  E
ENDDO  Mmore
RELEASE Mmore,Mmd
```

```
ELSE
    STORE F TO Gmore
ENDIF  M
ENDIF  P
ENDIF  N
ENDIF  S
ENDDO  Gmore
IF Gdel =  'Y'
    STORE  'N'  TO Gans
    @ 23,10 SAY  'WANT TO PERMANENTLY DELETE RECORDS(Y/N)'
    @ 23,49 GET Gans
    READ
    IF Gans =  'Y'
        PACK
    ELSE
        RECALL ALL
    ENDIF
        RELEASE Gans
ENDIF  Gdel
RELEASE  Gcmd,Gmore,Gdel,Gselect
```

Fig. 5-12. Search file for payroll system. (Continued from page 139.)

```
*    PAYCHEK.ED      -EDIT PROGRAM
STORE T TO Emore
* SET UP SCREEN VARIABLES
 STORE  last  TO  Mlast
 STORE  first  TO  Mfirst
 STORE  initial  TO  Minitial
 STORE  ssno  TO  Mssno
 STORE  vac  TO  Mvac
 STORE  term  TO  Mterm
 STORE  regpay  TO  Mregpay
 STORE  otpay  TO  Motpay
 STORE  sick  TO  Msick
 STORE  gross  TO  Mgross
 STORE  taxable  TO  Mtaxable
 STORE  whhold  TO  Mwhhold
 STORE  chkfica TO Mchkfica
 STORE  ins  TO  Mins
 STORE  pension  TO  Mpension
 STORE  net  TO  Mnet
DO WHILE Emore
ERASE
```

Fig. 5-13. Editing command file. (Continued on page 141.)

```
* GET SCREEN INPUT
 DO  PAYCHEK.IO
 @ 21,10 SAY  ' ENTER ANY CHANGES '
 READ
 STORE  'N'  TO Ecmd
 @ 21,10 SAY  ' RECALCULATE OR MORE CHANGES (Y/N)? '  GET Ecmd
 READ
* PUT SCREEN ENTRIES INTO FILE
 REPLACE  last  WITH  Mlast
 REPLACE  first  WITH  Mfirst
 REPLACE  initial  WITH  Minitial
 REPLACE  ssno  WITH  Mssno
 REPLACE  vac  WITH  Mvac
 REPLACE  term  WITH  Mterm
 REPLACE  regpay  WITH  Mregpay
 REPLACE  otpay  WITH  Motpay
 REPLACE  sick  WITH  Msick
 REPLACE  gross  WITH  Mgross
 REPLACE  taxable  WITH  Mtaxable
 REPLACE  whhold  WITH  Mwhhold
 REPLACE  chkfica WITH Mchkfica
 REPLACE  ins  WITH  Mins
 REPLACE  pension  WITH  Mpension
 REPLACE  net  WITH  Mnet
 IF  !(Ecmd)<> 'Y'
   STORE F TO Emore
 ENDIF
ENDDO
RELEASE Emore,Ecmd
RELEASE Mlast
RELEASE Mfirst
RELEASE Minitial
RELEASE Mssno
RELEASE Mvac
RELEASE Mterm
RELEASE Mregpay
RELEASE Motpay
RELEASE Msick
RELEASE Mgross
RELEASE Mtaxable
RELEASE Mwhhold
RELEASE Mchkfica
RELEASE Mins
RELEASE Mpension
RELEASE Mnet
```

```
* PAYCHEK.FMT
*  Print format for paychecks
@  2, 0 SAY Company
@  2,40 SAY Date()
@  2,56 SAY Checkno
@  3, 0 SAY TRIM(last)+' '+TRIM(first)+' '+ initial
@  3,56 SAY ssno
@  5, 0 SAY "PAY"
@  5,40 SAY "DEDUCTIONS"
@  6, 0 SAY "Regular"
@  6,16 SAY regpay
@  6,40 SAY "Fed. Inc. Tax"
@  6,56 SAY whhold
@  7, 0 SAY "Overtime"
@  7,16 SAY otpay
@  7,40 SAY "FICA"
@  7,56 SAY chkfica
@  8, 0 SAY "Sick Pay"
@  8,16 SAY sick
@  8,40 SAY "Insurance"
@  8,56 SAY ins
@  9, 2 SAY "TOTAL"
@  9,16 SAY gross
@  9,40 SAY "Pension"
@  9,56 SAY pension
@ 16, 0 SAY "NET PAY"
@ 16, 9 SAY net
@ 21, 0 SAY Company
@ 21,40 SAY "EAST BANK OF THE MISSISSIPPI"
@ 22,40 SAY "Lock and Dam Office"
@ 23,40 SAY "Dockside, TN 99999"
@ 25, 0 SAY checkno
@ 25,40 SAY Date()
@ 28, 8 SAY TRIM(last)+' '+TRIM(first)+' '+initial
@ 29,58 SAY net
@ 42,79 SAY ' '
@  1,0 SAY ' '
?
RETURN
```

Fig. 5-14. Format file for paycheck.

```
SUBMETROPOLIS WEEKLY SATELLITE                 00/00/00                4
TROLL WALTER W                                                 234-56-7890

PAY                                            DEDUCTIONS
Regular                400.00                  Fed. Inc. Tax       61.20
Overtime                25.00                  FICA                28.47
Sick Pay                 0.00                  Insurance            2.50
  TOTAL                425.00                  Pension              2.50




NET PAY    330.32
```

Please retain this portion for your records

```
SUBMETROPOLIS WEEKLY SATELLITE                 EAST BANK OF THE MISSISSIPPI
                                               Lock and Dam Office
                                               Dockside, TN 99999

          4                                    00/00/00
```

Pay to the Order of TROLL WALTER W

Amount 330.32

NOT NEGOTIABLE

Authorized Signature

Fig. 5-15. Sample paycheck.

```
X TRANSFIL.CMD
X Transfers data on paychecks printed to transaction file
SELECT SECONDARY
APPEND BLANK
  REPLACE   S.date WITH DATE()
  REPLACE   S.check WITH checkno
  REPLACE   S.last  WITH  P.last
  REPLACE   S.first  WITH  P.first
  REPLACE   S.initial  WITH  P.initial
  REPLACE   S.ssno  WITH  P.ssno
  REPLACE   S.vac  WITH  P.vac
  REPLACE   S.term  WITH  P.term
  REPLACE   S.regpay  WITH  P.regpay
  REPLACE   S.otpay  WITH  P.otpay
  REPLACE   S.sick  WITH  P.sick
  REPLACE   S.gross  WITH  P.gross
  REPLACE   S.taxable  WITH  P.taxable
  REPLACE   S.whhold  WITH  P.whhold
  REPLACE   S.chkfica WITH P.chkfica
  REPLACE   S.ins  WITH  P.ins
  REPLACE   S.pension  WITH  P.pension
  REPLACE   S.net  WITH  P.net
SELECT PRIMARY
RETURN
```

Fig. 5-16. Command file for transaction file.

```
DATE <='01/01/84'  .AND.  DATE >='03/31/84'
```

should give you a report of payroll taxes deducted during the first quarter of 1984. You then can make the necessary deposits in your account for these taxes. The IRS has varied requirements for the time and amounts of these deposits, so the program makes you specify your own dates.

To make things simpler, you might include a line in the procedure that stores these date specifications to a memory variable, which you might call **firstq.** Then when the computer asks for your conditions you merely could use the macro function to specify **&firstq.** You could use the same technique, of course, for other commonly used time periods.

The **Taxlist** report form is designed to add up a variety of totals for the period you specify. Make it a summary report with subtotals on the Social Security number—not because you need it, but to cut out much of the unneeded detail you'd otherwise get. The columns should be arranged like this:

```
8,GROSS                         EMPLOYEE; FICA; TO DATE
GROSS; SALARY
                                8, FICATD*COFICA
8, TAXABLE                      EMPLOYER; FICA; TO DATE
TAXABLE; PAY
                                8,WHHOLDTD
8, CKFICA                       INCOME; TAX; WITHHELD
```

```
*       WTWO.CMD
* Calculates and prints W-2 forms
ERASE
* Designate Transfil as the source of data
SELECT SECONDARY
USE TRANSFIL INDEX TRANSFIL
* Temporarily use Paychek to identify employee
SELECT PRIMARY
STORE 23 TO Wsize
STORE '                        '  TO Wslct
STORE 'Y' TO Wans
* Provide for individual printings.
@ 21,10 SAY 'PRINT INDIVIDUAL FORM? (Y/N)'  GET Wans
READ
@ 21,10
IF !(Wans)='Y'
  @ 21,10 SAY 'PLEASE ENTER SOCIAL SECURITY NUMBER'
  @ 23,10 GET Wslct
  READ
  @ 21,10
  @ 23,10
ELSE
  STORE 'T' TO Wslct
ENDIF
* Prepare to print
GOTO TOP
@ 23,10 SAY  ' PLEASE SET UP YOUR PRINTER '
SET CONSOLE OFF
WAIT
SET CONSOLE ON
* REPEAT UNTIL FILE ENDS
DO WHILE .NOT. EOF
  STORE P.ssno to Wslct
  IF Wslct <> ' '
* Go to Transfil for data.  Store to variables representing
*        positions on the form.
  SELECT SECONDARY
  STORE empid TO MQ1:02
  STORE company TO MQ1:03
  STORE cstreet TO MQ1:04
  STORE ccity TO MQ1:05
  STORE cstate TO MQ1:06
  STORE czip TO MQ1:07
```

Fig. 5-17. Command file for Form W-2. (Continued on page 146.)

```
    STORE ssno TO MQ1:08
* Add calculated values
  SUM S.whhold TO MQ1:09 FOR S.ssno=Wslct
  SUM S.taxable TO MQ1:10 FOR S.ssno=Wslct
* Determine maximum Social Security pay.  Calculate withholding
  SUM S.taxable TO MQ1:12 FOR S.ssno=Wslct
        IF MQ1:12 > ficamax
        STORE ficamax to MQ1:12
        ENDIF
  STORE MQ1:12*dedfica TO MQ1:11
* Identify employee
  STORE P.last TO MQ1:13
  STORE P.first TO MQ1:14
  STORE P.initial TO MQ1:15
 ELSE
* Skip invalid records
  SELECT PRIMARY
  SKIP
  LOOP
 ENDIF
*  Set print format
SET PRINT ON
 ?  '                                    '+STR(MQ1:02,        11,0)
 ?  ' '+MQ1:03
 ?  ' '+MQ1:04
 ?  ' '+MQ1:05
 ?  ' '+MQ1:06+' '+MQ1:07
 ?
 ?  ' '+MQ1:08+' '+STR(MQ1:09,     11,2)+'    '+STR(MQ1:10,     11,2);
        +' '+STR(MQ1:11,         11,2)

 ?  '                                    '+STR(MQ1:12,        11,2)
 ?  '      '+MQ1:13+' '+MQ1:14+' '+MQ1:15
 ?
 ?
 ?
 ?
 ?
 ?
 ?
 ?
 ?
 ?
```

Fig. 5-17. Command file for Form W-2. (Continued on page 147.)

```
      ?
      ?
      ?
   X Return  to topo
    SELECT PRIMARY
    SKIP
 ENDDO    NOT EOF
 SET PRINT OFF
 SET CONSOLE ON
 RELEASE Wsize,Wans,Wslct
    RELEASE MQ1:01
    RELEASE MQ1:02
    RELEASE MQ1:03
    RELEASE MQ1:04

    RELEASE MQ1:05
    RELEASE MQ1:06
    RELEASE MQ1:07
    RELEASE MQ1:08
    RELEASE MQ1:09
    RELEASE MQ1:10
    RELEASE MQ1:11
    RELEASE MQ1:12
    RELEASE MQ1:13
    RELEASE MQ1:14
    RELEASE MQ1:15
  RETURN
```

The Pay Register

Call form **Register** for the date of the last paychecks, and you'll print a list of the checks issued that week, including the detailed breakdown. This is a straight, totaled report covering these headings:

```
11,SSNO
SOCIAL SECURITY NO

15,TRIM(LAST)+' '+TRIM(FIRST)+' '+INITIAL
NAME

5,CHECKNO
CHECK NO.

7,REGPAY
REGULAR PAY

7,OTPAY
```

```
*       PAYCHEK.RPT
*   A command driven routine for producing payroll reports.
*   List existing report formats
ERASE
?
?
LIST FILES LIKE *.FRM
?
?'==============================================================
   ==============='
* Choose printer or disk file for report
STORE   '  '   TO Rlpt
DO WHILE !(Rlpt) <>  'Y'   .AND. !(Rlpt) <>   'N'
STORE  'Y'   TO Rlpt
@ 19,10 SAY  ' WANT REPORT SENT TO THE PRINTER? '   GET Rlpt
READ
ENDDO
   STORE  '  '   TO Rdsk
   DO WHILE !(Rdsk) <>  'Y'   .AND. !(Rdsk) <>   'N'
   STORE  'N'   TO Rdsk
@ 19,10 SAY  ' WANT REPORT SENT TO A FILE ?            GET Rdsk
READ
ENDDO
IF !(Rdsk)= 'Y'
STORE  '            '   TO Rfile
DO WHILE Rfile =  '           '
@ 20,10 SAY  ' ENTER FILE NAME '   GET Rfile
READ
ENDDO
STORE TRIM(Rfile) TO Rfile
ENDIF   RDSK
STORE  '           '   TO report
   DO WHILE report =  '      '
@ 21,10 SAY  ' ENTER REPORT NAME '   GET report
@ 22,10 SAY  ' SPECIFY CONDITIONS'   GET cond
READ
ENDDO
IF !(Rlpt) =   'Y'
@ 23,10 SAY  ' PLEASE SET UP PRINTER
SET CONSOLE OFF
WAIT
SET CONSOLE ON
SET PRINT ON
```

Fig. 5-18. Reporting file for payroll data. (Continued on page 149.)

```
ENDIF Rlpt
X  Open the disk file named earlier
IF !(Rdsk) =  'Y'
SET ALTERNATE TO &Rfile
SET ALTERNATE ON
ENDIF RDSK
ERASE
X Call for report form.  If it does not already exist,
X          dBASE will go through the report creation sequence.
REPORT FORM &report FOR &cond
SET PRINT OFF
SET ALTERNATE OFF
IF !(Rdsk) = 'Y'
   RELEASE Rdsk,Rfile
ENDIF
RELEASE Rlpt, report
```

```
O'TIME

7,OTHRPAY
OTHER

7,GROSS
GROSS PAY

7,WHHOLD
TAX; W'HELD

7,CKFICA
FICA

7,HEALTHDED+MMDED+DENTDED+LIFEDED
DEDUCT

7,NET
NET PAY
```

Notice that you can use TRIM to combine the employee's name into a single column. A semicolon in any title heading will send the next word to the next line; use it if you want to make that decision—otherwise dBASE will make it for you.

These are just examples of some of the reports you can create for yourself. You can work up forms of your own to such things as figuring total individual contributions to the pension plan or adding up total payroll costs. The basic technique is to set up the report format to call for the items you want to add.

```
*      PAYCHEK.GO      -STARTUP & INDEX PGM
*    USE THIS PGM TO START A KEYED DATA FILE
*    OR RE-INDEX AN EXISTING ONE
SET TALK OFF
SELECT PRIMARY
USE  PAYCHEK
INDEX ON   ssno+ last  TO  PAYCHEK
SELECT SECONDARY
USE TRANSFIL
INDES ON ssno + last to TRANSFIL
SELECT PRIMARY
```

Fig. 5-19. Reindexing command for payroll files, PAYCHEK.GO.

For the pension report, for example, you might set up columns for the name and contribution, giving a summary report with subtotals by Social Security number.

One Last Item

The final menu item is the brief **Paychek.GO**, Fig. 5-19. As explained earlier, this is the reindexing command that is the best way to save your skin. Use it the way citizens of certain cities, by legend, are urged to vote: early and often.

Chapter 6

Keeping
the Right Inventory

Nick Nader bought the first Corvair ever sold in the town of Greencastle Center, Vermont, and he still has it. "Nothing like it for gettin' up these mountains in the snow," Nader explained. "And it doesn't need any antifreeze."

Nick began to worry a few years later when a young man of the same name wrote a book about the Corvair, and he was quick to disavow any knowledge or common ancestry. He quietly began to fill his barn with spare parts for his favorite vehicle. The pace of his acquisitions picked up sharply after General Motors discontinued the Corvair, and the barn soon was filled with Monza fenders, Corsa taillights, and other Corvair exotica. Then one day the proverbial son home from college discovered the collection and exclaimed, "You've got a gold mine here."

Thus was born Nader and Son Corvair Parts, promising Delivery at Any Speed. Nick's sense of Yankee practicality, coupled with his son's newly acquired knowledge of modern business management, combined to establish a small but growing business, providing parts to fellow Corvair freaks who wanted to rebuild the surviving examples of GM's own Edsel.

Of course, father and son didn't always speak the same language. The son surveyed the well-stocked barn one day and pointed out that as orders kept rolling in there was less and less time to search through the barn for the requested parts. "What we need," said the son, "is a modern database system of inventory management."

"We need something worse than that," said the father. "We need a way to keep track of all this stuff."

It really didn't take them long to figure out they were talking about the same thing. Nader and Son soon found itself with a microcomputer equipped with dBASE II to manage its inventory and keep track of all that stuff.

Keeping the right inventory on hand is vital to nearly every small business. Keep your stock too low, and you often won't be able to meet the needs of your customers. When that happens, they'll go somewhere else. Maintain too high a level, and you have precious cash tied up in stock that isn't being sold. The worst possible combination is to have too large an investment in slow-moving items and too little money in the things most customers want.

This inventory management system is designed to help you keep track of what's moving—and what isn't. On one level, it's a basic method of keeping track of your stock and its value. On another, it's a source of periodic reports that can show you how rapidly each item in your inventory moves. With that knowledge you can weed out the slow-selling merchandise and make sure you always have enough of the hot stuff.

The system operates from a basic inventory record screen, as seen in Fig. 6-1, and from this database structure:

```
STRUCTURE FOR FILE:    STOCK.DBF
NUMBER OF RECORDS:     00006
DATE OF LAST UPDATE:   00/00/00
PRIMARY USE DATABASE
FLD         NAME        TYPE WIDTH      DEC
001         PARTNO        C    020
002         DESC          C    037
003         YEAR          C    019
004         MODEL         C    014
005         BODY          C    014
006         STATUS        C    008
007         DEPT          C    008
008         ONHAND        N    005
009         COST          N    008       002
010         DISC          N    002
011         MAX           N    008
012         MIN           N    008
013         REORD         N    008
014         SALES         N    008
015         RETURN        N    008
016         RECD          N    008
017         ORDQ          N    008
018         ORDNO         C    008
019         ORDDT         C    008
020         VENDOR        C    015
021         ALTERNATE     C    015
** TOTAL **                    00238
```

The key to the system is a *part number*. It meets this important need: one unique way to identify each item in the stock. Every item, and every variation in size, shape, and color should have its individual identifying number.

The description calls for a general identification, such as a bumper or spark plug. On the next line are places for the year, model, and body style the part is intended to fit. Collectively, these might correspond to a size listing in your own inventory.

```
                        INVENTORY STOCK RECORD

================================================================================
PART NO. :                 DESCRIPTION :
FITS YEAR :                MODEL :                      BODY :
USED/NOS/NEW :             DEPARTMENT :
                           ---------------------
                             Cost and Quantity
ON HAND :                  UNIT COST :                  DISCOUNT :
LIST PRICE :
MAXIMUM STOCK :            REORDER POINT :              QUANTITY :
SOLD :                     RETURNED :                   RECEIVED :
ON ORDER :                 ORDER NO :                   DATE :
                           ---------------------
                             Vendor Information

PRIMARY VENDOR :
ALTERNATE SOURCE :
```

Fig. 6-1. Inventory system screen display.

The business has grown since the Naders started selling parts from the barn, and now they obtain parts from several wholesalers and other sources. There is one entry for new or used parts, or for NOS items. (The latter stands for *New Original Stock,* an important item to some old car buffs. It refers to surviving new replacement parts made when the Corvair was still a current model.)

It is included to demonstrate how a good system can be tailored to the different inventory needs of different kinds of businesses. You probably don't want to classify your inventory the same way the Naders group does theirs—the purpose here is to demonstrate the possibilities.

In the **Department** entry, the Naders group their stock into mechanical parts, body parts, and interior trim. The next group of entries is fairly common to everyone. You have the quantity on hand, the cost of each item, and the normal wholesale discount. From this, the program can calculate the item's list price.

Then come the number received, sold, and returned as well as a record of pending orders. Also on the record is the primary source of such parts, and an alternate source in case the primary source can't meet the need.

THE MENU SELECTIONS

The command file in Fig. 6-2 and the index update utility in Fig. 6-3 produce the system menu shown in Fig. 6-4. This menu differs a little from previous menus, because the process of entering data is more centralized in a single group of commands, and because it offers a wider range of reports.

Another difference is that the file is in this passage of the command file:

```
STORE FILE('STOCKNO.NDX') TO index
IF .NOT. index
 DO STOCK.GO
STORE FILE ('STOCKDPT.NDX') TO index
IF .NOT. index
 DO STOCK.GO
STORE FILE ('STOCKVEN.NDX') TO index
```

```
* 	STOCK.CMD
* 	Main command and menu program for inventory system.
*
SET TALK OFF
SET FORMAT TO SCREEN
SET COLON OFF
SET BELL OFF
SET INTENSITY OFF
SELECT PRIMARY
STORE FILE('STOCKNO.NDX') TO index
IF .NOT. index
 DO STOCK.GO
STORE FILE ('STOCKDPT.NDX') TO index
IF .NOT. index
 DO STOCK.GO
STORE FILE ('STOCKVEN.NDX') TO index
IF .NOT. index
 DO STOCK.GO
 ERASE
 @ 21,10 SAY  ' FILE IS NOW BEING INDEXED '
ENDIF
USE STOCK   INDEX  STOCKNO, STOCKDPT, STOCKVEN
STORE T TO more
DO WHILE more
 ERASE
@  1, 0 SAY "Nader & Son Corvair Parts"
@  1,64 SAY Date()
@  2, 0 SAY "=================================================="
@  2,50 SAY "=============================="
@  3,29 SAY "INVENTORY SYSTEM MENU"
@  4,29 SAY "---------------------"
@  5,24 SAY "1:   Maintain Parts Listings"
@  6,24 SAY "2:   Print Standard Reports"
@  7,24 SAY "3:   Print Ad Hoc Reports"
@  8,24 SAY "4:   Reindex Database"
@  9,24 SAY "-----------------------------------"
@ 10,24 SAY "R:   Return to Previous Operation"
@ 11,24 SAY "X:   Return to Operating System"
@ 14,24 SAY "Please Enter Your Choice ==>_"
SET CONSOLE OFF
 WAIT TO option
 SET CONSOLE ON
DO CASE
```

Fig. 6-2. Menu command file. (Continued on page 155.)

```
CASE !(option)= '1'
    DO STOCK.GET
CASE !(option)= '2'
    DO SALES.GET
CASE !(option)= '3'
    DO REPORT.MEN
CASE !(option)='4'
    DO STOCK.RPT
CASE !(option)='5'
    @ 21,10 SAY  ' FILE IS NOW BEING INDEXED '
    DO STOCK.GO
CASE !(option)='R'
    CANCEL
CASE !(option)='X'
    QUIT
    ENDCASE
ENDDO
RELEASE more,option,index
RETURN
```

```
IF .NOT. index
 DO STOCK.GO
 ERASE
 @ 21,10 SAY  ' FILE IS NOW BEING INDEXED '
ENDIF
USE STOCK  INDEX  STOCKNO, STOCKDPT, STOCKVEN
```

It shows that the file is indexed on three different fields: the part number (**stockno**), the department (**stockdpt**), and the vendor from whom the part was obtained (**stockven**). This routine checks at the outset to make sure each of the three indexes is in order and calls the **GO** routine if any are not.

The main reason for all these indexes is that the system includes reports broken down by all three categories. For the report generator to work properly, the database must primarily be indexed on that category.

Also, there's no direct counterpart to the data addition function we had in the earlier files. If a new inventory item is received, it usually will have an existing part number in the files. Therefore, adding the new entry is an editing function, in which you alter an existing file. An addition process is called only if the program fails to find the number on file and you agree a new listing should be created for it.

All these functions are controlled by the main file management program, **Stock.Get,** Fig. 6-5. This is the same type of multifaceted program we used in the payroll system to edit, search for, and print records. The Naders will use it in a variety of ways.

POSTING ORDERS

When an order arrives or a customer inquires, the operator uses the S function of this file to check the available stock of this item. The screen design listing within the program sets up a blank screen and calls

```
*       STOCK.GO
*       USE TO START A KEYED DATA FILE
*       OR REINDEX AN EXISTING ONE
SET TALK OFF
SELECT PRIMARY
USE  STOCK
INDEX ON  partno TO  STOCKNO
INDEX ON  dept TO STOCKDEPT
INDEX ON  vendor TO STOCKVEN
RETURN
```

Fig. 6-3. Inventory system reindexing file.

for the part number; once you enter it, the program will find and display the rest of the information for that part.

The operator might find that there are six of these parts in stock, and can verify that they will fit the customer's year, model, and body style. If the part identified by the number doesn't fit the customer's car, the operator can take note of that and check for the source of the error.

Perhaps the part is out of stock, but a new supply is on order. The listing will point that out.

THE ODD REQUEST

This routine is useful, of course, only when the stock number is known. The Naders' catalogs and order blanks encourage customers to use the numbers, but old car nuts are more likely to phrase their requests as, "Do you have a new manifold pressure gauge for a '64 Spyder?"

It just happens that you *don't* know the part number of this item right off the top of your head. Instead, you use the searching function. It requires that you use dBASE query language to phrase a search for the things you do know.

```
Nader & Son Corvair Parts                                    Date()
================================================================
                      INVENTORY SYSTEM MENU
                      ---------------------

                1:   Maintain Parts Listings
                2:   Record Sales
                3:   Print Standard Reports
                4:   Print Ad Hoc Reports
                5:   Reindex Database
                ------------------------------------
                R:   Return to Previous Operation
                X:   Return to Operating System


                Please Enter Your Choice ==>_
```

Fig. 6-4. Inventory system menu.

```
*       STOCK.GET
*  General control program to search, update and display
*          inventory records.
STORE  ' T '   TO select
STORE T TO Gmore
STORE  'N'   TO Gdel
DO WHILE Gmore
ERASE
STORE  ' SEARCH '  TO mode
* DISPLAY CURRENT RECORD
IF &select
 DO   STOCK.OUT
ENDIF
STORE  ' '   TO command
@ 21,10 SAY  ' ENTER N FOR NEXT LISTING, P FOR PREVIOUS '
@ 22,10 SAY '      S TO SEARCH FILES, M FOR MORE COMMANDS '
IF select <>  ' T '
 @ 23,4 SAY 'XX'
ENDIF
@ 23,10 SAY  ' PRESS RETURN WHEN DONE '   GET command
READ
IF !(command)= 'S'
STORE T TO Smore
DO WHILE Smore
 ERASE
 STORE  ' SEARCH '  TO mode
* GET FIELDS TO SEARCH FOR
@ 02,000 SAY '====================='
@ 02,020 SAY '====================='
@ 02,040 SAY '====================='
@ 02,060 SAY '====================='
@ 03,000 SAY 'PART NO.'
 STORE  '                        '  TO  Mpartno
@ 03,009 GET Mpartno
@ 03,030 SAY 'DESCRIPTION'
@ 04,000 SAY 'FITS YEAR'
@ 04,030 SAY 'MODEL'
@ 04,060 SAY 'BODY'
@ 05,000 SAY 'USED/NOS/NEW'
@ 05,030 SAY 'DEPARTMENT'
@ 05,041 SAY Mdept
@ 06,030 SAY '---------------------'
@ 07,031 SAY 'Cost and Quantity'
```

Fig. 6-5. Inventory system file maintenance. (Continued on page 158.)

```
@ 03,000 SAY 'ON HAND'
@ 08,030 SAY 'UNIT COST'
@ 08,060 SAY 'DISCOUNT'
@ 09,000 SAY 'LIST PRICE'
@ 10,000 SAY 'MAXIMUM STOCK'
@ 10,030 SAY 'REORDER POINT'
@ 10,060 SAY 'QUANTITY'
@ 11,000 SAY 'SOLD'
@ 11,030 SAY 'RETURNED'
@ 11,060 SAY 'RECEIVED'
@ 12,000 SAY 'ON ORDER'
@ 12,030 SAY 'ORDER NO'
@ 12,060 SAY 'DATE'
@ 13,030 SAY '---------------------'
@ 14,031 SAY 'Vendor Information'
@ 15,000 SAY 'PRIMARY VENDOR'
@ 16,000 SAY 'ALTERNATE SOURCE'
 @ 21,10 SAY '   PLEASE ENTER INFORMATION TO SEARCH FOR  '
  IF select <>  ' T '
   @ 23,4 SAY 'XX'
  ENDIF
  READ
X EXIT FROM LOOP IF FOUND
 GOTO TOP
 STORE TRIM(Mpartno) TO key
 IF select=  ' T '
  FIND &key
  IF # <> 0
     STORE F TO Smore
  ELSE
   @ 22,10 SAY  '   NUMBER NOT FOUND  '
   @ 23,10 SAY  ' TRY AGAIN(Y/N)? '
   SET CONSOLE OFF
   WAIT TO retry
   SET CONSOLE ON
   IF !(retry) <>  'Y'
   STORE F TO Smore
  ENDIF  Y
  RELEASE retry
   ENDIF  # <> 0
 ELSE
  LOCATE FOR  partno+Mdept  = Mpartno+Mdept .AND. &select
   IF .NOT. EOF
 STORE F TO Smore
```

Fig. 6-5. Inventory system file maintenance. (Continued on page 159.)

```
      ELSE
        @ 22,10 SAY  '   NUMBER NOT FOUND  '
        @ 23,10 SAY  ' ADD NEW LISTING(Y/N)? '
        SET CONSOLE OFF
        WAIT TO retry
        SET CONSOLE ON
        IF !(retry) <>   'Y'
        STORE F TO Smore
        ELSE
        DO STOCK.ADD
      ENDIF  Y
      RELEASE retry
        ENDIF EOF
        ENDIF  select=T
      ENDDO  Smore
      RELEASE Smore
      RELEASE key
      ELSE
      IF !(command) =   'N'
        STORE T TO next
        DO WHILE next
           SKIP
           IF &select
             STORE F TO next
           ENDIF
           IF EOF
             STORE F TO next
             STORE  ' T '  TO select
             @ 23,4 SAY ' '
           ENDIF
        ENDDO
      RELEASE next
      ELSE
      IF !(command)= 'P'
         STORE  ' T '  TO select
         @ 23,4 SAY ' '
         SKIP -1
      ELSE
       IF !(command)= 'M'
      STORE T TO Mmore
      DO WHILE Mmore
      STORE  ' MORE '  TO mode
      STORE  ' '  TO Mmd
      @ 21,10 SAY  ' ENTER U TO UPDATE FILE, D TO DELETE,
```

```
 @ 22,10 SAY '          P TO PRINT, C TO SCAN FILE
  IF select <>  ' T '
   @ 23,4 SAY 'XX'
  ENDIF
  @ 23,10 SAY  ' PRESS RETURN WHEN DONE '  GET Mmd
  READ
  IF !(Mmd) = 'U'
     ERASE
IF select <>  ' T '
 @ 23,4 SAY 'XX'
ENDIF
X EDIT RECORD
     DO  STOCK.ED
ELSE
IF !(Mmd)= 'D'
     STORE  'N'  TO ans
  IF select <>  ' T '
   @ 23,4 SAY 'XX'
  ENDIF
@ 23,10 SAY  ' ARE YOU SURE(Y/N)?
@ 23,28 GET ans
     READ
IF !(ans)= 'Y'
     DELETE
     STORE  'Y'  TO Gdel
ENDIF
RELEASE ans
ELSE
IF !(Mmd)= 'P'
 @ 23,10 SAY  ' PLEASE SET UP PRINTER
 STORE '        '  TO mode
 SET CONSOLE OFF
 WAIT
 SET CONSOLE ON
 SET FORMAT TO PRINT
 DO  STOCK.OUT
 SET FORMAT TO SCREEN
ELSE
IF !(Mmd)='C'
 GOTO TOP
STORE '
TO select
@ 21,10 SAY 'PLEASE ENTER SELECTION CRITERIA
@ 22,10 SAY '    THEN PRESS RETURN
```

Fig. 6-5. Inventory system file maintenance. (Continued on page 161.)

```
@ 23,4 SAY 'XX'
@ 23,10 GET select
READ
LOCATE FOR &select
IF EOF
   @ 21,10 SAY 'NO MORE RECORDS CAN BE FOUND       '
   @ 22,10 SAY 'PLEASE PRESS RETURN TO CONTINUE       '
   @ 23,4 SAY '  '
   STORE  ' T '  TO select
   SET CONSOLE OFF
   WAIT
   SET CONSOLE ON
 ELSE
   DO STOCK.OUT
  ENDIF
 ELSE
 STORE F TO Mmore
ENDIF  F
ENDIF  P
ENDIF  D
ENDIF  E
ENDDO  Mmore
RELEASE Mmore,Mmd
ELSE
    STORE F TO Gmore
ENDIF  M
ENDIF  P
ENDIF  N
ENDIF  S
ENDDO   Gmore
IF Gdel =  'Y'
    STORE  'N'  TO ans
    @ 23,10 SAY   'WANT TO PERMANENTLY DELETE RECORDS(Y/N)?'
    @ 23,49 GET ans
    READ
    IF ans =  'Y'
        PACK
    ELSE
        RECALL ALL
    ENDIF
        RELEASE ans
ENDIF  Gdel
RELEASE  command,Gmore,Gdel,select
RELEASE mode
RETURN
```

```
* 	 STOCK.OUT
* OUTPUT ONLY FORM
@ 01,036 SAY mode
@ 02,000 SAY '====================='
@ 02,020 SAY '====================='
@ 02,040 SAY '====================='
@ 02,060 SAY '====================='
@ 03,000 SAY 'PART NO.'
@ 03,010 SAY partno
@ 03,030 SAY 'DESCRIPTION'
@ 03,043 SAY desc
@ 04,000 SAY 'FITS YEAR'
@ 04,011 SAY year
@ 04,030 SAY 'MODEL'
@ 04,037 SAY model
@ 04,060 SAY 'BODY'
@ 04,066 SAY body
@ 05,000 SAY 'USED/NOS/NEW'
@ 05,014 SAY status
@ 05,030 SAY 'DEPARTMENT'
@ 05,042 SAY dept
@ 06,030 SAY '--------------------'
@ 07,031 SAY 'Cost and Quantity'
@ 08,000 SAY 'ON HAND'
@ 08,009 SAY onhand
@ 08,030 SAY 'UNIT COST'
@ 08,041 SAY cost
@ 08,060 SAY 'DISCOUNT'
@ 08,070 SAY disc
@ 09,000 SAY 'LIST PRICE'
@ 09,012 SAY (cost*disc)+cost
@ 10,000 SAY 'MAXIMUM STOCK'
@ 10,015 SAY max
@ 10,030 SAY 'REORDER POINT'
@ 10,045 SAY min
@ 10,060 SAY 'QUANTITY'
@ 10,070 SAY reord
@ 11,000 SAY 'SOLD'
@ 11,006 SAY sales
@ 11,030 SAY 'RETURNED'
@ 11,040 SAY return
@ 11,060 SAY 'RECEIVED'
@ 11,070 SAY recd
```

Fig. 6-6. Inventory system output format file. (Continued from page 163.)

```
@ 12,000 SAY 'ON ORDER'
@ 12,010 SAY ordq
@ 12,030 SAY 'ORDER NO'
@ 12,040 SAY ordno
@ 12,060 SAY 'DATE'
@ 12,066 SAY orddt
@ 13,030 SAY '---------------------'
@ 14,031 SAY 'Vendor Information'
@ 15,000 SAY 'PRIMARY VENDOR'
@ 15,016 SAY vendor
@ 16,000 SAY 'ALTERNATE SOURCE'
@ 16,018 SAY alternate
```

After you punch C for the scanning function, you'll be asked for selection criteria. You might phrase the customer's request like this:

```
desc = 'manifold pressure gauge' .AND. year = '64'
```

This entry shortcuts a couple of specifications, relying a bit on your knowledge of your own product. The Naders certainly would know, for example, that in 1964 only the Spyder model was equipped with a manifold pressure gauge. The customer ordered a new gauge, but if the search turns up a good used one it's worth asking if the customer would be interested.

The purpose here is not to immerse you in Corvair trivia, but to demonstrate that a computer does not substitute for personal knowledge of your product. This is a way in which they can work in tandem. Literally, you supply the brains and the computer does the work.

If you find a match for the specifications you've entered, the computer will use the format file **Stock.Out,** Fig. 6-6, to display the results.

RECORDING SALES

Obviously every time you make a sale you must adjust your inventory. There are two basic methods of doing this. One records the sales in a separate transaction file, then uses the data in this file to update the inventory record every day, week, or whatever period is convenient. You would use a transaction file of similar structure to the inventory record and at each updating you would:

USE the transaction file
APPEND a new record of each sale
SUM the number of sales to a memory variable you might call **Msales**

At the end of the day or some other convenient period:

USE the main file and for each sale:
REPLACE the on-hand amount with **onhand-Msales** and the total sales amount with **sales+Msales.**

The advantage of this batch update method is that it leaves a permanent record of each sale in the transaction file, for auditing and preparing sales reports. The disadvantage is that your database will be precisely correct *only* when it has just been updated.

The Naders have adopted a method that updates their records more quickly. Many of their customers inquire by telephone if a particular part is in stock, so the system should provide the means for a quick, reliable response. This means any inventory changes should be posted immediately. Their system is similar to the batch technique, but instead of a separate transaction file it uses temporary memory variables.

The system uses the data entry form shown in Fig. 6-7. It searches for the part number and, if successful, includes a version of the editing process to take the new entries and update the figures. Figure 6-8 has the procedure. It calls the output form in Fig. 6-6 to display the results.

THE INCOMING SHIPMENT

Posting a new shipment makes use of a full screen editing process. It will require changes in the quantity on hand, plus perhaps changes in the cost per unit, the discount rate, the calculated list price, or even the prime supplier's name. Locate the part number, use M to reach the working level, and call for U to update the files. The record will be displayed with a chance to make any changes that are appropriate. The procedure: **Stock.Ed** (Fig. 6-9) controls the process, using the format file in Fig. 6-10 and the validation file in Fig. 6-11 to check values.

You can use this function, too, on those inevitable days when you find the physical inventory doesn't match the records in the computer.

There also is a provision to delete records, but use it with care. Even if you've decided a particular item is no longer worth carrying in inventory, you still may want to maintain a record of it. For example, you may decide it's not worthwhile to carry a certain expensive item for which you average less than one sale per year. Still, should you get one of those annual orders, it might be good still to have the vendor's name on record. That's one way to make a sale without the burden of an expensive, low-demand inventory item.

MAKING ADDITIONS

Sometimes the incoming shipment will be an item you do not now stock. In that case, the computer clearly won't be able to find the stock number in its search. Along with the options of searching again in a slightly different form, it will ask if you want to establish a new record for this item. A positive answer invokes the **Stock.Add** procedure, Fig. 6-12 (with the screen format of Fig. 6-10) and the default values found in Fig. 6-13.

```
                              ENTER SALES
==========================================================================

PART NO. :                          DESCRIPTION :
FITS YEAR :                         MODEL :                    BODY :
USED/NOS/NEW :                      DEPARTMENT :
                          ---------------------------

NO SOLD :                           CUSTOMER :
ORDER NO :                          PURCHASE ORDER NO :
```

Fig. 6-7. Sales screen display.

```
*       SALES.GET
* Records sales and updates inventory
ERASE
STORE  ' ENTER SALES '  TO mode
* DISPLAY CURRENT RECORD
STORE ' T ' TO select
IF &select
* Set up initial and values.  Provide enough spaces to match
* comparable items in Stock database.
STORE  '                              '  TO  Mpartno
STORE  '                         '  TO  Mdesc
STORE  '              '  TO  Myear
STORE  '            '  TO  Mmodel
STORE  '          '  TO  Mbody
STORE  '            '  TO  Mstatus
STORE  '          '  TO  Mdept
STORE  0    TO  Msale
STORE  '          '  TO  Mcust
STORE  '          '  TO  Mordno
STORE  '          '  TO  Mpono
ENDIF
STORE T TO Smore
DO WHILE Smore
  ERASE
  STORE  ' SEARCHING '  TO mode
* GET FIELDS TO SEARCH FOR
@ 02,000 SAY '===================='
@ 02,020 SAY '===================='
@ 02,040 SAY '===================='
@ 02,060 SAY '===================='
@ 03,000 SAY 'PART NO.'
@ 03,009 GET Mpartno
@ 03,040 SAY 'DESCRIPTION:'
@ 04,000 SAY 'FITS YEAR'
@ 04,040 SAY 'MODEL'
@ 04,060 SAY 'BODY'
@ 05,000 SAY 'USED/NOS/NEW'
@ 05,040 SAY 'DEPARTMENT'
@ 06,030 SAY '--------------------'
@ 07,000 SAY 'NO. SOLD'
@ 07,009 GET Msale
@ 07,040 SAY 'CUSTOMER'
@ 08,000 SAY 'ORDER NO'
```

Fig. 6-8. File maintenance for sales records. (Continued on page 166.)

```
@ 08,040 SAY 'PURCHASE ORDER NO'
 IF select <>  ' T '
  @ 23,4 SAY 'XX'
 ENDIF
 READ
X If found, go to editing program to enter changes.
X EXIT FROM LOOP IF FOUND
 GOTO TOP
 STORE TRIM(Mpartno) TO key
 IF select=  ' T '
  FIND &key
IF # <> 0
    STORE F TO Smore
    REPLACE onhand with onhand - msale
    REPLACE sales with sales + msale
 ELSE
  @ 22,10 SAY  '  NUMBER NOT FOUND  '
  @ 23,10 SAY  ' TRY AGAIN(Y/N)? '
  SET CONSOLE OFF
  WAIT TO retry
  SET CONSOLE ON
  IF !(retry) <>  'Y'
  STORE F TO Smore
 ENDIF  Y
 RELEASE retry
  ENDIF  # <> 0
 ELSE
  LOCATE FOR  partno = Mpartno .AND. &select
  IF .NOT. EOF
   STORE F TO Smore
 ELSE
  @ 22,10 SAY  '  NUMBER NOT FOUND  '
  @ 23,10 SAY  ' TRY AGAIN(Y/N)? '
  SET CONSOLE OFF
  WAIT TO retry
  SET CONSOLE ON
  IF !(retry) <>  'Y'
  STORE F TO Smore
ENDIF  Y
 RELEASE retry
  ENDIF EOF
 ENDIF   select=T
ENDDO   Smore
```

Fig. 6-8. File maintenance for sales records. (Continued on page 167.)

```
    RELEASE Smore
    RELEASE key
    STORE 'UPDATE' TO mode
    DO STOCK.OUT
    RELEASE mode
    RETURN
```

This works much like the earlier procedure for adding names to the payroll, but in the inventory system it is called only when there is not already an entry on file for the part number.

The validation file listed in Fig. 6-11 is worth some extra attention. It shows several ways to screen out clearly inaccurate listings.

```
* VALIDATE  Myear
STORE T TO Vmore
DO WHILE Vmore
IF  Myear    >=  '60'   .AND.   Myear <= '69' .OR. IF Myear = '
  !(All)'
  STORE F TO Vmore
  ELSE
  @ 23,0 SAY   '

  @ 23,0 SAY   ' None This Year   MUST BE 60 to 69'
@ 04,010 GET Myear
READ
ENDIF
ENDDO   Myear
```

This sequence checks the model years listed in new entries. It is designed to accept only the years in which the Corvair was manufactured. If you've entered some other year it gives you a chance to correct the entry.

By the way, the blank line inserted at 23,0 is to erase any previous message that might be left there, so you don't get a confusing overwrite.

```
IF  Mbody  =  '2DR' .OR. IF Mbody = '4DR';
        .OR. IF Mbody = '!(conv)' .OR> if Mbody ='!(all)'
  STORE F TO Vmore
ELSE
  @ 23,0 SAY   '
  @ 23,0 SAY   ' ONLY BODY STYLES WERE 2DR, 4DR AND CONV        '
@ 04,065 GET Mbody
```

Conveniently for our purposes, Corvairs were made in only three body styles. This sequence insists on one of the three. It goes a step beyond the previous routine, though, because it also provides for an "all" listing, in either capital or lowercase letters. This will be convenient, for example, if you have an engine part that has absolutely nothing to do with the body style.

```
*       STOCK.ED
*       Edit and revise inventory listings.
STORE T TO Emore
 STORE ' EDIT '  TO mode
* SET UP SCREEN VARIABLES
 STORE  partno  TO  Mpartno
 STORE  desc  TO  Mdesc
 STORE  year  TO  Myear
 STORE  model  TO  Mmodel
 STORE  body  TO  Mbody
 STORE  status  TO  Mstatus
 STORE  dept  TO  Mdept
 STORE  onhand  TO  Monhand
 STORE  cost  TO  Mcost
 STORE  disc  TO  Mdisc
 STORE  max  TO  Mmax
 STORE  min  TO  Mmin
 STORE  reord  TO  Mreord
 STORE  sales  TO  Msales
 STORE  return  TO  Mreturn
 STORE  recd  TO  Mrecd
 STORE  ordq  TO  Mordq
 STORE  ordno  TO  Mordno
 STORE  orddt  TO  Morddt
 STORE  vendor  TO  Mvendor
 STORE  alternate  TO  Malternate
DO WHILE Emore
ERASE
* GET SCREEN INPUT
 DO  STOCK.IO
 @ 21,10 SAY  ' ENTER ALL CHANGES '
 READ
* VALIDATE INPUT
 DO  STOCK.VAL
 STORE 'N'  TO Ecmd
 @ 21,10 SAY  ' ANY MORE CHANGES (Y/N)? '  GET Ecmd
 READ
* PUT SCREEN ENTRIES INTO FILE
 REPLACE  partno  WITH  Mpartno
 REPLACE  desc  WITH  Mdesc
 REPLACE  year  WITH  Myear
 REPLACE  model  WITH  Mmodel
 REPLACE  body  WITH  Mbody
```

Fig. 6-9. Editing file for sales records. (Continued on page 169.)

```
    REPLACE   status  WITH  Mstatus
    REPLACE   dept  WITH  Mdept
    REPLACE   onhand  WITH  Monhand
    REPLACE   cost  WITH  Mcost
    REPLACE   disc  WITH  Mdisc
    REPLACE   max  WITH  Mmax
    REPLACE   min  WITH  Mmin
    REPLACE   reord  WITH  Mreord
    REPLACE   sales  WITH  Msales
    REPLACE   return  WITH  Mreturn
    REPLACE   recd  WITH  Mrecd
    REPLACE   ordq  WITH  Mordq
    REPLACE   ordno  WITH  Mordno
    REPLACE   orddt  WITH  Morddt
    REPLACE   vendor  WITH  Mvendor
    REPLACE   alternate  WITH  Malternate
    IF  !(Ecmd)<> 'Y'
      STORE F TO Emore
    ENDIF
  ENDDO
ENDDO
RELEASE mode,Emore,Ecmd
RELEASE Mpartno
RELEASE Mdesc
RELEASE Myear
RELEASE Mmodel
RELEASE Mbody
RELEASE Mstatus
RELEASE Mdept
RELEASE Monhand
RELEASE Mcost
RELEASE Mdisc
RELEASE Mmax
RELEASE Mmin
RELEASE Mreord
RELEASE Msales
RELEASE Mreturn
RELEASE Mrecd
RELEASE Mordq
RELEASE Mordno
RELEASE Morddt
RELEASE Mvendor
RELEASE Malternate
```

```
*       STOCK.IO
* Format screen for editing input and output
@ 01,036 SAY mode
@ 02,000 SAY '===================='
@ 02,020 SAY '===================='
@ 02,040 SAY '===================='
@ 02,060 SAY '===================='
@ 03,000 SAY 'PART NO.'
@ 03,009 GET Mpartno
@ 03,030 SAY 'DESCRIPTION'
@ 03,042 GET Mdesc
@ 04,000 SAY 'FITS YEAR'
@ 04,010 GET Myear
@ 04,030 SAY 'MODEL'
@ 04,036 GET Mmodel
@ 04,060 SAY 'BODY'
@ 04,065 GET Mbody
@ 05,000 SAY 'USED/NOS/NEW'
@ 05,013 GET Mstatus
@ 05,030 SAY 'DEPARTMENT'
@ 05,041 GET Mdept
@ 06,030 SAY '--------------------'
@ 07,031 SAY 'Cost and Quantity'
@ 08,000 SAY 'ON HAND'
@ 08,008 GET Monhand
@ 08,030 SAY 'UNIT COST'
@ 08,040 GET Mcost PICTURE '99999.99'
@ 08,060 SAY 'DISCOUNT'
@ 08,069 GET Mdisc PICTURE '.99'
@ 09,000 SAY 'LIST PRICE'
@ 09,012 SAY (cost*disc
@ 10,000 SAY 'MAXIMUM STOCK'
@ 10,014 GET Mmax
@ 10,030 SAY 'REORDER POINT'
@ 10,044 GET Mmin
@ 10,060 SAY 'QUANTITY'
@ 10,069 GET Mreord
@ 11,000 SAY 'SOLD'
@ 11,005 GET Msales
@ 11,030 SAY 'RETURNED'
@ 11,039 GET Mreturn
@ 11,060 SAY 'RECEIVED'
@ 11,069 GET Mrecd
```

Fig. 6-10. Format file for sales data input. (Continued on page 171.)

```
      @ 12,000 SAY 'ON ORDER'
      @ 12,009 GET Mordq
      @ 12,030 SAY 'ORDER NO'
      @ 12,039 GET Mordno
      @ 12,060 SAY 'DATE'
      @ 12,065 GET Morddt PICTURE '99/99/99'
      @ 13,030 SAY '--------------------'
      @ 14,031 SAY 'Vendor Information'
      @ 15,000 SAY 'PRIMARY VENDOR'
      @ 15,015 GET Mvendor
      @ 16,000 SAY 'ALTERNATE SOURCE'
      @ 16,017 GET Malternate
      RETURN
```

```
IF  Mstatus  =  'NEW' .OR. IF Mstatus = 'USED'
   STORE F TO Vmore
ELSE
IF  Mstatus  =  'NOS      '
   STORE F TO Vmore
ELSE
  @ 23,0 SAY  '
  @ 23,0 SAY  ' Check Status -PROPER VALUES ARE: NEW, USED
    OR NOS       '
@ 05,013 GET Mstatus
```

As you remember, there are three types of parts in the old car market. This simply makes sure you've listed one of the three.

```
IF  Mdept  =  'BODY' .OR. IF Mdept = 'MECH'
   STORE F TO Vmore
ELSE
IF  Mdept  =  'INTERIOR'
   STORE F TO Vmore
ELSE
  @ 23,0 SAY  '
  @ 23,0 SAY  ' Check Dept. -PROPER VALUES ARE BODY, MECH AND
    INTERIOR '
@ 05,041 GET Mdept
```

The Nader catalog is divided into body, mechanical, and interior trim sections for the convenience of customers. This sequence makes sure no part escapes the system—and thus escapes its proper catalog listing.

```
X VALIDATE  Monhand
STORE T TO Vmore
DO WHILE Vmore
```

```
*       STOCK.VAL
* A validation program to check entries against established
*     ranges of values.
* VALIDATE  Myear
STORE T TO Vmore
DO WHILE Vmore
IF  Myear   >=  '60'   .AND.  Myear <= '69' .OR. IF Myear = '!(All)'
  STORE F TO Vmore
  ELSE
  @ 23,0 SAY  '                                                        '
  @ 23,0 SAY  ' None This Year  MUST BE 60 to 69'
@ 04,010 GET Myear
READ
ENDIF
ENDDO  Myear
STORE T TO Vmore
DO WHILE Vmore
IF  Mbody  =  '2DR' .OR. IF Mbody = '4DR';
        .OR. IF Mbody = '!(conv)' .OR> if Mbody ='!(all)'
  STORE F TO Vmore
ELSE
  @ 23,0 SAY  '                                                       '
  @ 23,0 SAY  ' ONLY BODY STYLES WERE 2DR, 4DR AND CONV        '
@ 04,065 GET Mbody
READ
ENDIF
ENDIF
ENDDO  Mbody
STORE T TO Vmore
DO WHILE Vmore
IF  Mstatus  =  'NEW' .OR. IF Mstatus = 'USED'
  STORE F TO Vmore
ELSE
IF  Mstatus  =  'NOS      '
  STORE F TO Vmore
ELSE
  @ 23,0 SAY  '                                                      '
  @ 23,0 SAY  ' Check Status -PROPER VALUES ARE: NEW, USED OR NOS        '
@ 05,013 GET Mstatus
READ
ENDIF
ENDIF
ENDDO  Mstatus
```

Fig. 6-11. Validation file for sales information. (Continued on page 173.)

```
STORE T TO Vmore
DO WHILE Vmore
IF  Mdept  =  'BODY' .OR. IF Mdept = 'MECH'
   STORE F TO Vmore
ELSE
IF  Mdept  =  'INTERIOR'
   STORE F TO Vmore
ELSE
 @ 23,0 SAY  '
 @ 23,0 SAY  ' Check Dept. -PROPER VALUES ARE BODY, MECH AND INTERIOR '
@ 05,041 GET Mdept
READ
ENDIF
ENDIF
ENDDO  Mdept
* VALIDATE  Monhand
STORE T TO Vmore
DO WHILE Vmore
IF  Monhand   >=  Mmin   .AND.  Monhand <= Mmax
 STORE F TO Vmore
 ELSE
 @ 23,0 SAY  '
 @ 23,0 SAY  '   -MUST BE: >=' Mmin 'and <=' Mmax
@ 08,008 GET Monhand
READ
ENDIF
ENDDO  Monhand
STORE T TO Vmore
DO WHILE Vmore
SELECT SECONDARY
USE  vendor     INDEX   vendor
STORE  Mvendor  TO find
FIND &find
RELEASE find
IF # <> 0
   SELECT PRIMARY
   STORE F TO Vmore
ELSE
   SELECT PRIMARY
 @ 23,0 SAY  '
 @ 23,0 SAY  ' CANNOT FIND IN VENDOR FILE   '
@ 15,015 GET Mvendor
```

```
   READ
   ENDIF
   ENDDO  Mvendor
   STORE T TO Vmore
   DO WHILE Vmore
   SELECT SECONDARY
   USE  alternat  INDEX  alternat
   STORE  Malternate  TO find
   FIND &find
   RELEASE find
   IF # <> 0
      SELECT PRIMARY
      STORE F TO Vmore
   ELSE
      SELECT PRIMARY
   @ 23,0 SAY  '                                                    '
   @ 23,0 SAY  ' CANNOT FIND IN VENDOR FILE'
   @ 16,017 GET Malternate
   READ
   ENDIF
   ENDDO  Malternate
   RELEASE Vmore
   RETURN
```

Fig. 6-11. Validation file for sales information. Continued from page 173.

```
IF  Monhand   >=  Mmin  .AND.  Monhand <= Mmax
 STORE F TO Vmore
 ELSE
 @ 23,0 SAY  '
 @ 23,0 SAY  '  -MUST BE: >=' Mmin 'and <=' Mmax
@ 08,008 GET Monhand
```

Here, the validation system gives you some management assistance. An analysis of your sales level and of the turnover level of your inventory—something we'll discuss later in more detail—can help you determine the maximum stock level you should maintain for each item. Your supplier's normal packaging practices or your analysis of an economical order quantity can help you determine the level at which you should order new stock.

These two levels appear as the minimum and maximum entries in your database; the validation program picks them up for processing as memory variables. Between the two is an acceptable range for your stock level. This routine flags quantities that are outside the range.

```
SELECT SECONDARY
USE  vendor     INDEX  vendor
STORE  Mvendor  TO find
FIND &find
RELEASE find
IF # <> 0
```

```
    SELECT PRIMARY
    STORE F TO Vmore
ELSE
    SELECT PRIMARY
  @ 23,0 SAY   '
  @ 23,0 SAY   ' CANNOT FIND IN VENDOR FILE    '
@ 15,015 GET Mvendor
```

Consider this: you have a large order for a particular item, and your inventory is too small to fill it. You check the vendor listing, then go to your separate file of vendor names and addresses to find out where to reach this source of supply. Gasp! Lost sales! The vendor isn't there.

This sequence heads off trouble by creating the problem at an earlier, more manageable time—when you first enter the data. This sequence calls the vendor list as a secondary file and checks for the listed vendor's name. If it is not found, an error message will alert you to one of two possibilities:

1) An error in the entry you're now making.
2) A legitimate but unlisted vendor whose name should be added to the vendor file.

Either way, it's better to know now, when you can correct the problem, than later when you suddenly need this source of supply. A companion routine makes the same check for your alternate supplier.

WRITING REPORTS

Nader and Son periodically issues a catalog for their customers. Actually, it's little more than a listing of parts in the inventory, plus their prices. In fact, it can be produced with the dBASE report generator.

This is where they begin to put the collected information in their inventory records to good use. There are many reports that can be created from the assembled inventory database, and the catalog is just one of them. In fact, there are enough to justify a separate submenu of these reports alone. It looks like Fig. 6-14.

The menu offers a series of reports, including the catalog and several kinds of management analyses. It also provides a mechanism for creating reports of your own design. Figure 6-15 is the command file to create the menu.

Getting Out the Catalog

The father-and-son parts business originally established its dBASE system to keep track of its stock on hand. The Naders soon found out, though, that there were other benefits as well. The reports they could generate from the information inside their computer ranged from a price list to some valuable management tools.

A big benefit where sales are concerned is the ability to generate a complete and current price list. The business is able to update its list regularly and easily. The company offers a current price list to anyone who sends a stamped envelope. The computer insures that the lists sent out are fully up to date, and if the company has any new items in stock, the customers need not wait in ignorance for them to appear on some future list. The prices can be kept up to date, too.

Creating the catalog is as simple as generating a properly·configured dBASE report:

```
*       STOCK.ADD
* Creates inventory files for newly stocked items
STORE T TO Amore
DO WHILE Amore
* SET UP DEFAULT VALUES
 DO  STOCK.FAU
ERASE
STORE  ' ADD '  TO mode
 * GET DATA TO ADD
DO  STOCK.IO
@ 21,10 SAY  ' ADD NEW INVENTORY LISTINGS AS NEEDED'
@ 22,10 SAY  ' WHEN DONE ENTER BLANKS FOR  partno '
READ
* ARE WE DONE?
IF Mpartno <> '                           '
* PERFORM VALIDATION
 DO  STOCK.VAL
 APPEND BLANK
* PUT SCREEN DATA INTO FILE
 REPLACE  partno  WITH  Mpartno
 REPLACE  desc  WITH  Mdesc
 REPLACE  year  WITH  Myear
 REPLACE  model  WITH  Mmodel
 REPLACE  body  WITH  Mbody
 REPLACE  status  WITH  Mstatus
 REPLACE  dept  WITH  Mdept
 REPLACE  onhand  WITH  Monhand
 REPLACE  cost  WITH  Mcost
 REPLACE  disc  WITH  Mdisc
 REPLACE  max  WITH  Mmax
 REPLACE  min  WITH  Mmin
 REPLACE  reord  WITH  Mreord
 REPLACE  sales  WITH  Msales
 REPLACE  return  WITH  Mreturn
 REPLACE  recd  WITH  Mrecd
 REPLACE  ordq  WITH  Mordq
 REPLACE  ordno  WITH  Mordno
 REPLACE  orddt  WITH  Morddt
 REPLACE  vendor  WITH  Mvendor
 REPLACE  alternate  WITH  Malternate
ELSE
     STORE F TO Amore
```

Fig. 6-12. Command file for additions to inventory. (Continued on page 177.)

```
        ENDIF
        ENDDO
        RELEASE mode,Amore
        X RELEASE INPUT FIELDS
        RELEASE Mpartno
        RELEASE Mdesc
        RELEASE Myear
        RELEASE Mmodel
        RELEASE Mbody
        RELEASE Mstatus
        RELEASE Mdept
        RELEASE Monhand
        RELEASE Mcost
        RELEASE Mdisc
        RELEASE Mmax
        RELEASE Mmin
        RELEASE Mreord
        RELEASE Msales
        RELEASE Mreturn
        RELEASE Mrecd
        RELEASE Mordq
        RELEASE Mordno
        RELEASE Morddt
        RELEASE Mvendor
        RELEASE Malternate
        RETURN
```

. REPORT FORM CATALOG
ENTER OPTIONS, M=LEFT MARGIN, L=LINES/PAGE, W=PAGE WIDTH
PAGE HEADING? (Y/N) Y
ENTER PAGE HEADING: NADER AND SON CORVAIR PARTS; Delivery at
     Any Speed;
     Catalog No. 1
DOUBLE SPACE REPORT? (Y/N) M
ARE TOTALS REQUIRED? (Y/N) Y
SUBTOTALS IN REPORT? (Y/N) Y
ENTER SUBTOTALS FIELD: DEPT
SUMMARY REPORT ONLY? (Y/N) N
EJECT PAGE AFTER SUBTOTALS? (Y/N) N
ENTER SUBTOTAL HEADING: DEPARTMENT:
COL   WIDTH,CONTENTS
001   12,PARTNO
ENTER HEADING: PART; NUMBER

```
002       20,DESC
ENTER HEADING: DESCRIPTION
003       10,YEAR
004        5,STATUS
ENTER HEADING: NEW/USED/NOW
ENTER HEADING: FITS YEARS
005       10,MODEL
ENTER HEADING: FITS MODELS
006       10,BODY
ENTER HEADING: FITS BODY; STYLE
007        7,COST+(COST*DISC)
ENTER HEADING: PRICE
ARE TOTALS REQUIRED? (Y/N) N
```

Notice the use of semicolons to control where the words are broken; among other things, we've created a three-line heading. There is a calculated value in the report, and to segregate the listings by department we have called for subtotals on that field—even though there's nothing to add. With a few sample items in the database, the report looks like Fig. 6-16.

The Naders' entire barnfull would take several pages, of course. As the business expands they might want to go to a slicker catalog, particularly for the new items they carry all the time. Still, this list is an efficient, useful way to get a complete, current price list into the customers' hands.

Evaluating Suppliers

Since the Naders only recently started buying new parts from wholesale vendors, they would like some way to know whether they're getting good results from these vendors. The second report, shown in Fig. 6-17, is designed to help analyze that. It shows costs, sales, and revenues, broken down by vendor. The details:

```
. REPORT FORM VENDOR
ENTER OPTIONS, M=LEFT MARGIN, L=LINES/PAGE, W=PAGE WIDTH
PAGE HEADING? (Y/N) Y
ENTER PAGE HEADING: VENDOR ANALYSIS
DOUBLE SPACE REPORT? (Y/N) N
ARE TOTALS REQUIRED? (Y/N) Y
SUBTOTALS IN REPORT? (Y/N) Y
ENTER SUBTOTALS FIELD: VENDOR
SUMMARY REPORT ONLY? (Y/N) N
EJECT PAGE AFTER SUBTOTALS? (Y/N) N
ENTER SUBTOTAL HEADING: SUPPLIER:
COL       WIDTH,CONTENTS
001       12,PARTNO
ENTER HEADING: PART; NUMBER
002       20,DESCR
ENTER HEADING: DESCRIPTION
003        6,ONHAND
ENTER HEADING: ON HAND
```

```
*       STOCK.FAU
*   -DEFAULT VALUES PROGRAM
STORE   '                                 '  TO  Mpartno
STORE   '                                           '  TO  Mdesc
STORE   '                        '  TO  Myear
STORE   '            '  TO  Mmodel
STORE   '            '  TO  Mbody
STORE   '        '  TO  Mstatus
STORE   '        '  TO  Mdept
STORE   0  TO  Monhand
STORE   0.00  TO  Mcost
STORE   .40  TO  Mdisc
STORE   0  TO  Mmax
STORE   0  TO  Mmin
STORE   0  TO  Mreord
STORE   0  TO  Msales
STORE   0  TO  Mreturn
STORE   0  TO  Mrecd
STORE   0  TO  Mordq
STORE   '        '  TO  Mordno
STORE   '00/00/00'  TO  Morddt
STORE   '           '  TO  Mvendor
STORE   '           '  TO  Malternate
RETURN
```

Fig. 6-13. Default file for inventory system.

```
*  REPORT.PRN
*
Nader & Son Corvair Parts                                    Date()
==================================================================
                        REPORT MENU
                        -----------
            1:  Print Catalog
            2:  Inventory Listed by Vendor
            3:  List of Items on Order
            4:  Prepare Orders to Restore Stock
            5:  Turnover Analysis
            ------------------------------
            R:  Return to Previous Function
            X:  Exit to Operating System


            Please Enter Your Choice ==>_
```

Fig. 6-14. Submenu display for inventory reports.

```
* Menu format and command program for standard reports
USE STOCK INDEX STOCKVEND
STORE T TO more
DO WHILE more
ERASE
@  1, 0 SAY "Nader & Son Corvair Parts"
@  1,64 SAY Date()
@  2, 0 SAY "=================================================="
@  2,50 SAY "=============================="
@  3,24 SAY "REPORT MENU"
@  4,24 SAY "-----------"
@  5,16 SAY "1:  Print Catalog"
@  6,16 SAY "2:  Inventory Listed by Vendor"
@  7,16 SAY "3:  List of Items on Order"
@  8,16 SAY "4:  Prepare Orders to Restore Stock"
@  9,16 SAY "5:  Turnover Analysis"
@ 10,16 SAY "-----------------------------"
@ 11,16 SAY "R:  Return to Previous Function"
@ 12,16 SAY "X:  Exit to Operating System"
@ 15,16 SAY "Please Enter Your Choice ==>"
SET CONSOLE OFF
WAIT TO CHOICE
SET CONSOLE ON
DO CASE
        CASE CHOICE = '1'
                USE STOCK INDEX STOCKDEPT
                REPORT FORM CATALOG
        CASE CHOICE = '2'
                USE STOCK INDEX STOCKVEN
                REPORT FORM VENDOR
        CASE CHOICE = '3'
                USE STOCK INDEX STOCKVEN
                REPORT FORM ORDER FOR vendor # 0
        CASE CHOICE = '4'
                USE STOCK INDEX STOCKNO
                REPORT FORM REORDER FOR onhand+ordq < min;
                        .OR. onhand+ordq > max
        CASE CHOICE = '5'
                USE STOCK INDEX STOCKNO
                REPORT FORM TURNS
        CASE CHOICE = 'R'
                CANCEL
        CASE CHOICE = 'X'
                QUIT
ENDCASE
ENDDO
RETURN
```

Fig. 6-15. Command file for report menu, REPORT.MEN.

```
PAGE NO. 00001

                    NADER AND SON CORVAIR PARTS
                       Delivery at Any Speed
                         Catalog No. 1

   PART            DESCRIPTION      NEW/  FITS YEARS     FITS      FITS BODY   PRICE
   NUMBER                           USED/                MODELS      STYLE
                                    NOS


X DEPARTMENT: BODY
23-4567          PR HEADLITE RIMS   USED  60 - 64        ALL        ALL        14.40
56-7890          WHEEL COVERS       NOS   65-69          ALL        ALL        21.00
678-90           FENDER SKIRTS, PR  NEW   60 - 64        ALL        ALL        63.00


X DEPARTMENT: INTERIOR
12-3456          RIGHT DOOR PANEL   USED  65             MONZA      2DR CONV   18.00
598-7654         CARPET SET, BLACK  NEW   65 -69         ALL        4 DR      119.14


X DEPARTMENT: MECH
34-5678          IDLER ARM ASSEMBLY NEW   60 64          ALL        ALL        37.80
```

Fig. 6-16. Catalog report.

```
ARE TOTALS REQUIRED? (Y/N) N
004        6,SALES
ENTER HEADING: SOLD
ARE TOTALS REQUIRED? (Y/N) Y
005        6,COST
ENTER HEADING: UNIT COST
ARE TOTALS REQUIRED? (Y/N) N
006        6,SALES*(COST+(COST*DISC))
ENTER HEADING: REVE-;NUE
ARE TOTALS REQUIRED? (Y/N) Y
```

A glance at this report will tell you such things as whether these products are selling, and you can compute some figures on the amount of revenue you've received in relation to the cost of your inventory. It's a good way to identify the most profitable products and suppliers.

The fender skirts are moving surprisingly well, but there is a lot of money tied up in carpets that no one seems to be buying. Perhaps it's time to advertise a discount.

There's one pair of items for which no vendor is listed; these are used parts from the stash in the barn. It can be interesting to know how well these are selling. However, if you want to consider only the new items bought from active suppliers, go into the **Report.Men** file, locate the line that calls the **Vendor** report, and change it to:

```
. REPORT FORM VENDOR FOR VENDOR <> ' '
```

```
                        VENDOR ANALYSIS

     PART           DESCRIPTION        ON     SOLD    UNIT   REVE-
     NUMBER                            HAND            COST   NUE

  X SUPPLIER:
  12-3456        RIGHT DOOR PANEL       1      1     15.00   18.00
  23-4567        PR HEADLITE RIMS       1      0     12.00    0.00
  XX SUBTOTAL XX
                                               1             18.00


  X SUPPLIER: A-GRAPE CORVAIR
  678-90         FENDER SKIRTS, PR      3      2     45.00  126.00
  XX SUBTOTAL XX
                                               2            126.00


  X SUPPLIER: CHARLIE TROY
  598-7654       CARPET SET, BLACK      3      0     85.10  0.0000
  XX SUBTOTAL XX
                                               0            0.0000


  X SUPPLIER: MOTOR CENTER
  56-7890        WHEEL COVERS           2      3     15.00   63.00
  XX SUBTOTAL XX
                                               3             63.00


  X SUPPLIER: VINTAGE VANTAGE
  34-5678        IDLER ARM ASSEMBLY     4      2     27.00   75.60
  XX SUBTOTAL XX
                                               2             75.60

  XX TOTAL XX
                                               8            282.60
```

Fig. 6-17. Vendor analysis report.

```
PAGE NO. 00001


           PART              DESCRIPTION        ON      ON
           NUMBER                               HAND    ORDER

        X VENDOR: A-GRAPE CORVAIR
        678-90          FENDER SKIRTS, PR         3       1
        XX SUBTOTAL XX
                                                          1



        X VENDOR: MOTOR CENTER
        56-7890         WHEEL COVERS              2       5
        XX SUBTOTAL XX
                                                          5


        XX TOTAL XX
                                                          6
```

Fig. 6-18. Stock item report.

This will make the program pass up those used parts for which no active vendor is listed.

Keeping Track of Orders

The next report keeps track of another aspect of vendor performance, the number of outstanding orders:

```
    REPORT FORM ORDER FOR VENDOR # ′ ′
ENTER OPTIONS, M=LEFT MARGIN, L=LINES/PAGE, W=PAGE WIDTH
PAGE HEADING? (Y/N)Y

ENTER HEADING:  SUMMARY REPORT: PARTS ON ORDER
DOUBLE SPACE REPORT? (Y/N) N
ARE TOTALS REQUIRED? (Y/N) Y
SUBTOTALS IN REPORT? (Y/N) Y
ENTER SUBTOTALS FIELD: VENDOR
SUMMARY REPORT ONLY? (Y/N) N
EJECT PAGE AFTER SUBTOTALS? (Y/N) N
ENTER SUBTOTAL HEADING: VENDOR:
COL     WIDTH,CONTENTS
001     12,PARTNO
ENTER HEADING: PART; NUMBER
002     20, DESC
ENTER HEADING: DESCRIPTION
```

```
PAGE NO. 00001

              STOCK AND ON ORDER: EXCEPTION REPORT

   PART        VENDOR       DESCRIPTION        ON     SOLD   AVAIL-   MINI-   MAXI-
   NUMBER                                      HAND           ABLE     MUM     MUM

   598-7654    CHARLIE      CARPET SET, BLACK   3       0      3        0       1
               TROY
```

Fig. 6-19. Exception report.

```
003       6,ONHAND
ENTER HEADING: ON HAND
ARE TOTALS REQUIRED? (Y/N)  N
004       6,ORDQ
ENTER HEADING: ON ORDER
ARE TOTALS REQUIRED? (Y/N)  Y
```

The command line in the report menu calls only for those parts for which the quantity on order is not zero. (You can use $<>$ 0 to express that idea, or you can use # 0, because dBASE reads both the same way.) The report produced is shown in Fig. 6-18.

If the boom in fender skirts continues, we have another set on order. We're also in the process of replenishing our supply of wheel covers. Should these items run low, we can tell our customers that more have already been ordered. If we notice high demand or low stock levels, this report also can tell us whether an order already has been placed.

```
PAGE NO. 00001


                               TURNOVER ANALYSIS

   PART NUMBER    ON      COST    SOLD   REVENUE   RETURN   TURNS
                  HAND                                        AT
                                                          CURRENT
                                                           STOCK

   12-3456         1     15.00     1      18.00    0.83       1
   23-4567         1     12.00     0       0.00
   678-90          3     45.00     2     126.00    1.07       0
   598-7654        3     85.10     0       0.00
   56-7890         2     15.00     3      63.00    0.47       1
   34-5678         4     27.00     2      75.60    1.42       0
```

Fig. 6-20. Turnover analysis report.

```
X       STOCK.RPT
X    REPORT PROGRAM
?
LIST FILES LIKE X.FRM
?
?'====================================================================================='
?
STORE    '    '    TO print
DO WHILE !(print) <>   'Y'   .AND. !(print) <>   'N'
STORE   'Y'   TO print
@ 21,10 SAY   ' WANT REPORT SENT TO THE PRINTER? '   GET print
READ
ENDDO
  STORE   ' '   TO disk
  DO WHILE !(disk) <>   'Y'   .AND. !(disk) <>   'N'
  STORE   'N'   TO disk
@ 21,10 SAY   ' WANT REPORT SENT TO A FILE ?          '   GET disk
READ
ENDDO
IF !(disk)= 'Y'
STORE   '              '   TO file
DO WHILE file =   '            '
@ 22,10 SAY   ' ENTER FILE NAME '   GET file
READ
ENDDO
STORE TRIM(file) TO file
ENDIF   disk
STORE   '            '   TO report
  DO WHILE report =   '     '
@ 23,10 SAY   ' ENTER REPORT NAME '   GET report
READ
ENDDO
IF !(print) =   'Y'
@ 23,10 SAY   ' PLEASE SET UP PRINTER              '
SET CONSOLE OFF
WAIT
SET CONSOLE ON
SET PRINT ON
ENDIF print
IF !(disk) =   'Y'
SET ALTERNATE TO &file
SET ALTERNATE ON
ENDIF disk
ERASE
REPORT FORM &report
SET PRINT OFF
SET ALTERNATE OFF
IF !(disk) = 'Y'
  RELEASE disk,file
ENDIF
RELEASE print, report
```

Fig. 6-21. Reporting commands for inventory system.

```
✗ VENDOR.PRN
                              VENDOR DATA LIST
===================================================================================
VENDOR ==>

 STREET ==>

 CITY ==>

 STATE ==>

 ZIP ==>

 CONTACT ==>

 TELEPHONE ==>
```

Fig. 6-22. Screen display for vendor records.

Placing the Order

The next report is a variety of *exception report,* a report which flags things that are out of line. Here, the menu program command line has been keyed to tell us when the number of parts are *available*—those in stock plus those on order—is either lower than our established maximum stock level or higher than the minimum. On one hand it flags parts for which new orders should be made to replenish the stock; on the other, it identifies stock levels that exceed those we would like to carry. The format below produces a report such as that shown in Fig. 6-19.

```
ENTER OPTIONS, M=LEFT MARGIN, L=LINES/PAGE, W=PAGE WIDTH
PAGE HEADING? (Y/N) Y
ENTER HEADING:   STOCK AND ON ORDER: EXCEPTION REPORT
DOUBLE SPACE REPORT? (Y/N) N
ARE TOTALS REQUIRED? (Y/N) N
COL       WIDTH,CONTENTS
001       12, PARTNO
ENTER HEADING: PART; NUMBER
002       10, VENDOR
ENTER HEADING: VENDOR
003       20, DESC
ENTER HEADING: DESCRIPTION
004        6, ONHAND
ENTER HEADING: ON HAND
005        6, SALES
ENTER HEADING: SOLD
006        6, ONHAND+ORDQ
ENTER HEADING: AVAIL-ABLE
007        6, MIN
ENTER HEADING: MINI-;MUM
008        6, MAX
ENTER HEADING: MAXI-;MUM
```

```
*      VENDOR.CMD
* MAIN MENU PROGRAM FOR VENDOR FILE
*   DATABASE NAME IS    VENDOR
*   DATABASE IS KEYED
SET TALK OFF
SET FORMAT TO SCREEN
SELECT PRIMARY
USE VENDOR INDEX VENDOR
STORE FILE('VENDOR.NDX') TO Vindex
IF .NOT. Vindex
 DO VENDOR.GO
 ERASE
 @ 21,10 SAY  ' FILE IS NOW BEING INDEXED '
ENDIF
USE VENDOR      INDEX   VENDOR
STORE T TO Vmore
DO WHILE Vmore
 ERASE
@ 1,30 SAY 'VENDOR FILE MENU'
@ 2,0  SAY '========================================'
@ 2,40 SAY '========================================'
@ 3,16 SAY '1:  Maintain Vendor Files'
@ 4,16 SAY '2:  Find Vendor Information'
@ 5,16 SAY '----------------------------------'
@ 6,16 SAY 'R:  Return to Previous Operation'
@ 7,16 SAY 'X:  Return to Operating System
@ 9,16 SAY 'Please Enter Your Choice ==>'_
SET CONSOLE OFF
WAIT TO choice
SET CONSOLE ON
DO CASE
        CASE choice = '1'
              DO VENDOR.ADD
        CASE choice = '2'
              DO VENDOR.GET
        CASE CHOICE = 'R'
              CANCEL
        CASE CHOICE = 'X'
              QUIT
ENDCASE
ENDDO
RELEASE Vmore,command,Vindex
```

Fig. 6-23. Command file for screen display.

```
*       VENDOR.GO
*   STARTUP & INDEX PGM
SET TALK OFF
SELECT PRIMARY
USE  VENDOR
INDEX ON   vendor  TO  A:VENDOR
```

Fig. 6-24. Reindexing file for vendor files.

```
*       VENDOR.ADD
*   ADD NEW VENDOR RECORDS
STORE T TO more
DO WHILE more
ERASE
STORE  ' ADD '  TO mode
* GET DATA TO ADD
DO  VENDOR.IO
READ
* ARE WE DONE?
IF Mvendor <> '                              '
 APPEND BLANK
* PUT SCREEN DATA INTO FILE
 REPLACE  vendor  WITH  Mvendor
 REPLACE  vstreet  WITH  Mvstreet
 REPLACE  vcity  WITH  Mvcity
 REPLACE  vstate  WITH  Mvstate
 REPLACE  vzip  WITH  Mvzip
 REPLACE  vcont  WITH  Mvcont
 REPLACE  vphone  WITH  Mvphone
ELSE
    STORE F TO more
ENDIF
ENDDO
RELEASE mode,more
* RELEASE INPUT FIELDS
RELEASE Mvendor
RELEASE Mvstreet
RELEASE Mvcity
RELEASE Mvstate
RELEASE Mvzip
RELEASE Mvcont
RELEASE Mvphone
```

Fig. 6-25. Adding new vendors to files.

```
*       VENDOR.GET
*  Retrieve and examine vendor records
ERASE
STORE ' GET '  TO mode
* DISPLAY CURRENT RECORD
IF &select
 DO  VENDOR.OUT
ENDIF
STORE T TO more
DO WHILE more
 ERASE
 STORE ' SEARCH '  TO mode
* GET FIELDS TO SEARCH FOR
@ 02,000 SAY '==================='
@ 02,020 SAY '==================='
@ 02,040 SAY '==================='
@ 02,060 SAY '==================='
@ 03,000 SAY 'VENDOR ==>'
 STORE '                         '  TO Mvendor
@ 03,011 GET Mvendor
@ 04,000 SAY 'STREET ==>'
@ 05,000 SAY 'CITY ==>'
@ 06,000 SAY 'STATE ==>'
@ 07,000 SAY 'ZIP ==>'
@ 08,000 SAY 'CONTACT ==>'
@ 09,000 SAY 'TELEPHONE ==>'
 IF select <> ' T '
  @ 23,4 SAY '**'
 ENDIF
 READ
* EXIT FROM LOOP IF FOUND
 GOTO TOP
 STORE TRIM(Mvendor) TO key
 IF select= ' T '
  FIND &key
  IF # <> 0
     STORE F TO more
 ELSE
  @ 22,10 SAY '  NOT FOUND  '
  @ 23,10 SAY ' TRY AGAIN(Y/N)? '
  SET CONSOLE OFF
  WAIT TO retry
  SET CONSOLE ON
```

Fig. 6-26. Search commands for vendor records. (Continued on page 190.)

```
      IF !(retry) <>  'Y'
       STORE F TO more
    ENDIF   Y
    RELEASE retry
     ENDIF   # <> 0
    ELSE
      LOCATE FOR  vendor  = Mvendor .AND. &select
      IF .NOT. EOF
        STORE F TO more
    ELSE
      @ 22,10 SAY  '   NOT FOUND  '
      @ 23,10 SAY  ' TRY AGAIN(Y/N)? '
      SET CONSOLE OFF
      WAIT TO retry
      SET CONSOLE ON
      IF !(retry) <>  'Y'
       STORE F TO more
    ENDIF   Y
    RELEASE retry
     ENDIF EOF
    ENDIF   select=T
  ENDDO  more
  RELEASE more
  RELEASE key
  RELEASE mode
```

Fig. 6-26. Search commands for vendor records. (Continued from page 189.)

Sure enough, there are those carpets again. We've made it official—as far as the computer is concerned—that we're vastly overstocked on these items.

Setting Stock Levels

Of course, the minimum and maximum stock levels with which we've dealt so far have been arbitrary figures, plugged into the database for the sake of illustration. How can you determine the actual figures to use?

You can do it with the help of the final report (Fig. 6-20) in this group, although the most important word is *help*. As you might be aware, a major recent development in corporate data processing is the "decision support system." Note carefully that it's not called a "decision *making* system." The idea behind those systems, and this report, is to give you the information you need to make your own decisions. The computer will help, but it won't make the decisions for you.

```
ENTER OPTIONS, M=LEFT MARGIN, L=LINES/PAGE, W=PAGE WIDTH
PAGE HEADING? (Y/N) Y
ENTER PAGE HEADING: TURNOVER ANALYSIS
DOUBLE SPACE REPORT? (Y/N) N
ARE TOTALS REQUIRED? (Y/N) N
```

```
COL      WIDTH,CONTENTS
001      12, PARTNO
ENTER HEADING: PART NUMBER
002       6, ONHAND
ENTER HEADING: ON HAND
003       6, COST
ENTER HEADING: COST
004       6, SALES
ENTER HEADING: SOLD
005       7, SALES*(COST+(COST*DISC/100))
ENTER HEADING: REVENUE
006       7, COST*ONHAND/(SALES*(COST+(COST*DISC/100)))
ENTER HEADING: RETURN
007       7, SALES/ONHAND
ENTER HEADING: TURNS AT CURRENT STOCK
```

```
*       VENDOR.IO
*   INPUT/OUTPUT SCREEN
@ 01,036 SAY mode
@ 02,000 SAY '===================='
@ 02,020 SAY '===================='
@ 02,040 SAY '===================='
@ 02,060 SAY '===================='
@ 03,000 SAY 'VENDOR ==>'
@ 03,011 GET Mvendor
@ 04,000 SAY 'STREET ==>'
@ 04,011 GET Mvstreet
@ 05,000 SAY 'CITY ==>'
@ 05,009 GET Mvcity
@ 06,000 SAY 'STATE ==>'
@ 06,010 GET Mvstate
@ 07,000 SAY 'ZIP ==>'
@ 07,008 GET Mvzip
@ 08,000 SAY 'CONTACT ==>'
@ 08,012 GET Mvcont
@ 09,000 SAY 'TELEPHONE ==>'
@ 09,014 GET Mvphone PICTURE '(XXX)999-9999'
@ 20,000 SAY '--------------------'
@ 20,020 SAY '------- PLEASE ENTER'
@ 20,041 SAY 'YOUR CHOICE --------'
@ 20,061 SAY '--------------------'
```

Fig. 6-27. Format for vendor file entries.

```
*       VENDOR.OUT
*       OUTPUT FORM
@ 01,036 SAY mode
@ 02,000 SAY '======================'
@ 02,020 SAY '======================'
@ 02,040 SAY '======================'
@ 02,060 SAY '======================'
@ 03,000 SAY 'VENDOR ==>'
@ 03,012 SAY vendor
@ 04,000 SAY 'STREET ==>'
@ 04,012 SAY vstreet
@ 05,000 SAY 'CITY ==>'
@ 05,010 SAY vcity
@ 06,000 SAY 'STATE ==>'
@ 06,011 SAY vstate
@ 07,000 SAY 'ZIP ==>'
@ 07,009 SAY vzip
@ 08,000 SAY 'CONTACT ==>'
@ 08,013 SAY vcont
@ 09,000 SAY 'TELEPHONE ==>'
@ 09,015 SAY vphone
```

Fig. 6-28. Format file for output from vendor records.

You'd need a database full of parts and a year-long sales history to make this report work properly, but there are some important figures here. The first is the amount of revenue you've received from various items. The fender skirts are the hot seller in dollar volume, with the idler arms second, and the wheel covers third.

The next column takes a little different perspective. It states the value of your inventory as a percentage of the return gained from that product—the lower the number, the higher the relative return. Take notice, though, that a good percentage may be attached to the modest income from a low-value part. You have to consider both the amounts and the percentages to make good judgments.

The final item is a *turnover ratio*. If your annual sales are about three times your normal inventory level, you are carrying three *turns*, a figure that's considered right for many retail businesses. The right number of turns depends on the nature of the business and its products; trade associations and other sources of advice probably can help you determine the right ratio for your purposes. Whatever it is, you can compare it with figures in the final column—a low number of turns means a slow-moving item.

Using these figures, particularly the return percentage and the turnover ratio, you can determine the ideal stock level for every item. From that ideal, consider such things as your normal sales volume, the length of time it takes to receive an order, and the number of items in a normal wholesale lot. Use these factors to establish minimum and maximum figures for your stock level; then EDIT the database or use the editing portion of the **Stock.Get** command to insert those figures. Run this report regularly, and make adjustments as the figures indicate.

You can create your own ad hoc reports using the commands in Fig. 6-21.

KEEPING TRACK OF VENDORS

In keeping with the principle that a database should be concerned with only one subject, the parts inventory lists only the vendor's name. Further information on the vendor's identity is provided in a separate **Vendor** database, linked through the name to the inventory records. Should you need to include detailed vendor information with your stock data you can SELECT the **Vendor** file as a secondary database. This record also can be linked to the accounts payable system.

In most respects, it's a simple system, consisting of basic contact information as shown by the screen in Fig. 6-22.

The remaining command files are basic instructions, beginning with Fig. 6-23, for calling and maintaining the file. Most are simplified versions of procedures you've seen already.

Figure 6-24 updates the indexing on a single item, the vendor's name. You can add new vendors to the list with the commands in Fig. 6-25, and you can search and edit the file with the sequence in Fig. 6-26. The two format files (Figs. 6-27 and 6-28) handle the input and output of, respectively, memory variables and database items.

Chapter 7

Paying the Bills

The growth of Nick Nader's parts collection into an increasingly sophisticated small business gave the senior partner one big cause for worry. Nick is a man who believes in paying his bills. The idea that every order from a parts supplier represented another bill to be paid made him extremely uncomfortable.

It isn't that he was worried about being unable to pay. If he couldn't pay he wouldn't order, it was simple as that. But as he asked his son one day, "What if we forget to pay one of the bills?"

"Don't worry, Pop," his son tried to reassure him. "We'll use that dBASE program we set up for inventory control, and turn it into an accounts payable system. It'll keep track of all our outstanding bills and when they're due. It can even be set up to identify any discounts we can earn for paying early."

The latter idea appealed to Nick's thrifty nature, so he agreed to let his son proceed with the project. "Just remember," he warned. "That computer should learn to speak our language, not the other way 'round."

"I'll try," said the son. "Now the first thing we have to do is to add a touch of sophistication to the **Vendor** file we created for the inventory system. In fact, all we need to do is to add one item so the new file looks like this."

```
STRUCTURE FOR FILE:   VENDOR.DBF
NUMBER OF RECORDS:    00000
DATE OF LAST UPDATE:  00/00/00
PRIMARY USE DATABASE
FLD         NAME        TYPE WIDTH      DEC
001    VENDOR          C     010
002    FULL            C     020
003    VSTREET         C     020
```

```
004        VCITY              C      015
005        VSTATE             C      002
006        VZIP               C      005
007        VCONT              C      015
008        VPHONE             C      013
** TOTAL **                          00101
```

As the younger Nader explained the situation, most of the files to be created in the accounts payable system would be keyed to an identification of the vendor. It would quickly become clumsy to have to enter the suppliers' full names every time, so the new database calls for a short, common name to serve as the

```
% PAYABLE.CMD
% Menu file for accounts payable system
ERASE
SET TALK OFF
SET BELL OFF
SET INTENSITY OFF
SET FORMAT TO SCREEN
@  1, 0 SAY "Nader & Son Corvair Parts"
@  1,64 SAY Date()
@  2, 0 SAY "================================================="
@  2,50 SAY "==================================="
@  3,28 SAY "ACCOUNTS PAYABLE MENU"
@  4,28 SAY "--------------------------"
@  5,24 SAY "1:  Add Vendor Files"
@  6,24 SAY "2:  Edit Vendor Files"
@  7,24 SAY "3:  Delete Vendor Files"
@  8,24 SAY "4:  Print Vendor Mailing List"
@  9,24 SAY "5:  Add Vouchers to Transaction File"
@ 10,24 SAY "6:  Select Vouchers for Payment"
@ 11,24 SAY "7:  Maintain Transaction File"
@ 12,24 SAY "8:  Maintain Voucher File"
@ 13,24 SAY "9:  Report on Pending Vouchers"
@ 14,24 SAY "10: Report on Paid Vouchers"
@ 15,24 SAY "----------------------------------------"
@ 16,24 SAY "R:  Return to previous Operation"
@ 17,24 SAY "X:  Return to Operating System"
@ 19,24 SAY "Please Enter Your Choice ==>_"
SET CONSOLE OFF
WAIT TO choice
SET CONSOLE ON
DO CASE
CASE choice = '1'
DO VENDOR.CMD
```

Fig. 7-1. Accounts payable menu command file. (Continued on page 196.)

```
              DO VENDOR.ADD
           CASE choice = '2'
              DO VENDOR.CMD
              DO VENDOR.ED
           CASE choice = '3'
              DO VENDOR.CMD
              DO VENDOR.DEL
           CASE choice = '4'
              DO VENDOR.CMD
              DO VENDOR.LBL
           CASE choice = '5'
              DO TRANS.CMD
              DO TRANS.ADD
           CASE choice = '6'
              DO TRANS.CMD
              DO TRANS.PAY
           CASE choice = '7'
              DO TRANS.CMD
              DO TRANS.GET
           CASE choice = '8'
              DO VOUCHER.CMD
              DO VOUCHER.GET
           CASE choice = '9'
              DO TRANS.CMD
              DO TRANS.RPT
           CASE choice = '10'
              DO VOUCHER.CMD
              DO TRANS.RPT
           CASE choice = 'R'
           CANCEL
           CASE choice = 'X'
           QUIT
           RETURN
```

Fig. 7-1. Accounts payable menu command file. (Continued from page 195.)

identifier, and as the link between related files. That's the **Vendor** field in the revised database. The **Full** field then contains the suppliers' full names for purposes of statements and mailing lists.

"I could give every vendor a number," the son pointed out, but if you want a plain-language system I'm sure you'd rather call them by name. Take that guy who stuck us with all the carpets. What would you rather call him Troy or, say, No. 356?"

"Neither," said the father. He had to acknowledge, though, that "Old Reprobate" wouldn't work too well in a database, and that his son did have the right idea. The revised **Vendor** file, then, became the first element of the new payables system.

The junior Nader decided, too, that if his father wanted a more communicative system he shouldn't

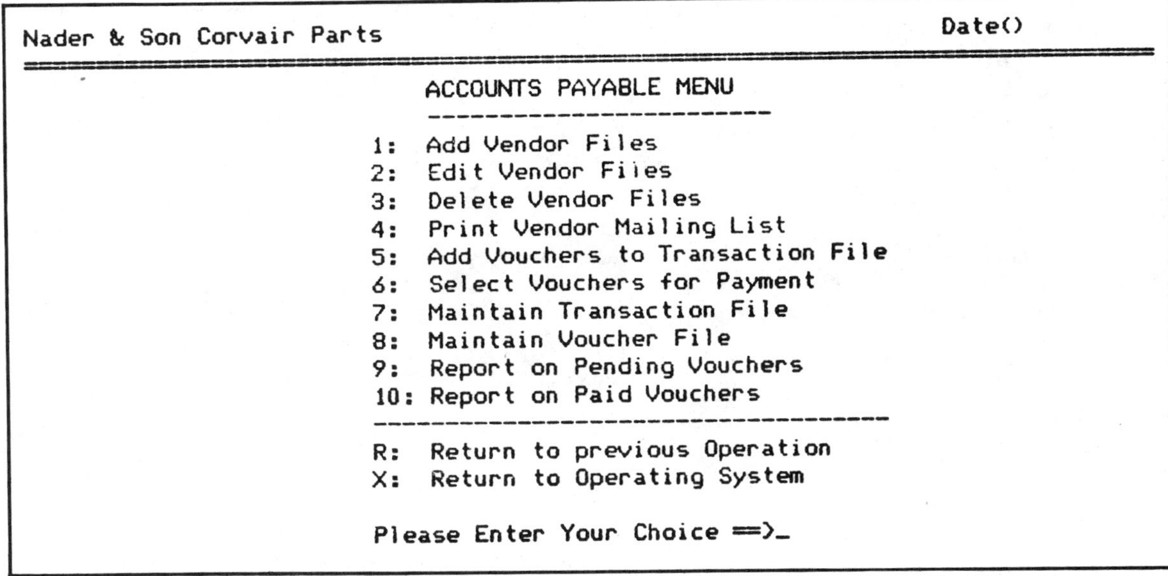

Fig. 7-2. Accounts payable menu display.

rely so heavily on the all-purpose **Get** program, derived from Fox & Geller's QUICKCODE, that he'd used before. Instead, he'd break up these functions and give each a separate listing in the command and menu program. The result is the command file, Fig. 7-1, producing the menu display in Fig. 7-2.

Vendor.Cmd, Fig. 7-3, sets up and indexes the **Vendor** file. Adding new listings is the job of the first file maintenance routine, **Vendor.Add**, Fig. 7-4. The second file maintenance program, Fig. 7-5, edits existing files. A third, Fig. 7-6, deletes obsolete files. Both of the last two call the **Vendor.Get** program, Fig. 7-7, to find the files to be changed or deleted. Figures 7-8 and 7-9 are the screen formats for the file maintenance functions. They produce the layout seen in Fig. 7-10.

```
*       VENDOR.CMD
*    DATABASE NAME IS     VENDOR
*    DATABASE IS KEYED
SET TALK OFF
SET FORMAT TO SCREEN
STORE FILE('VENDOR.NDX') TO index
IF .NOT. index
 @ 21,10 SAY  ' FILE IS NOW BEING INDEXED '
SELECT PRIMARY
USE  VENDOR
INDEX ON    vendor  TO  vendor
 ERASE
ENDIF
USE VENDOR     INDEX  VENDOR
RELEASE index
RETURN
```

Fig. 7-3. Command file for vendor records.

```
*       VENDOR.ADD
STORE T TO Amore
DO WHILE Amore
*   Set default values
STORE '             ' TO Mvendor
STORE '                    ' TO  Mvfull
STORE '                   ' TO  Mvstreet
STORE '              ' TO  Mvcity
STORE ' ' TO  Mvstate
STORE '     ' TO  Mvzip
STORE '                ' TO  Mvcont
STORE '(   )000-0000' TO  Mvphone
  ERASE
STORE ' ADD ' TO mode
* GET DATA TO ADD
DO  VENDOR.IO
READ
* ARE WE DONE?
IF Mvendor <> '             '
 APPEND BLANK
* PUT SCREEN DATA INTO FILE
 REPLACE  vendor  WITH  Mvendor
 REPLACE  vfull  WITH  Mvfull
 REPLACE  vstreet  WITH  Mvstreet
 REPLACE  vcity  WITH  Mvcity
 REPLACE  vstate  WITH  Mvstate
 REPLACE  vzip  WITH  Mvzip
 REPLACE  vcont  WITH  Mvcont
 REPLACE  vphone  WITH  Mvphone
ELSE
    STORE F TO Amore
ENDIF
ENDDO
RELEASE mode,Amore
* RELEASE INPUT FIELDS
RELEASE Mvendor
RELEASE Mvfull
RELEASE Mvstreet
RELEASE Mvcity
RELEASE Mvstate
RELEASE Mvzip
RELEASE Mvcont
RELEASE Mvphone
RETURN
```

Fig. 7-4. Adding to vendor file.

The "delete" operation will make the operator confirm at least twice that you really want to eliminate the file. The first prompt requires a positive answer before dBASE will make the record for deletion. The second demands further confirmation before it will make the ultimate PACK.

The **Vendor.Lbl** program, Fig. 7-11, gives you the means to produce a mailing list or a set of labels for sending orders or payments to the vendors. It gives you the chance to specify the size of each label. (A common type holds six lines, but there are many exceptions.) You also can scan the file to select vendors with certain characteristics. The file is indexed to produce a list in ZIP code order.

```
*       VENDOR.ED
* Edit vendor file records
 STORE  ' EDIT '  TO MQ:MODE
* LOCATE FILE TO BE CHANGED
DO VENDOR.GET
* SET UP SCREEN VARIABLES
 STORE  vendor  TO  Mvendor
 STORE  vfull  TO  Mvfull
 STORE  vstreet  TO  Mvstreet
 STORE  vcity  TO  Mvcity
 STORE  vstate  TO  Mvstate
 STORE  vzip  TO  Mvzip
 STORE  vcont  TO  Mvcont
 STORE  vphone  TO  Mvphone
ERASE
* GET SCREEN INPUT
 DO  VENDOR.IO
 READ
* PUT SCREEN ENTRIES INTO FILE
 REPLACE  vendor  WITH  Mvendor
 REPLACE  vfull  WITH  Mvfull
 REPLACE  vstreet  WITH  Mvstreet
 REPLACE  vcity  WITH  Mvcity
 REPLACE  vstate  WITH  Mvstate
 REPLACE  vzip  WITH  Mvzip
 REPLACE  vcont  WITH  Mvcont
 REPLACE  vphone  WITH  Mvphone
RELEASE Mvendor
RELEASE Mvfull
RELEASE Mvstreet
RELEASE Mvcity
RELEASE Mvstate
RELEASE Mvzip
RELEASE Mvcont
RELEASE Mvphone
```

Fig. 7-5. Edit vendor records.

```
* Vendor.Del
* Delete suppliers from vendor file
STORE 'DELETE' TO mode
* Find record to be deleted
DO VENDOR.GET
@ 23,10 SAY 'DELETE THIS RECORD(Y/N)? ' GET delete
READ
IF !(delete)= 'Y'
    STORE 'N' TO ans
  ENDIF
@ 23,10 SAY ' ARE YOU SURE(Y/N)?
@ 23,28 GET ans
    READ
IF !(ans)= 'Y'
    DELETE
    STORE 'Y' TO confirm
ENDIF
RELEASE ans
IF confirm = 'Y'
    STORE 'N' TO ans
    @ 23,10 SAY 'WANT TO PERMANENTLY DELETE RECORDS(Y/N)'
    @ 23,49 GET ans
    READ
    IF ans = 'Y'
        PACK
    ELSE
        RECALL ALL
    ENDIF
        RELEASE ans
ENDIF  confirm
RELEASE  confirm
RELEASE mode
```

Fig. 7-6. Delete vendor records.

ENTERING THE VOUCHERS

When the company receives an invoice from a supplier, the operator should check on whether the invoiced shipment has arrived in satisfactory order. If so, a voucher for the payment is added to the **Transaction** file:

```
STRUCTURE FOR FILE:   TRANS.DBF
NUMBER OF RECORDS:    00000
DATE OF LAST UPDATE: 00/00/00
PRIMARY USE DATABASE
FLD       NAME        TYPE WIDTH    DEC
```

```
*       VENDOR.GET
* Search program for file maintenance
ERASE
STORE  ' GET '  TO mode
* DISPLAY CURRENT RECORD
STORE 'T' TO select
IF &select
 DO  VENDOR.OUT
ENDIF
STORE T TO more
DO WHILE more
  ERASE
  STORE  ' SEARCH '  TO mode
* GET FIELDS TO SEARCH FOR
@ 02,000 SAY '===================='
@ 02,020 SAY '===================='
@ 02,040 SAY '===================='
@ 02,060 SAY '===================='
@ 03,000 SAY 'VENDOR ==>'
  STORE  '                ' TO  Mvendor
@ 03,011 GET Mvendor
@ 04,000 SAY 'FULL NAME ==>'
@ 05,000 SAY 'STREET ==>'
@ 06,000 SAY 'CITY ==>'
@ 07,000 SAY 'STATE ==>'
@ 08,000 SAY 'ZIP ==>'
@ 09,000 SAY 'CONTACT ==>'
@ 10,000 SAY 'TELEPHONE ==>'
  IF select <>  ' T '
   @ 23,4 SAY '**'
  ENDIF
  READ
* EXIT FROM LOOP IF FOUND
  GOTO TOP
  STORE TRIM(Mvendor) TO key
  IF select=  ' T '
   FIND &key
   IF # <> 0
      STORE F TO more
  ELSE
   @ 22,10 SAY  '  NOT FOUND  '
   @ 23.10 SAY  ' TRY AGAIN(Y/N)? '
  SET CONSOLE OFF
WAIT TO retry;
```

Fig. 7-7. Search for vendor data. (Continued on page 202.)

```
      SET CONSOLE ON
      IF !(retry;) <>   'Y'
       STORE F TO more
     ENDIF  Y
     RELEASE retry;
      ENDIF  # <> 0
     ELSE
      LOCATE FOR  vendor   = Mvendor .AND. &select
      IF .NOT. EOF
        STORE F TO more
     ELSE
       @ 22,10 SAY  '   NOT FOUND  '
       @ 23,10 SAY  ' TRY AGAIN(Y/N)? '
       SET CONSOLE OFF
       WAIT TO retry;
       SET CONSOLE ON
       IF !(retry;) <>   'Y'
        STORE F TO more
     ENDIF  Y
     RELEASE retry;
      ENDIF EOF
     ENDIF  select=T
    ENDDO  more
    RELEASE more
    RELEASE key
    RELEASE mode
    RETURN
```

Fig. 7-7. Search for vendor data. (Continued from page 201.)

001	VENDOR	C	011	
002	INVNO	C	011	
003	DUEDATE	C	008	
004	DUEAMT	N	011	002
005	DISDATE	C	008	
006	DISAMT	N	011	002
007	ACCT	C	007	
008	PDDATE	C	008	
009	CHECKNO	N	005	
010	PDAMT	N	007	002
** TOTAL **			00088	

The command file for the transaction sequence is Fig. 7-12. The data entry and editing screen for this file is shown in Fig. 7-13. It's the one Nader and Son use when they receive yet another shipment of Corvair carpets. "At least they're red this time," the son said.

"Ayuh," said the elder Nader. "Had a call about them yesterday. Thanks to your computer there, I was able to say we had some comin'."

```
*       VENDOR.IO
*   Input/output screen for vendor file maintenance.
@ 01,036 SAY mode
@ 02,000 SAY '===================='
@ 02,020 SAY '===================='
@ 02,040 SAY '===================='
@ 02,060 SAY '===================='
@ 03,000 SAY 'VENDOR ==>'
@ 03,011 GET Mvendor
@ 04,000 SAY 'FULL NAME ==>'
@ 04,014 GET Mvfull
@ 05,000 SAY 'STREET ==>'
@ 05,011 GET Mvstreet
@ 06,000 SAY 'CITY ==>'
@ 06,009 GET Mvcity
@ 07,000 SAY 'STATE ==>'
@ 07,010 GET Mvstate
@ 08,000 SAY 'ZIP ==>'
@ 08,008 GET Mvzip
@ 09,000 SAY 'CONTACT ==>'
@ 09,012 GET Mvcont
@ 10,000 SAY 'TELEPHONE ==>'
@ 10,014 GET Mvphone PICTURE '(XXX)999-9999'
```

Fig. 7-8. Format screen for entering vendor data.

To roll out their red carpet officially, the Naders welcomed the shipment by punching up the routine for adding the item to their payable **Transaction** file. Figure 7-14 is the main file. Figure 7-15 provides the screen display.

It isn't necessary in this case, but you can call Fig. 7-16, which checks to make sure the supplier's name is listed in the **Vendor** file:

```
SELECT SECONDARY
USE  vendor      INDEX  vendor
STORE  Mvendor  TO search
FIND &search
RELEASE search
IF # <> 0
    SELECT PRIMARY
    STORE F TO Vmore
ELSE
    SELECT PRIMARY
  @ 23,0 SAY  '                                        '
  @ 23,0 SAY  ' CANNOT FIND IN VENDOR FILE '
@ 08,000 GET Mvendor
```

```
*        VENDOR.OUT
*     Output form for vendor file mainetnance
@ 01,036 SAY mode
@ 02,000 SAY '======================'
@ 02,020 SAY '======================'
@ 02,040 SAY '======================'
@ 02,060 SAY '======================'
@ 03,000 SAY 'VENDOR ==>'
@ 03,012 SAY vendor
@ 04,000 SAY 'FULL NAME ==>'
@ 04,015 SAY vfull
@ 05,000 SAY 'STREET ==>'
@ 05,012 SAY vstreet
@ 06,000 SAY 'CITY ==>'
@ 06,010 SAY vcity
@ 07,000 SAY 'STATE ==>'
@ 07,011 SAY vstate
@ 08,000 SAY 'ZIP ==>'
@ 08,009 SAY vzip
@ 09,000 SAY 'CONTACT ==>'
@ 09,013 SAY vcont
@ 10,000 SAY 'TELEPHONE ==>'
@ 10,015 SAY vphone
```

Fig. 7-9. Output screen for vendor data.

This routine calls **Vendor** as a secondary file, indexes it on the vendor's short identification. If it fails to find a match, i.e., if it turns up a zero for a record number, it posts the warning and asks you to try again. This feature lets you keep going if the mismatch was due to a typing error.

WHO GETS PAID?

The voucher will wait in the **Transaction** file until it comes time to write the checks. Then you must

```
                              ADD
======================================================================
VENDOR ==>
FULL NAME ==>
STREET ==>
CITY ==>
STATE ==>
ZIP ==>
CONTACT ==>
TELEPHONE ==>
```

Fig. 7-10. Screen display for vendor data.

```
* Vendor.Lbl
* Prints mailing list and labels from vendor file
STORE '          '  TO mode
STORE 10 TO size
STORE   '

TO select
STORE 'Y' TO reply
@ 21,10 SAY 'DO YOU WISH TO SCAN FILE? (Y/N)'  GET reply
READ
@ 21,10
IF !(reply)='Y'
 @ 21,10 SAY 'PLEASE ENTER SELECTION CRITERIA'
 @ 23,10 GET select
 READ
 @ 21,10
 @ 23,10
ELSE
 STORE 'T' TO select
ENDIF
@ 21,10 SAY  ' HOW MANY LINES PER LABEL/FORM?  '
@ 22,10 SAY  ' (ENTER 0 TO GET PAGE EJECTS) '
@ 23,10 SAY  ' PLEASE COUNT THE SPACE BETWEEN LABELS  '  GET size
READ
GOTO TOP
@ 23,10 SAY  ' PLEASE SET UP YOUR PRINTER
SET CONSOLE OFF
WAIT
SET CONSOLE ON
* REPEAT UNTIL FILE ENDS
DO WHILE .NOT. EOF
  IF &select
   STORE vcont TO item1
   STORE vfull TO item2
   STORE vstreet TO item3
   STORE vcity TO item4
   STORE vstate TO item5
   STORE vzip TO item6
  ELSE
   SKIP
   LOOP
  ENDIF
 SET PRINT ON
  ?  ' '+item1
```

Fig. 7-11. Label printing commands for vendor data. (Continued on page 206.)

```
    ?  ' '+item2
    ?  ' '+item3
    ?  ' '+item4+' '+item5+' '+item6
   STORE 0 TO count
 * IF LABEL IS LARGER, SKIP SOME LINES
  IF size >    4
   DO WHILE count < (size -    4 )

     ? '  '
      STORE count + 1 TO count
    ENDDO  count
   ELSE
   IF size = 0
    EJECT
   ENDIF  0
   ENDIF  >
   SKIP
  ENDDO   NOT EOF
  SET PRINT OFF
  SET CONSOLE ON
  RELEASE size,count,reply,select
    RELEASE item1
    RELEASE item2
    RELEASE item3
    RELEASE item4
    RELEASE item5
    RELEASE item6
  RETURN
```

Fig. 7-11. Label printing commands for vendor data. (Continued from page 205.)

sort through the **Transaction** file to identify the bills to be paid. This is a sorting and editing routine that uses **Trans.Pay**, Fig. 7-17 and the screen file in Fig. 7-15. You can search for the file by the vendor's identification and enter the appropriate information on the payment.

dBASE will then transfer all the bills paid to the main **Voucher** file. The completed record will be marked for deletion, and once you've verified that the check is correct it will complete the job.

The **Transaction** and **Voucher** files are identical in structure, but there's a difference in the way they're used. The **Transaction** file stores vouchers that are *waiting* to be acted upon. The **Voucher** file holds those on which action has been *completed*.

This system also includes a general searching and editing routine for the **Transaction** file. It appears in Fig. 7-18 with the screen layout command in Fig. 7-19. It's much like the similar routines in earlier chapters.

It does illustrate, though, that you have this option in dBASE: you can use this general editing routine to maintain your records, or you can break out parts of it for specific purposes. The voucher payment routine is an example; so are the specialized procedures for maintaining the **Vendor** file.

```
*       TRANS.CMD
*   Control program for payable transaction file
*   DATABASE NAME IS    TRANS
*   DATABASE IS KEYED
SET TALK OFF
SET FORMAT TO SCREEN
SELECT PRIMARY
STORE FILE('TRANS.NDX') TO index
IF .NOT. index
SET TALK OFF
@ 21,10 SAY 'FILE IS NOW BEING INDEXED'
SELECT PRIMARY
USE   TRANS
INDEX ON    vendor  TO  TRANSVEND
INDEX ON    duedate TO TRANSDUE
INDEX ON    disdate TO TRANSDIS
INDEX ON    acct TO TRANSACCT
 ERASE
ENDIF
USE TRANS   INDEX  TRANSVEND, TRANSDUE, TRANSDIS, TRANSACCT
RELEASE index
RETURN
```

Fig. 7-12. Command listing for transaction file.

THE VOUCHER FILE

There's a similar editing routine for the **Voucher** file itself. It lets you make searches and corrections and, if you'd like, print a record of any entry. Figures 7-20 through 7-24 follow what (by now) should be a familiar pattern. Use this sequence to make any necessary changes to the permanent **Voucher** file. Most additions, though, will be made from the **Transaction** file, and most reports will be generated in the same way.

The main job of this junction is to help you pay the bills. That includes, of course, selecting the bills for payment and issuing the checks. A good system should do more, though, and this one helps you decide

```
                                    ADD
=======================================================================

              ACCOUNTS PAYABLE:   VOUCHER TRANSACTION FILE
              ---------------------------------------------

VENDOR         INVOICE        STANDARD                  DISCOUNT                 ACCOUNT
               NUMBER      --------------------      --------------------
                           DATE        AMOUNT        DATE        AMOUNT
  :              :          :        :  :            :         :  :              :      :
                                     ----------
DATE PAID :        :            CHECK NO :        :            AMOUNT :  '      :
```

Fig. 7-13. Transaction file screen display.

which bills to pay, whether it is to your advantage to take advantage of discounts, and how much cash you will need to meet your coming obligations.

You can call a series of reports from the **Trans.Rpt** program, Fig. 7-25. The first is a general report that uses the **Transaction** file to list currently open vouchers by vendor. We'll call the report **Open**, and it looks like this:

```
ENTER OPTIONS, M=LEFT MARGIN, L=LINES/PAGE, W=PAGE WIDTH W=45
PAGE HEADING? (Y/N) Y
ENTER PAGE HEADING: ACCOUNTS PAYABLE; OPEN VOUCHERS
DOUBLE SPACE REPORT? (Y/N) N
ARE TOTALS REQUIRED? (Y/N) Y
SUBTOTALS IN REPORT? (Y/N) Y
ENTER SUBTOTALS FIELD: VENDOR
SUMMARY REPORT ONLY? (Y/N) N
EJECT PAGE AFTER SUBTOTALS? (Y/N) N
ENTER SUBTOTAL HEADING: VENDOR:
COL      WIDTH,CONTENTS
001      8,invno
ENTER HEADING: INVOICE NO
002      8,duedate
ENTER HEADING: DATE DUE
003      7,dueamt
ENTER HEADING: AMOUNT DUE
ARE TOTALS REQUIRED? (Y/N) Y
004      8,disdate
ENTER HEADING: DISCOUNT DATE
005      7,disamt
ENTER HEADING: AMOUNT
ARE TOTALS REQUIRED? (Y/N) Y
```

This form produces a basic report of payments due shown in Fig. 7-26.

The next two reports are designed, first, to assess your cash needs as the bills come due and, second, to let you compare payment options. The first totals, by due date, the open vouchers in the file. The second does much the same thing, but it breaks down the report on the basis of the last days to earn discounts. In both cases the reports let you compare the relative advantages and disadvantages of paying earlier to earn the discount. Here are the near-twins, named **Cashdue** and **Cashdis**, starting with the full payment option offering later payment dates:

```
ENTER OPTIONS, M=LEFT MARGIN, L=LINES/PAGE, W=PAGE WIDTH W=45
PAGE HEADING? (Y/N) Y
ENTER PAGE HEADING: ACCOUNTS PAYABLE; CASH REQUIREMENTS;
BY DUE DATE
DOUBLE SPACE REPORT? (Y/N) N
ARE TOTALS REQUIRED? (Y/N) Y
SUBTOTALS IN REPORT? (Y/N) Y
ENTER SUBTOTALS FIELD: duedate
```

```
SUMMARY REPORT ONLY? (Y/N) N
EJECT PAGE AFTER SUBTOTALS? (Y/N) N
ENTER SUBTOTAL HEADING: DUE DATE:
COL        WIDTH,CONTENTS
001        10,vendor
ENTER HEADING: VENDOR
002        8,invno
ENTER HEADING: INVOICE NO
003        7,dueamt
ENTER HEADING: AMOUNT DUE
ARE TOTALS REQUIRED? (Y/N) Y
004        8,disdate
ENTER HEADING: DISCOUNT DATE
005        7,disamt
ENTER HEADING: AMT W/ DISC
ARE TOTALS REQUIRED? (Y/N) Y
```

This produces the report shown in Fig. 7-27.

```
*         TRANS.ADD
*  Adds new invoices to voucher transaction file
STORE T TO Amore
DO WHILE Amore
* GET DEFAULT VALUES
STORE  '            '  TO  Mvendor
STORE  '            '  TO  Minvno
STORE  '00/00/00'  TO  Mduedate
STORE  0.00  TO  Mdueamt
STORE  '00/00/00'  TO  Mdisdate
STORE  0.00  TO  Mdisamt
STORE  '          '  TO  Macct
STORE  '00/00/00'  TO  Mpddate
STORE  0  TO  Mcheckno
STORE  0.00  TO  Mpdamt
  ERASE
STORE  ' ADD '  TO mode
* GET DATA TO ADD
DO  TRANS.IO
@ 21,10 SAY  ' ADD VOUCHERS TO FILE '
@ 22,10 SAY  ' WHEN DONE ENTER BLANKS FOR VENDOR '
READ
* ARE WE DONE?
IF Mvendor  <>  '            '
  APPEND BLANK
* PUT SCREEN DATA INTO FILE
```

Fig. 7-14. Adding records to transaction file. (Continued on page 210.)

```
        REPLACE  vendor   WITH  Mvendor
        REPLACE  invno   WITH  Minvno
        REPLACE  duedate  WITH  Mduedate
        REPLACE  dueamt  WITH  Mdueamt
        REPLACE  disdate  WITH  Mdisdate
        REPLACE  disamt  WITH  Mdisamt
        REPLACE  acct  WITH  Macct
        REPLACE  pddate  WITH  Mpddate
        REPLACE  checkno  WITH  Mcheckno
        REPLACE  pdamt  WITH  Mpdamt
    ELSE
        STORE F TO Amore
    ENDIF
    ENDDO
    RELEASE mode,Amore
    * RELEASE INPUT FIELDS
    RELEASE Mvendor
    RELEASE Minvno
    RELEASE Mduedate
    RELEASE Mdueamt
    RELEASE Mdisdate
    RELEASE Mdisamt
    RELEASE Macct
    RELEASE Mpddate
    RELEASE Mcheckno
    RELEASE Mpdamt
```

Fig. 7-14. Adding records to transaction file. (Continued from page 209.)

Or the discount version, which generates the report in Fig. 7-28.

```
ENTER OPTIONS, M=LEFT MARGIN, L=LINES/PAGE, W=PAGE WIDTH W=45
PAGE HEADING? (Y/N) Y
ENTER PAGE HEADING: ACCOUNTS PAYABLE; CASH REQUIREMENTS;
BY DISCOUNT DAT
DOUBLE SPACE REPORT? (Y/N) N
ARE TOTALS REQUIRED? (Y/N) Y
SUBTOTALS IN REPORT? (Y/N) Y
ENTER SUBTOTALS FIELD: disdate
SUMMARY REPORT ONLY? (Y/N) n
EJECT PAGE AFTER SUBTOTALS? (Y/N) N
ENTER SUBTOTAL HEADING: DISCOUNT DATE:
COL     WIDTH,CONTENTS
001      10, vendor
```

ENTER HEADING: VENDOR
002   8, invno
ENTER HEADING: INVOICE NO
003   7, disamt
ENTER HEADING: DISC. AMT
ARE TOTALS REQUIRED? (Y/N) Y
004   8, duedate
ENTER HEADING: DATE DUE
005   7, dueamt
ENTER HEADING: AMOUNT DUE
ARE TOTALS REQUIRED? (Y/N) Y

```
    *     TRANS.IO
@ 01,036 SAY mode
@ 02,000 SAY '====================='
@ 02,020 SAY '====================='
@ 02,040 SAY '====================='
@ 02,060 SAY '====================='
@ 03,018 SAY 'ACCOUNTS PAYABLE:   VOUCHER TRANSACTION FILE'
@ 04,018 SAY '----------------------------------------------'
@ 05,000 SAY 'VENDOR          INVOICE'
@ 05,028 SAY 'STANDARD'
@ 05,052 SAY 'DISCOUNT'
@ 05,072 SAY 'ACCOUNT'
@ 06,012 SAY 'NUMBER'
@ 06,024 SAY '--------------------'
@ 06,048 SAY '--------------------'
@ 07,024 SAY 'DATE         AMOUNT'
@ 07,048 SAY 'DATE         AMOUNT'
@ 08,000 GET Mvendor
@ 08,012 GET Minvno
@ 08,024 GET Mduedate PICTURE '99/99/99'
@ 08,036 GET Mdueamt PICTURE '9999.99'
@ 08,048 GET Mdisdate PICTURE '99/99/99'
@ 08,060 GET Mdisamt PICTURE '9999.99'
@ 08,072 GET Macct
@ 09,035 SAY '----------'
@ 10,000 SAY 'DATE PAID'
@ 10,010 GET Mpddate PICTURE '99/99/99'
@ 10,032 SAY 'CHECK NO'
@ 10,041 GET Mcheckno
@ 10,060 SAY 'AMOUNT'
@ 10,067 GET Mpdamt PICTURE '9999.99'
```

Fig. 7-15. Input format for transaction file operations.

```
* TRANS.VAL
*  Validation Program:   Checks vouchers against vendor file
STORE T TO Vmore
DO WHILE Vmore
SELECT SECONDARY
USE vendor      INDEX  vendor
STORE  '&Mvendor'  TO Mvendor
FIND &Mvendor
RELEASE search
IF # <> 0
   SELECT PRIMARY
   STORE F TO Vmore
ELSE
   SELECT PRIMARY
 @ 23,0 SAY  '
 @ 23,0 SAY  ' CANNOT FIND IN VENDOR FILE '
@ 08,000 GET Mvendor
READ
ENDIF
ENDDO  Mvendor
```

Fig. 7-16. Validation file for transaction file input.

Take a look at that Vantage entry, for example. Is it worthwhile to take the discount? It appears that you could wait for nearly another month for only a five-dollar penalty. The decision is yours, but a close look at figures like these can help you get more mileage from your hard-earned (of course) cash.

A second report-generating sequence from the main menu lets you generate ad hoc reports from the **Voucher** file of paid bills.

WRITING CHECKS

On the basis of your cash requirement reports you can make better selections of which vouchers to select for payment. The final step, naturally, is to write the checks.

With the necessary reports in hand, make your decisions and punch item 6 from the main payables menu. It will present you with a blank version of the data entry form and ask for the vendor's identification. The routine which does this is this part of the program:

```
@ 05,000 SAY 'VENDOR          INVOICE'
@ 05,028 SAY 'STANDARD'
@ 05,052 SAY 'DISCOUNT'
@ 05,072 SAY 'ACCOUNT'
@ 06,012 SAY 'NUMBER'
@ 06,024 SAY '--------------------'
@ 06,048 SAY '--------------------'
@ 07,024 SAY 'DATE        AMOUNT'
@ 07,048 SAY 'DATE        AMOUNT'
  STORE '               '  TO  Mvendor
@ 08,000 GET Mvendor
```

```
*       TRANS.PAY
*     Select Records for Payment
ERASE
STORE 'Y' TO continue
  DO WHILE !(continue) = 'Y'
STORE  ' LOCATE '  TO mode
* DISPLAY CURRENT RECORD
STORE 'T' TO select
IF &select
 DO  TRANS.OUT
ENDIF
STORE T TO Smore
DO WHILE Smore
 ERASE
 STORE  ' SEARCH '  TO mode
* GET FIELDS TO SEARCH FOR
@ 01,035 SAY mode
@ 02,000 SAY '====================='
@ 02,020 SAY '====================='
@ 02,040 SAY '====================='
@ 02,060 SAY '====================='
@ 03,018 SAY 'ACCOUNTS PAYABLE:  VOUCHER TRANSACTION FILE'
@ 04,018 SAY '------------------------------------------------'
@ 05,000 SAY 'VENDOR         INVOICE'
@ 05,028 SAY 'STANDARD'
@ 05,052 SAY 'DISCOUNT'
@ 05,072 SAY 'ACCOUNT'
@ 06,012 SAY 'NUMBER'
@ 06,024 SAY '-------------------'
@ 06,048 SAY '-------------------'
@ 07,024 SAY 'DATE          AMOUNT'
@ 07,048 SAY 'DATE          AMOUNT'
 STORE  '              '  TO  Mvendor
@ 08,000 GET Mvendor
@ 09,035 SAY '----------'
@ 10,000 SAY 'DATE PAID'
@ 10,032 SAY 'CHECK NO'
@ 10,060 SAY 'AMOUNT'
 IF select <> ' T '
  @ 23,4 SAY '**'
 ENDIF
 READ
```

Fig. 7-17. Paying vouchers. (Continued on page 214.)

```
* EXIT FROM LOOP IF FOUND
GOTO TOP
STORE TRIM(Mvendor) TO key
IF select=  ' T '
 FIND &key
 IF # <> 0
    STORE F TO Smore
  ELSE
    @ 22,10 SAY  '   NOT FOUND  '
    @ 23,10 SAY  ' TRY AGAIN(Y/N)? '
    SET CONSOLE OFF
    WAIT TO retry
    SET CONSOLE ON
    IF !(retry) <>  'Y'
    STORE F TO Smore
  ENDIF  Y
  RELEASE retry
   ENDIF  # <> 0
  ELSE
   LOCATE FOR  vendor   = Mvendor .AND. &select
   IF .NOT. EOF
     STORE F TO Smore
  ELSE
    @ 22,10 SAY  '   NOT FOUND  '
    @ 23,10 SAY  ' TRY AGAIN(Y/N)? '
    SET CONSOLE OFF
    WAIT TO retry
    SET CONSOLE ON
    IF !(retry) <>  'Y'
    STORE F TO Smore
  ENDIF  Y
  RELEASE retry
   ENDIF EOF
  ENDIF  select=T
ENDDO  Smore
RELEASE Smore
RELEASE mode
STORE T TO Emore
 STORE  ' TO PAY' TO mode
* SET UP SCREEN VARIABLES
SELECT SECONDARY
USE VENDOR INDEX VENDOR
FIND &key
```

Fig. 7-17. Paying vouchers. (Continued on page 215.)

```
SELECT PRIMARY
 STORE   vendor   TO  Mvendor
 STORE   S.vfull to Mvfull
 STORE   S.vstreet to Mvstreet
 STORE   S.vcity to Mvcity
 STORE   S.vstate to Mvstate
 STORE   S.vzip to Mvzip
 STORE   invno  TO  Minvno
 STORE   duedate  TO  Mduedate
 STORE   dueamt  TO  Mdueamt
 STORE   disdate  TO  Mdisdate
 STORE   disamt  TO  Mdisamt
 STORE   acct  TO  Macct
 STORE   pddate  TO  Mpddate
 STORE   checkno  TO  Mcheckno
 STORE   pdamt  TO  Mpdamt
DO WHILE Emore
ERASE
X GET SCREEN INPUT
 DO  TRANS.IO
 @ 21,10 SAY  ' ENTER PAYMENT DETAILS '
 READ
 STORE  'N'  TO command
 @ 21,10 SAY  ' ANY MORE ENTRIES (Y/N)? '   GET command
 READ
 IF  !(command)<> 'Y'
  STORE F TO Emore
 ENDIF
ENDDO
SELECT PRIMARY
X Print Checks
@ 23, 10 SAY 'READY TO PRINT CHECKS(Y/N)?'
SET CONSOLE OFF
WAIT TO REPLY
SET CONSOLE ON
IF !(reply) = 'Y'
 @ 23,10 SAY  ' PLEASE SET UP PRINTER
 STORE '        '  TO mode
 SET CONSOLE OFF
 WAIT
 SET CONSOLE ON
 SET FORMAT TO PRINT
 X  Prints checks for accounts payable
```

```
SET MARGIN TO    0
@  1, 8 SAY "Nader & Son Corvair Parts"
@  2, 8 SAY "Box 110"
@  3, 8 SAY "Greencastle Ctr., Vt. 01234"
@  5, 8 SAY "PAID TO:"
@  5,17 SAY mvfull
@  6, 8 SAY "INVOICE NO:"
@  6,20 SAY minvno
@  7, 8 SAY "CHECK NO:"
@  7,18 SAY mcheckno
@  8, 8 SAY "AMOUNT:"
@  8,16 SAY mpdamt
@ 20, 8 SAY "Nader & Son Corvair Parts"
@ 20,56 SAY "Green Mountain Bank"
@ 21, 8 SAY "Box 110"
@ 22, 8 SAY "Greencastle Ctr., Vt. 01234"
@ 27, 8 SAY mvfull
@ 28, 8 SAY mvstreet
@ 28,64 SAY mpdamt
@ 29, 8 SAY mvcity
@ 30, 8 SAY mvstate
@ 30,17 SAY mvzip
@ 42,0 SAY ' '
?
SET FORMAT TO SCREEN
DELETE ALL FOR pdamt <> 0
@ 23,10 SAY 'IS CHECK CORRECT(Y/N)?
SET CONSOLE OFF
WAIT TO verify
SET CONSOLE ON
        IF !(verify) = 'Y'
        STORE 'N' TO continue
        PACK
        ENDIF
* TRANSFER DATA TO VOUCHER FILE
SELECT SECONDARY
USE VOUCHER INDEX VOUCHER
APPEND BLANK
 REPLACE  vendor  WITH  Mvendor
 REPLACE  invno  WITH  Minvno
 REPLACE  duedate  WITH  Mduedate
 REPLACE  dueamt  WITH  Mdueamt
 REPLACE  disdate  WITH  Mdisdate
```

Fig. 7-17. Paying vouchers. (Continued on page 217.)

```
       REPLACE   disamt   WITH   Mdisamt
       REPLACE   acct   WITH   Macct
       REPLACE   pddate   WITH   Mpddate
       REPLACE   checkno   WITH   Mcheckno
       REPLACE   pdamt   WITH   Mpdamt
     RELEASE mode,Emore,command
     RELEASE Mvendor
     RELEASE Minvno
     RELEASE Mduedate
     RELEASE Mdueamt
     RELEASE Mdisdate
     RELEASE Mdisamt
     RELEASE Macct
     RELEASE Mpddate
     RELEASE Mcheckno
     RELEASE Mpdamt
     RELEASE key
     @ 23,10 SAY 'MORE PAYMENTS(Y/N)?
     SET CONSOLE OFF
     WAIT TO continue
     SET CONSOLE ON
     ENDDO
     DO PAYABLE.CMD
     RETURN
```

Hold it right there. We interrupt this screen format to set up **Mvendor** as a character variable and then to GET it on the screen. When you fill in the blank for **Vendor,** you are creating this variable.

You could use this technique for any variable for which you wish to search. Perhaps you'd prefer to locate the voucher by number instead of the vendor's name. Use the STORE and GET lines for the invoice number entry instead (you can take the coordinates from the IO or OUT files). You could do this twice, forcing yourself to specify both the vendor and a date, for example. (Useful if a vendor is likely to have more than one unpaid voucher on file.)

```
@ 09,035 SAY '-----------'
@ 10,000 SAY 'DATE PAID'
@ 10,032 SAY 'CHECK NO'
@ 10,060 SAY 'AMOUNT'
```

Notice that the variables you *don't* specify as objects of your search don't appear on this particular screen. You'll be given a blank screen, and you'll be able to fill in only the items for which you are hunting.

Whatever item(s) you use as your search keys, enter a valid one and the program will locate any corresponding open voucher. You'll then be asked to enter the date, check number, and amount to be paid. dBASE then will make a second search, this time opening the **Vendor** file as a secondary database. Your search criteria have already been stored to the memory variable **key**, and the routine proceeds from there:

```
*       TRANS.GET
*  Search and edit program for payable transaction file.
ERASE
STORE  ' GET '  TO mode
* DISPLAY CURRENT RECORD
IF &select
 DO  TRANS.OUT
ENDIF
STORE T TO Smore
DO WHILE Smore
 ERASE
 STORE  ' SEARCH '  TO mode
* GET FIELDS TO SEARCH FOR
@ 01,000 SAY '--------------------'
@ 01,020 SAY '---------------'
@ 01,046 SAY '------------------'
@ 01,066 SAY '--------------'
@ 02,000 SAY '======================'
@ 02,020 SAY '==================='
@ 02,040 SAY '=================='
@ 02,060 SAY '=================='
@ 03,018 SAY 'ACCOUNTS PAYABLE:  VOUCHER TRANSACTION FILE'
@ 04,018 SAY '-------------------------------------------'
@ 05,000 SAY 'VENDOR          INVOICE'
@ 05,028 SAY 'STANDARD'
@ 05,052 SAY 'DISCOUNT'
@ 05,072 SAY 'ACCOUNT'
@ 06,012 SAY 'NUMBER'
@ 06,024 SAY '------------------'
@ 06,048 SAY '------------------'
@ 07,024 SAY 'DATE         AMOUNT'
@ 07,048 SAY 'DATE         AMOUNT'
 STORE  '            '  TO  Mvendor
@ 08,000 GET Mvendor
 STORE  '00/00/00'  TO  Mduedate
@ 08,024 GET Mduedate PICTURE '99/99/99'
 STORE  '00/00/00'  TO  Mdisdate
@ 08,048 GET Mdisdate PICTURE '99/99/99'
 STORE  '        '  TO  Macct
@ 08,072 GET Macct
@ 09,035 SAY '----------'
```

Fig. 7-18. Searching vendor records. (Continued on page 219.)

```
@ 10,000 SAY 'DATE PAID'
@ 10,032 SAY 'CHECK NO'
@ 10,060 SAY 'AMOUNT'
 IF select <>  ' T '
  @ 23,4 SAY 'XX'
 ENDIF
 READ
X EXIT FROM LOOP IF FOUND
 GOTO TOP
 STORE TRIM(Mvendor) TO key
 IF select=  ' T '
  FIND &key
  IF # <> 0
     STORE F TO Smore
STORE T TO Emore
 STORE  ' EDIT '  TO mode
X SET UP SCREEN VARIABLES
 STORE  vendor  TO  Mvendor
 STORE  invno  TO  Minvno
 STORE  duedate  TO  Mduedate
 STORE  dueamt  TO  Mdueamt
 STORE  disdate  TO  Mdisdate
 STORE  disamt  TO  Mdisamt
 STORE  acct  TO  Macct
 STORE  pddate  TO  Mpddate
 STORE  checkno  TO  Mcheckno
 STORE  pdamt  TO  Mpdamt
DO WHILE Emore
ERASE
X GET SCREEN INPUT
 DO  TRANS.IO
 @ 21,10 SAY  ' ENTER ALL CHANGES '
 READ
 STORE  'N'  TO Ecmd
 @ 21,10 SAY  ' ANY MORE CHANGES (Y/N)? '  GET Ecmd
 READ
X PUT SCREEN ENTRIES INTO FILE
 REPLACE  vendor  WITH  Mvendor
 REPLACE  invno  WITH  Minvno
 REPLACE  duedate  WITH  Mduedate
```

```
      REPLACE   dueamt   WITH   Mdueamt
      REPLACE   disdate  WITH   Mdisdate
      REPLACE   disamt   WITH   Mdisamt
      REPLACE   acct   WITH   Macct
      REPLACE   pddate   WITH   Mpddate
      REPLACE   checkno   WITH   Mcheckno
      REPLACE   pdamt   WITH   Mpdamt
     IF   !(Ecmd)<> 'Y'
       STORE F TO Emore
     ENDIF
    ENDDO
    RELEASE mode,Emore,Ecmd
    RELEASE Mvendor
    RELEASE Minvno
    RELEASE Mduedate
    RELEASE Mdueamt
    RELEASE Mdisdate
    RELEASE Mdisamt
    RELEASE Macct
    RELEASE Mpddate
    RELEASE Mcheckno
    RELEASE Mpdamt
     ELSE
       @ 22,10 SAY   '   NOT FOUND   '
       @ 23,10 SAY   ' TRY AGAIN(Y/N)? '
       SET CONSOLE OFF
       WAIT TO retry
       SET CONSOLE ON
       IF !(retry) <>   'Y'
       STORE F TO Smore
     ENDIF   Y
     RELEASE retry
      ENDIF   # <> 0
     ENDIF   select=T
    ENDDO   Smore
    RELEASE Smore
    RELEASE key
    RELEASE mode
    RETURN
```

Fig. 7-18. Searching vendor records. Continued from page 219.

```
*    TRANS.OUT
*    Output form for transaction file
@ 01,036 SAY mode
@ 02,000 SAY '===================='
@ 02,020 SAY '===================='
@ 02,040 SAY '===================='
@ 02,060 SAY '===================='
@ 03,018 SAY 'ACCOUNTS PAYABLE:  VOUCHER TRANSACTION FILE'
@ 04,018 SAY '-------------------------------------------'
@ 05,000 SAY 'VENDOR         INVOICE'
@ 05,028 SAY 'STANDARD'
@ 05,052 SAY 'DISCOUNT'
@ 05,072 SAY 'ACCOUNT'
@ 06,012 SAY 'NUMBER'
@ 06,024 SAY '------------------'
@ 06,048 SAY '------------------'
@ 07,024 SAY 'DATE        AMOUNT'
@ 07,048 SAY 'DATE        AMOUNT'
@ 08,001 SAY vendor
@ 08,013 SAY invno
@ 08,025 SAY duedate
@ 08,037 SAY dueamt
@ 08,049 SAY disdate
@ 08,061 SAY disamt
@ 08,073 SAY acct
@ 09,035 SAY '----------'
@ 10,000 SAY 'DATE PAID'
@ 10,011 SAY pddate
@ 10,032 SAY 'CHECK NO'
@ 10,042 SAY checkno
@ 10,060 SAY 'AMOUNT'
@ 10,068 SAY pdamt
```

Fig. 7-19. Output file for vendor records.

```
* SET UP SCREEN VARIABLES
SELECT SECONDARY
USE VENDOR INDEX VENDOR
FIND &key
SELECT PRIMARY
 STORE  vendor  TO  Mvendor
 STORE  S.vfull to Mvfull
 STORE  S.vstreet to Mvstreet
 STORE  S.vcity to Mvcity
```

```
STORE   S.vstate to Mvstate
STORE   S.vzip to Mvzip
```

The S. prefixes indicate that the program will go to the secondary file to retrieve the vendor's full name and address for the check. It then goes back to the primary record, the voucher to be paid, for the remaining items of information:

```
STORE   invno   TO  Minvno
STORE   duedate  TO  Mduedate
STORE   dueamt  TO  Mdueamt
STORE   disdate  TO  Mdisdate
STORE   disamt  TO  Mdisamt
STORE   acct  TO  Macct
STORE   pddate  TO  Mpddate
STORE   checkno  TO  Mcheckno
STORE   pdamt  TO  Mpdamt
```

The program uses the IO routine to accept your entries for the date, check number, and amount to be paid; gives you a chance to make changes or corrections; and returns to the main program and a routine which prints the checks:

```
*      VOUCHER.CMD
*  Command and index program for voucher file
*  DATABASE NAME IS   VOUCHER
*  DATABASE IS KEYED
SET DEFAULT TO B
SET TALK OFF
SET FORMAT TO SCREEN
SELECT PRIMARY
STORE FILE('VOUCHER.NDX') TO index
IF .NOT. index
 ERASE
 @ 21,10 SAY  ' FILE IS NOW BEING INDEXED '
SET TALK OFF
SELECT PRIMARY
USE  VOUCHER
INDEX ON    vendor+ duedate+ disdate+ acct+ pddate  TO  VOUCHER
ENDIF
USE VOUCHER    INDEX  VOUCHER
RELEASE index
RETURN
```

Fig. 7-20. Voucher command file.

```
*       VOUCHER.GET
* Search and edit program for voucher files
STORE  ' T '  TO select
STORE T TO Gmore
STORE  'N'  TO delete
DO WHILE Gmore
ERASE
STORE  ' GET '  TO mode
* DISPLAY CURRENT RECORD
IF &select
 DO  VOUCHER.OUT
ENDIF
STORE  ' '  TO command
@ 21,10 SAY  ' ENTER N FOR NEXT, P FOR PREVIOUS '
@ 22,10 SAY  '       S FOR SEARCH, M FOR MORE COMMANDS '
IF select <>  ' T '
 @ 23,4 SAY '**'
ENDIF
@ 23,10 SAY  ' PRESS RETURN WHEN DONE '  GET command
READ
IF !(command)= 'S'
STORE T TO Smore
DO WHILE Smore
 ERASE
 STORE  ' SEARCH '  TO mode
* GET FIELDS TO SEARCH FOR
@ 02,000 SAY '====================='
@ 02,020 SAY '====================='
@ 02,040 SAY '====================='
@ 02,060 SAY '====================='
@ 03,024 SAY 'ACCOUNTS PAYABLE:  VOUCHER FILE'
@ 04,024 SAY '----------------------------------'
@ 05,000 SAY 'VENDOR        INVOICE'
@ 05,028 SAY 'STANDARD'
@ 05,052 SAY 'DISCOUNT'
@ 05,072 SAY 'ACCOUNT'
@ 06,012 SAY 'NUMBER'
@ 06,024 SAY '-------------------'
@ 06,048 SAY '-------------------'
@ 07,024 SAY 'DATE          AMOUNT'
@ 07,048 SAY 'DATE          AMOUNT'
 STORE  '              '  TO Mvendor
```

Fig. 7-21. Search and edit voucher listings. (Continued on page 224.)

```
@ 08,000 GET Mvendor
 STORE  '00/00/00'  TO  Mdisdate
@ 09,035 SAY '----------'
@ 10,000 SAY 'DATE PAID'
@ 10,030 SAY 'CHECK NO'
@ 10,060 SAY 'AMOUNT'
 @ 21,10 SAY  '   PLEASE ENTER VALUES TO SEARCH FOR  '
  IF select <>  ' T '
   @ 23,4 SAY 'XX'
  ENDIF
  READ
* EXIT FROM LOOP IF FOUND
 GOTO TOP
 STORE TRIM(Mvendor) TO key
 IF select=  ' T '
  FIND &key
  IF # <> 0
     STORE F TO Smore
 ELSE
  @ 22,10 SAY  '  NOT FOUND  '
  @ 23,10 SAY  ' TRY AGAIN(Y/N)? '
  SET CONSOLE OFF
  WAIT TO retry
  SET CONSOLE ON
  IF !(retry) <>  'Y'
  STORE F TO Smore
 ENDIF  Y
 RELEASE retry
  ENDIF  # <> 0
 ELSE
  LOCATE FOR  vendor  = Mvendor .AND. &select
  IF .NOT. EOF
   STORE F TO Smore
 ELSE
  @ 22,10 SAY  '   NOT FOUND  '
  @ 23,10 SAY  ' TRY AGAIN(Y/N)? '
  SET CONSOLE OFF
  WAIT TO retry
  SET CONSOLE ON
  IF !(retry) <>  'Y'
  STORE F TO Smore
 ENDIF  Y
 RELEASE retry
```

Fig. 7-21. Search and edit voucher listings. (Continued on page 225.)

```
     ENDIF EOF
   ENDIF  select=T
ENDDO  Smore
RELEASE Smore
RELEASE key
ELSE
IF !(command) =   'N'
  STORE T TO next
  DO WHILE next
     SKIP
      IF &select
        STORE F TO next
      ENDIF
      IF EOF
        STORE F TO next
        STORE  ' T '  TO select
        @ 23,4 SAY ' '
      ENDIF
  ENDDO
  RELEASE next
ELSE
IF !(command)= 'P'
     STORE  ' T '  TO select
     @ 23,4 SAY '  '
     SKIP -1
ELSE
  IF !(command)= 'M'
  STORE T TO Mmore
  DO WHILE Mmore
  STORE  ' MORE '  TO mode
  STORE  ' '  TO Mmd
  @ 21,10 SAY  ' ENTER E TO EDIT, D TO DELETE,
  @ 22,10 SAY '        P TO PRINT, C TO SCAN
  IF select <>  ' T '
   @ 23,4 SAY 'XX'
  ENDIF
  @ 23,10 SAY  ' PRESS RETURN WHEN DONE ' GET Mmd

  READ
  IF !(Mmd) = 'E'
     ERASE
  IF select <>  ' T '
   @ 23,4 SAY 'XX'
```

```
ENDIF
X EDIT RECORD
     DO  VOUCHER.ED
ELSE
IF !(Mmd)= 'D'
     STORE  'N'  TO answer
  IF select <>  ' T '
   @ 23,4 SAY 'XX'
  ENDIF
@ 23,10 SAY  ' ARE YOU SURE(Y/N)?
@ 23,28 GET answer
     READ
IF !(answer)= 'Y'
     DELETE
     STORE  'Y'  TO delete
ENDIF
RELEASE answer
ELSE
IF !(Mmd)= 'P'
  @ 23,10 SAY  ' PLEASE SET UP PRINTER
  STORE '       '  TO mode
  SET CONSOLE OFF
  WAIT
  SET CONSOLE ON

 SET FORMAT TO PRINT
 DO  VOUCHER.OUT
 SET FORMAT TO SCREEN
ELSE
IF !(Mmd)='C'
 GOTO TOP
 STORE  '
 TO select

 @ 21,10 SAY 'PLEASE ENTER SELECTION CRITERIA
 @ 22,10 SAY '   DO NOT PRESS RETURN UNTIL FINISHED
 @ 23,4 SAY 'XX'
 @ 23,10 GET select
 READ
 LOCATE FOR &select
 IF EOF
    @ 21,10 SAY 'NO MORE RECORDS CAN BE FOUND
```

Fig. 7-21. Search and edit voucher listings. (Continued on page 227.)

```
    @ 22,10 SAY 'PLEASE PRESS RETURN TO CONTINUE             '
    @ 23,4 SAY '   '
    STORE  ' T '  TO select
    SET CONSOLE OFF
    WAIT
    SET CONSOLE ON
 ELSE
   DO VOUCHER.OUT
  ENDIF
 ELSE
 STORE F TO Mmore
ENDIF   F
ENDIF   P
ENDIF   D
ENDIF   E
ENDDO   Mmore
RELEASE Mmore,Mmd
ELSE
    STORE F TO Gmore
ENDIF   M
ENDIF   P
ENDIF   N
ENDIF   S
ENDDO    Gmore
IF delete =  'Y'
    STORE  'N'  TO answer
    @ 23,10 SAY  'WANT TO PERMANENTLY DELETE RECORDS(Y/N)'
    @ 23,49 GET answer
    READ
    IF answer =  'Y'
        PACK
    ELSE
        RECALL ALL
    ENDIF
        RELEASE answer
ENDIF  delete
 RELEASE  command,Gmore,delete,select
 RELEASE mode
 RETURN
```

```
*       VOUCHER.ED
*   Edits Voucher File
STORE T TO Emore
 STORE  ' EDIT '  TO mode
* SET UP SCREEN VARIABLES
 STORE  vendor  TO  Mvendor
 STORE  invno  TO  Minvno
 STORE  duedate  TO  Mduedate
 STORE  dueamt  TO  Mdueamt
 STORE  disdate  TO  Mdisdate
 STORE  disamt  TO  Mdisamt
 STORE  acct  TO  Macct
 STORE  pddate  TO  Mpddate
 STORE  checkno  TO  Mcheckno
 STORE  amount  TO  Mamount
DO WHILE Emore
ERASE
* GET SCREEN INPUT
 DO  VOUCHER.IO
 @ 21,10 SAY  ' ENTER ALL CHANGES '
 READ
 STORE  'N'  TO Ecommand
 @ 21,10 SAY  ' ANY MORE CHANGES (Y/N)? '   GET Ecommand
 READ
* PUT SCREEN ENTRIES INTO FILE
 REPLACE  vendor  WITH  Mvendor
 REPLACE  invno  WITH  Minvno
 REPLACE  duedate  WITH  Mduedate
 REPLACE  dueamt  WITH  Mdueamt
 REPLACE  disdate  WITH  Mdisdate
 REPLACE  disamt  WITH  Mdisamt
 REPLACE  acct  WITH  Macct
 REPLACE  pddate  WITH  Mpddate
 REPLACE  checkno  WITH  Mcheckno
 REPLACE  amount  WITH  Mamount
 IF  !(Ecommand)<> 'Y'
   STORE F TO Emore
 ENDIF
ENDDO
RELEASE mode,Emore,Ecommand
RELEASE Mvendor
RELEASE Minvno
RELEASE Mduedate
RELEASE Mdueamt
RELEASE Mdisdate
RELEASE Mdisamt
RELEASE Macct
RELEASE Mpddate
RELEASE Mcheckno
RELEASE Mamount
RETURN
```

Fig. 7-22. Edit voucher listings.

```
    *       VOUCHER.IO
    *    Input/Output Screen for voucher file
    @ 01,036 SAY mode
    @ 02,000 SAY '======================'
    @ 02,020 SAY '======================'
    @ 02,040 SAY '======================'
    @ 02,060 SAY '======================'
    @ 03,024 SAY 'ACCOUNTS PAYABLE:  VOUCHER FILE'
    @ 04,024 SAY '------------------------------'
    @ 05,000 SAY 'VENDOR        INVOICE'
    @ 05,028 SAY 'STANDARD'
    @ 05,052 SAY 'DISCOUNT'
    @ 05,072 SAY 'ACCOUNT'
    @ 06,012 SAY 'NUMBER'
    @ 06,024 SAY '-----------------'
    @ 06,048 SAY '-----------------'
    @ 07,024 SAY 'DATE       AMOUNT'
    @ 07,048 SAY 'DATE       AMOUNT'
    @ 08,000 GET Mvendor
    @ 08,012 GET Minvno
    @ 08,024 GET Mduedate PICTURE '99/99/99'
    @ 08,036 GET Mdueamt PICTURE '9999.99'
    @ 08,048 GET Mdisdate PICTURE '99/99/99'
    @ 08,060 GET Mdisamt PICTURE '9999.99'
    @ 08,072 GET Macct
    @ 09,035 SAY '----------'
    @ 10,000 SAY 'DATE PAID'
    @ 10,010 GET Mpddate PICTURE '99/99/99'
    @ 10,030 SAY 'CHECK NO'
    @ 10,039 GET Mcheckno
    @ 10,060 SAY 'AMOUNT'
    @ 10,067 GET Mamount PICTURE '9999.99'
    RETURN
```

Fig. 7-23. Input screen for voucher file maintenance.

```
* GET SCREEN INPUT
 DO  TRANS.IO
 @ 21,10 SAY  ' ENTER PAYMENT DETAILS '
 READ
 STORE  'N'  TO command
 @ 21,10 SAY  ' ANY MORE ENTRIES (Y/N)? '  GET command
READ
 IF  !(command)<> 'Y'
  STORE F TO Emore
 ENDIF
```

```
ENDDO
SELECT PRIMARY
* Print Checks
@ 23, 10 SAY 'READY TO PRINT CHECKS(Y/N)?'
SET CONSOLE OFF
WAIT TO REPLY
SET CONSOLE ON
IF !(reply) = 'Y'
 @ 23,10 SAY ' PLEASE SET UP PRINTER '
STORE '        '  TO mode
SET CONSOLE OFF
WAIT
SET CONSOLE ON
SET FORMAT TO PRINT
```

You'll be asked, first, to verify again that the information on the screen should be printed as a check and, second, that the printer is ready to go. Then the program swings into the check-printing routine:

```
*   Prints checks for accounts payable
SET MARGIN TO   O
@  1, 8 SAY "Nader & Son Corvair Parts"
@  2, 8 SAY "Box 110"
@  3, 8 SAY "Greencastle Ctr., Vt. 01234"
@  5, 8 SAY "PAID TO:"
@  5,17 SAY mvfull
@  6, 8 SAY "INVOICE NO:"
@  6,20 SAY minvno
@  7, 8 SAY "CHECK NO:"
@  7,18 SAY mcheckno
@  8, 8 SAY "AMOUNT:"
@  8,16 SAY mpdamt
@ 20, 8 SAY "Nader & Son Corvair Parts"
@ 20,56 SAY "Green Mountain Bank"
@ 21, 8 SAY "Box 110"
@ 22, 8 SAY "Greencastle Ctr., Vt. 01234"
@ 27, 8 SAY mvfull
@ 28, 8 SAY mvstreet
@ 28,64 SAY mpdamt
@ 29, 8 SAY mvcity
@ 30, 8 SAY mvstate
@ 30,17 SAY mvzip
@ 42,0 SAY ' '
?
SET FORMAT TO SCREEN
```

This format is designed to use the same check format as the payroll check in Chapter Five. To fit your own format, measure the distance of the various elements from the top and left sides. The normal printer settings are 10 horizontal spaces and 6 vertical lines per inch.

```
*       VOUCHER.OUT
*   Output form for voucher file
@ 01,036 SAY mode
@ 02,000 SAY '===================='
@ 02,020 SAY '===================='
@ 02,040 SAY '===================='
@ 02,060 SAY '===================='
@ 03,024 SAY 'ACCOUNTS PAYABLE:  VOUCHER FILE'
@ 04,024 SAY '------------------------------'
@ 05,000 SAY 'VENDOR         INVOICE'
@ 05,028 SAY 'STANDARD'
@ 05,052 SAY 'DISCOUNT'
@ 05,072 SAY 'ACCOUNT'
@ 06,012 SAY 'NUMBER'
@ 06,024 SAY '-------------------'
@ 06,048 SAY '-------------------'
@ 07,024 SAY 'DATE        AMOUNT'
@ 07,048 SAY 'DATE        AMOUNT'
@ 08,001 SAY vendor
@ 08,013 SAY invno
@ 08,025 SAY duedate
@ 08,037 SAY dueamt
@ 08,049 SAY disdate
@ 08,061 SAY disamt
@ 08,073 SAY acct
@ 09,035 SAY '----------'
@ 10,000 SAY 'DATE PAID'
@ 10,011 SAY pddate
@ 10,030 SAY 'CHECK NO'
@ 10,040 SAY checkno
@ 10,060 SAY 'AMOUNT'
@ 10,068 SAY amount
RETURN
```

Fig. 7-24. Output screen for vouchers.

```
DELETE ALL FOR pdamt <> 0
@ 23,10 SAY 'IS CHECK CORRECT(Y/N)?
SET CONSOLE OFF
WAIT TO verify
SET CONSOLE ON
    IF !(verify) = 'Y'
    STORE 'N' TO continue
    PACK
    ENDIF
```

```
*     TRANS.RPT
*       REPORT PROGRAM FROM TRANSACTION FILE
?
LIST FILES LIKE *.FRM
?
?'===================================================================='
STORE    '  '   TO print
DO WHILE !(print) <>  'Y'   .AND. !(print) <>   'N'
STORE  'Y'  TO print
@ 21,10 SAY  ' WANT REPORT SENT TO THE PRINTER? '   GET print
READ
ENDDO
   STORE  ' '  TO disk
   DO WHILE !(disk) <>  'Y'   .AND. !(disk) <>  'N'
   STORE  'N'  TO disk
@ 21,10 SAY  ' WANT REPORT SENT TO A FILE ?          '   GET disk
READ
ENDDO
IF !(disk)= 'Y'
STORE  '              '  TO file
DO WHILE file = '            '
@ 22,10 SAY  ' ENTER FILE NAME '  GET file
READ
ENDDO
STORE TRIM(file) TO file
ENDIF   RDSK
STORE  '          '  TO report
   DO WHILE report = '      '
@ 23,10 SAY  ' ENTER REPORT NAME '  GET report
READ
ENDDO
IF !(print) =  'Y'
@ 23,10 SAY  ' PLEASE SET UP PRINTER             '
SET CONSOLE OFF
WAIT
SET CONSOLE ON
SET PRINT ON
ENDIF RLPT
IF !(disk) =   'Y'
SET ALTERNATE TO &file
SET ALTERNATE ON
ENDIF RDSK
ERASE
REPORT FORM &report
SET PRINT OFF
SET ALTERNATE OFF
IF !(disk) = 'Y'
   RELEASE disk,file
ENDIF
   RELEASE print, report
   RETURN
```

Fig. 7-25. Report activities in transaction file.

```
PAGE NO. 00001

            ACCOUNTS PAYABLE
             OPEN VOUCHERS


INVOICE   DATE DUE  AMOUNT  DISCOUNT   AMOUNT
   NO                  DUE      DATE

X VENDOR: A-GRAPE
12-456    04/01/84   50.00 03/15/84    45.00
XX SUBTOTAL XX
                     50.00             45.00


X VENDOR: CENTER
456       05/10/84   75.00 04/10/84    45.00
XX SUBTOTAL XX
                     75.00             45.00


X VENDOR: TROY
84-84     04/01/84   85.10 03/15/84    80.50
XX SUBTOTAL XX
                     85.10             80.50


X VENDOR: VANTAGE
999       06/10/84  100.00 05/15/84    95.00
XX SUBTOTAL XX
                    100.00             95.00

XX TOTAL XX
                    310.10            265.50
```

Fig. 7-26. Typical open vouchers report.

The **Transaction** file is intended to hold only unpaid vouchers and to serve as a data resource while you are processing their payment. The program now searches for any that have been paid—whose payment amounts are something other than zero—and marks them for deletion. This normally will be the voucher for the check you just wrote.

Now there's one final prompt, to check the check. If it's right, press the Y key. You'll send the transaction entry into limbo with a final, irrevocable PACK. The data isn't entirely lost, though, because the next routine takes the matching items still in memory and records them in a new record among the paid vouchers:

```
* TRANSFER DATA TO VOUCHER FILE
SELECT SECONDARY
USE VOUCHER INDEX VOUCHER
APPEND BLANK
 REPLACE    vendor   WITH   Mvendor
 REPLACE    invno    WITH   Minvno
 REPLACE    duedate  WITH   Mduedate
 REPLACE    dueamt   WITH   Mdueamt
 REPLACE    disdate  WITH   Mdisdate
 REPLACE    disamt   WITH   Mdisamt
 REPLACE    acct   WITH   Macct
 REPLACE    pddate   WITH   Mpddate
 REPLACE    checkno   WITH   Mcheckno
 REPLACE    pdamt   WITH   Mpdamt
```

```
PAGE NO. 00001


              ACCOUNTS PAYABLE
              CASH REQUIREMENTS
                BY DUE DATE


    VENDOR     INVOICE   AMOUNT   DISCOUNT AMT W/
                 NO        DUE      DATE     DISC


 X DUE DATE: 04/01/84
 TROY       84-84      85.10 03/15/84    80.50
 A-GRAPE    12-456     50.00 03/15/84    45.00
 XX SUBTOTAL XX
                      135.10           125.50


 X DUE DATE: 05/10/84
 CENTER      456       75.00 04/10/84    45.00
 XX SUBTOTAL XX
                       75.00            45.00


 X DUE DATE: 06/10/84
 VANTAGE     999      100.00 05/15/84    95.00
 XX SUBTOTAL XX
                      100.00            95.00

 XX TOTAL XX
                      310.10           265.50
```

Fig. 7-27. Cash requirements report, by due date.

```
PAGE NO. 00001

             ACCOUNTS PAYABLE
             CASH REQUIREMENTS
             BY DISCOUNT DATE

   VENDOR    INVOICE    DISC    DATE DUE AMOUNT
               NO     AMOUNT               DUE


 * DISCOUNT DATE: 03/15/84
 TROY        84-84      80.50 04/01/84    85.10
 A-GRAPE     12-456     45.00 04/01/84    50.00
 ** SUBTOTAL **
                       125.50            135.10



 * DISCOUNT DATE: 04/10/84
 CENTER      456        45.00 05/10/84    75.00
 ** SUBTOTAL **
                        45.00             75.00



 * DISCOUNT DATE: 05/15/84
 VANTAGE     999        95.00 06/10/84   100.00
 ** SUBTOTAL **
                        95.00            100.00


 ** TOTAL **
                       265.50            310.10
```

Fig. 7-28. Cash requirements report, by discount date.

The program then will do the necessary housecleaning, and will give you the choice of either processing another check or returning to the payables menu.

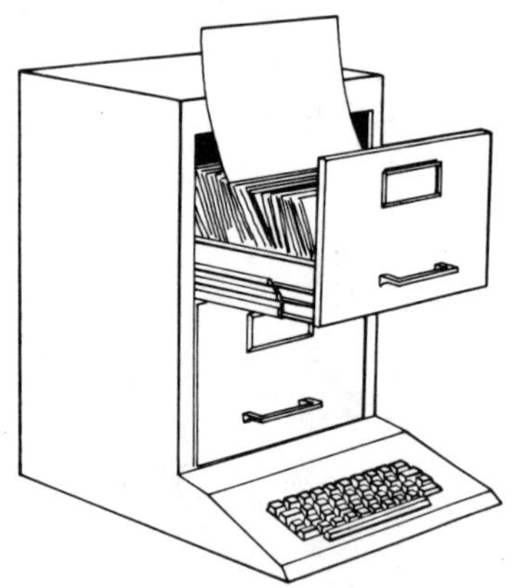

Chapter 8

Collecting *Your* Bills

Before you can pay your payables you must receive your receivables. On that fundamental basis we're about to meet some of the most important people in the world, your customers.

They're the people, of course, who buy what you have to sell. They're also the people from whom you must collect before you can claim those elusive things called profits. This system is designed to help you do both.

It is built around a master file of your customers' records. From this file you can generate sales letters and mailing labels to build up business. You can sort through your customer lists to develop selective lists of hot prospects for a particular product or service. Combined with a word processing program, this system can write personalized mailings to the customers you select—no matter whether you select some or all of them.

In other words, it's more than a standard accounts receivable system. It includes the means to get the accounts in the first place.

MAKING THE COLLECTIONS

Then it gives you the means to collect on your sales. There is a system of invoices and periodic statements, and the means to produce management reports that tell you who is—and isn't—paying.

This, then, is the system that brings in the money, and helps you do a more effective job of it. It stops a little short of going out and collecting those overdue bills. You have to do that yourself. It can show you, though, where to go knocking, and it can alert you to problems before they become serious.

Figure 8-1 is the menu for this system, and Fig. 8-2 is the command file that creates and operates it. Activate the system with the command:

```
.  DO RECEIVE
```

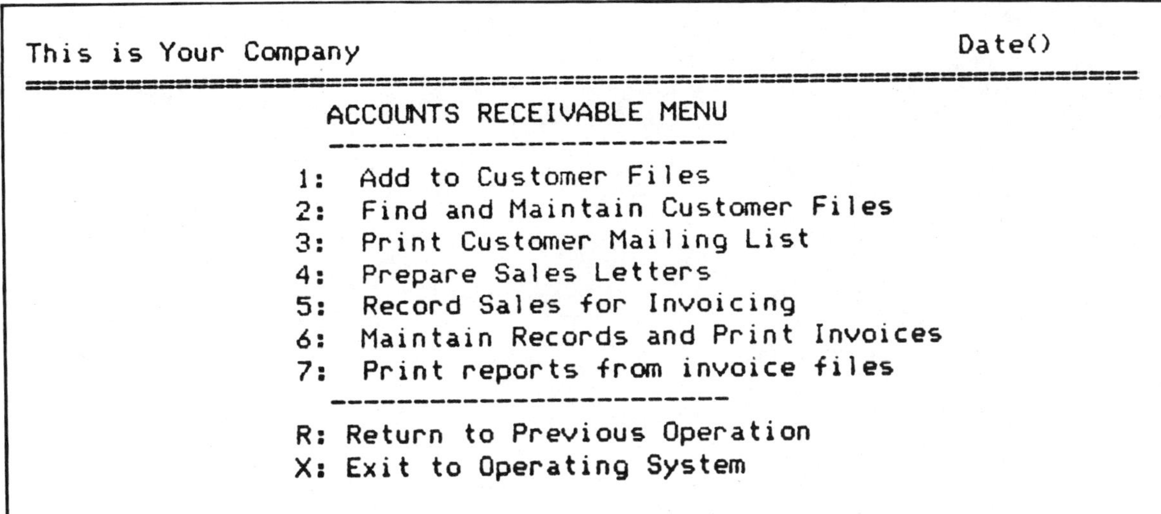

Fig. 8-1. Accounts receivable menu display.

```
X RECEIVE.CMD
X Menu file for receivable system
SET MARGIN TO    0
@  0, 0 SAY "This is Your Company"
@  0,56 SAY "Date()"
@  1, 0 SAY "======================================================="
@  1,50 SAY "============================="
@  2,18 SAY "ACCOUNTS RECEIVABLE MENU"
@  3,18 SAY "------------------------"
@  4,16 SAY "1:   Add to Customer Files"
@  5,16 SAY "2:   Find and Maintain Customer Files"
@  6,16 SAY "3:   Print Customer Mailing List"
@  7,16 SAY "4:   Prepare Sales Letters"
@  8,16 SAY "5:   Record Sales for Invoicing"
@  9,16 SAY "6:   Maintain Records and Print Invoices"
@ 10,16 SAY "7:   Print reports from invoice files"
@ 11,18 SAY "------------------------"
@ 12,16 SAY "R: Return to Previous Operation"
@ 13,16 SAY "X: Exit to Operating System"
SET CONSOLE OFF
WAIT TO choice
SET CONSOLE ON
DO CASE
CASE choice = '1')$[DO CUSTOMER.CMD
DO CUSTOMER.ADD
```

Fig. 8-3. Menu format command line. (Continued on page 238.)

```
          CASE choice = '2'
          DO CUSTOMER.CMD
          DO CUSTOMER.GET
          CASE choice = '3'
          DO CUSTOMER.CMD
          DO MAILLIST.LBL
          CASE choice = '4'
          DO CUSTOMER.CMD
          DO CUSTOMER.WS
          CASE choice = '5'
          DO INVOICE.CMD
          DO INVOICE.ADD
          CASE choice = '6'
          DO INVOICE.CMD
          DO INVOICE.GET
          CASE choice = '7'
          DO INVOICE.CMD
          DO INVOICE.RPT
          CASE choice = 'R'
          CANCEL
          CASE choice = 'X'
          QUIT
          ENDCASE
          RETURN
```

First, though, let's meet those customers.

THE BASIC RECORD

The basic customer records are in a dBASE file structured like this:

```
STRUCTURE FOR FILE:   CUSTOMER.DBF
NUMBER OF RECORDS:     00000
DATE OF LAST UPDATE: 00/00/00
PRIMARY USE DATABASE
FLD        NAME       TYPE WIDTH    DEC
001     CUSTID        C     011
002     NAME          C     020
003     STREET        C     015
004     CITY          C     010
005     STATE         C     006
006     ZIP           C     005
007     CONTACT       C     023
```

```
                                    CUSTOMER RECORD
                                    ===============
ACCOUNT ID    CUSTOMER NAME          STREET                        CITY        STATE  ZIP
----------    -------------          ------                        ----        --     ----



                                -----------------
CONTACT                    PHONE        OPEN OR BALANCE          BALANCE
-------                    -----        ----------------         -------
```

Fig. 8-3. Customer record display.

```
008        PHONE          C       013
009        TYPE           C       023
010        BALANCE        N       011       002
** TOTAL **                       00138
```

The file has a matching data entry and reporting format, as seen in Fig. 8-3. It is a basic record: the customer's identity and location, plus a column for how much the customer currently owes you. It includes a "short form" identification listing like the one we used for the vendor file.

When you call one of the customer functions from the main receivable menu, it first will go through the command sequence in Fig. 8-4. This includes the indexing feature presented as a separate procedure in some of the earlier systems; this is another place where you have a choice.

```
*      CUSTOMER.CMD
* Setup and indexing program for customer records.
*    DATABASE NAME IS    CUSTOMER
*    DATABASE IS KEYED
SET TALK OFF
SET FORMAT TO SCREEN
SELECT PRIMARY
USE CUSTOMER INDEX CUSTOMER, CUSTZIP
STORE FILE('CUSTOMER.NDX') TO index
ERASE
IF .NOT. index
  @ 21,10 SAY  ' FILE IS NOW BEING INDEXED '
SET TALK OFF
SELECT PRIMARY
USE  CUSTOMER
INDEX ON    custid  TO  CUSTOMER
INDEX ON    zip TO CUSTZIP
ENDIF
USE CUSTOMER  INDEX  CUSTOMER, CUSTZIP
RELEASE index
RETURN
```

Fig. 8-4. Command file for customer display.

```
*        CUSTOMER.ADD
* Add names to customer file
STORE T TO Amore
DO WHILE Amore
* SET UP DEFAULT VALUES
 DO  CUSTOMER.FAU
ERASE
STORE  ' ADD '   TO mode
* GET DATA TO ADD
DO  CUSTOMER.IO
@ 21,10 SAY  ' MAKE AS MANY ENTRIES AS YOU WANT '
@ 22,10 SAY  ' WHEN DONE ENTER BLANK RECORD      '
READ
* ARE WE DONE?
IF Mcustid <>  '            '
 APPEND BLANK
* PUT SCREEN DATA INTO FILE
 REPLACE   custid  WITH  Mcustid
 REPLACE   name  WITH  Mname
 REPLACE   street  WITH  Mstreet
 REPLACE   city  WITH  Mcity
 REPLACE   state  WITH  Mstate
 REPLACE   zip  WITH  Mzip
 REPLACE   contact  WITH  Mcontact
 REPLACE   phone  WITH  Mphone
 REPLACE   type  WITH  Mtype
 REPLACE   balance  WITH  Mbalance
ELSE
    STORE F TO Amore
ENDIF
ENODO
RELEASE mode,Amore
* RELEASE INPUT FIELDS
RELEASE Mcustid
RELEASE Mname
RELEASE Mstreet
RELEASE Mcity
RELEASE Mstate
RELEASE Mzip
RELEASE Mcontact
RELEASE Mphone
RELEASE Mtype
RELEASE Mbalance
RETURN
```

Fig. 8-5. Add customers to records.

```
*       CUSTOMER.FAU
*   DEFAULT VALUES PROGRAM
STORE   '             '  TO  Mcustid
STORE   '                  '  TO  Mname
STORE   '                   '  TO  Mstreet
STORE   '           '  TO  Mcity
STORE   '       '  TO  Mstate
STORE   '      '  TO  Mzip
STORE   '                        '  TO  Mcontact
STORE   '(   )000-0000'  TO  Mphone
STORE   '              '  TO  Mtype
STORE   0.00  TO  Mbalance
```

Fig. 8-6. Default file for customer record entries.

```
*       CUSTOMER.IO
*   INPUT/OUTPUT SCREEN FOR CUSTOMER RECORDS
@ 01,036 SAY mode
@ 02,000 SAY '===================='
@ 02,020 SAY '===================='
@ 02,040 SAY '===================='
@ 02,060 SAY '===================='
@ 03,032 SAY 'CUSTOMER RECORD'
@ 04,032 SAY '==============='
@ 05,000 SAY 'ACCOUNT ID  CUSTOMER'
@ 05,021 SAY 'NAME         STREET'
@ 05,056 SAY 'CITY         STATE  ZIP'
@ 06,000 SAY '----------  --------'
@ 06,020 SAY '-----        ------'
@ 06,056 SAY '----      --      -----'
@ 07,000 GET Mcustid
@ 07,012 GET Mname
@ 07,033 GET Mstreet
@ 07,056 GET Mcity
@ 07,067 GET Mstate
@ 07,074 GET Mzip
@ 09,032 SAY '---------------'
@ 10,000 SAY 'CONTACT'
@ 10,024 SAY 'PHONE            OPEN OR BALANCE'
@ 10,064 SAY 'BALANCE'
@ 11,000 SAY '-------'
@ 11,024 SAY '-----         ---------------'
@ 11,064 SAY '-------'
@ 12,000 GET Mcontact
@ 12,024 GET Mphone PICTURE '(XXX)999-9999'
@ 12,040 GET Mtype
@ 12,064 GET Mbalance PICTURE '99999999.99'
```

Fig. 8-7. Input/output format for customer records.

The first of the menu options for the customer system is to add new names to the file. Figures 8-5 through 8-10 have the details; they're similar to the data entry programs and screen formats of the other systems. The simple process: it presents you with a blank screen, and you fill in the blanks. The entries then are appended to the customer file.

The searching and maintenance file also is similar to those you've seen before, but there is one feature that's more important here than it might have been in the earlier systems. This is the ability to print out a copy of each customer's record. Use the M option at the first level and the P option at the second, and the system will prompt you the rest of the way.

The value of this feature: when you're about to make a sales or collection call you can have the printout right at hand to discuss the customer's status. You might want to add to the database and input screens a comment line, where you could enter such things as previous collection contacts or preferences that you can turn into sales leads.

THE SALES TOOL

More useful, though, is the ability to massage your customer list to make it a real sales tool. You can use the full list to send out periodic mailings of catalogs or sale brochures. Or, search your invoice files for customers who've bought particular kinds of merchandise. Then use this procedure to direct a custom mailing specifically to them.

The first element in this system is the program that turns your customer list into mailing labels. It is shown in Fig. 8-11. Let's run through it.

The program will give you several prompts. The first asks whether you want to scan the database on the basis of some selective criteria you've developed. You might, for example, use this feature to set up a mailing list of every customer in the music business. When asked for the selection criteria, use the dBASE query language to specify:

```
DEMOLITION $NAME
```

This calls for any entry where the word DEMOLITION appears in the field NAME. We've loaded a few fanciful listings into the Customer database; such a search would turn up this one:

```
PHIL PHILLIPS
UPTOWN DEMOLITION
21 HUDSON ST
BOSTON MA          02107
```

You can use ZIP codes to specify certain areas of the country. For example, ZIP = '02' should get you a list of customers from the Boston metropolitan area.

Another prompt will ask you about the label size. The program is set to start a new label every six lines. This fits a standard 1-inch label (as the prompt suggests, the dimension includes the space between labels). If you are using another size, the prompt gives you the opportunity to change this default dimension. A "0" entry at this point will eject the form after each label—useful for printing envelopes.

Then we get to the heart of the matter:

```
* REPEAT UNTIL FILE ENDS
DO WHILE .NOT. EOF
  IF &select
    STORE contact TO line1
    STORE name TO line2
    STORE street TO line3
    STORE TRIM(city)+' '+state+' '+zip TO line4
```

```
*       CUSTOMER.GET
*  Search, edit and print customer records
STORE  ' T '  TO select
STORE T TO Gmore
STORE  'N'  TO delete
DO WHILE Gmore
ERASE
STORE  ' GET '  TO mode
* DISPLAY CURRENT RECORD
IF &select
 DO  CUSTOMER.OUT
ENDIF
STORE  ' '  TO command
@ 21,10 SAY  ' ENTER N FOR NEXT RECORD, P FOR PREVIOUS
@ 22,10 SAY  '       S FOR SEARCH, M FOR MORE COMMANDS '
IF select <>  ' T '
 @ 23,4 SAY '**'
ENDIF
@ 23,10 SAY  ' PRESS RETURN WHEN DONE '   GET command
READ
IF !(command)= 'S'
STORE T TO Smore
DO WHILE Smore
 ERASE
 STORE  ' SEARCH '  TO mode
* GET FIELDS TO SEARCH FOR
@ 02,000 SAY '====================='
@ 02,020 SAY '====================='
@ 02,040 SAY '====================='
@ 02,060 SAY '====================='
@ 03,032 SAY 'CUSTOMER RECORD'
@ 04,032 SAY '==============='
@ 05,000 SAY 'ACCOUNT ID  CUSTOMER'
@ 05,021 SAY 'NAME          STREET'
@ 05,056 SAY 'CITY        STATE  ZIP'
@ 06,000 SAY '----------   --------'
@ 06,020 SAY '-----        -------'
@ 06,056 SAY '----         -----  ---'
 STORE  '              '  TO  Mcustid
@ 07,000 GET Mcustid
@ 09,032 SAY '----------------'
@ 10,000 SAY 'CONTACT'
@ 10,024 SAY 'PHONE             OPEN OR BALANCE
```

Fig. 8-8. Search file for customer records. (Continued on page 244.)

```
@ 10,064 SAY 'BALANCE'
@ 11,000 SAY '-------'
@ 11,024 SAY '-----             ----------------'
@ 11,064 SAY '-------'
 @ 21,10 SAY  '  PLEASE ENTER VALUES TO SEARCH FOR  '
  IF select <>  ' T '
  @ 23,4 SAY 'XX'
ENDIF
READ
X EXIT FROM LOOP IF FOUND
 GOTO TOP
 STORE TRIM(Mcustid) TO key
 IF select=  ' T '
  FIND &key
  IF # <> 0
     STORE F TO Smore
 ELSE
  @ 22,10 SAY  '  NOT FOUND  '
  @ 23,10 SAY  ' TRY AGAIN(Y/N)? '
  SET CONSOLE OFF
  WAIT TO retry
  SET CONSOLE ON
  IF !(retry) <>  'Y'
  STORE F TO Smore
 ENDIF  Y
 RELEASE retry
  ENDIF  # <> 0
 ELSE
  LOCATE FOR  custid  = Mcustid .AND. &select
  IF .NOT. EOF
   STORE F TO Smore
 ELSE
  @ 22,10 SAY  '  NOT FOUND  '
  @ 23,10 SAY   ' TRY AGAIN(Y/N)? '
  SET CONSOLE OFF
  WAIT TO retry
  SET CONSOLE ON
  IF !(retry) <>  'Y'
  STORE F TO Smore
 ENDIF  Y
 RELEASE retry
  ENDIF EOF
```

Fig. 8-8. Search file for customer records. (Continued on page 245.)

```
  ENDIF   select=T
ENDDO  Smore
RELEASE Smore
RELEASE key
ELSE
IF !(command) =   'N'
 STORE T TO next
 DO WHILE next
    SKIP
    IF &select
      STORE F TO next
    ENDIF
    IF EOF
      STORE F TO next
      STORE  ' T '  TO select
       @ 23,4 SAY '  '
     ENDIF
 ENDDO
 RELEASE next
ELSE
IF !(command)= 'P'
    STORE  ' T '  TO select
    @ 23,4 SAY '  '
    SKIP -1
ELSE
 IF !(command)= 'M'
 STORE T TO Mmore
 DO WHILE Mmore
 STORE  ' MORE '  TO mode
 STORE  ' '  TO Mmd
 @ 21,10 SAY  ' ENTER E TO EDIT, D TO DELETE,              '
 @ 22,10 SAY '         P TO PRINT RECORD, C TO SCAN       '
 IF select <>  ' T '
  @ 23,4 SAY 'XX'
 ENDIF
 @ 23,10 SAY  ' PRESS RETURN WHEN DONE            ' GET Mmd
 READ
 IF !(Mmd) = 'E'
    ERASE
IF select <>  ' T '
 @ 23,4 SAY 'XX'
ENDIF
```

```
* EDIT RECORD
     DO  CUSTOMER.ED
ELSE
IF !(Mmd)= 'D'
    STORE  'N'  TO answer
  IF select <>  ' T '
   @ 23,4 SAY 'XX'
  ENDIF
@ 23,10 SAY  ' ARE YOU SURE(Y/N)?
@ 23,28 GET answer
    READ
IF !(answer)= 'Y'
    DELETE
    STORE  'Y'  TO delete
ENDIF
RELEASE answer
ELSE
IF !(Mmd)= 'P'
 @ 23,10 SAY  ' PLEASE SET UP PRINTER
 STORE '        '  TO mode
 SET CONSOLE OFF
 WAIT
 SET CONSOLE ON
 SET FORMAT TO PRINT
 DO  CUSTOMER.OUT
 SET FORMAT TO SCREEN
ELSE
IF !(Mmd)='C'
 GOTO TOP
 STORE  '
TO select
@ 21,10 SAY 'PLEASE ENTER SELECTION CRITERIA
@ 22,10 SAY '   DO NOT PRESS RETURN UNTIL FINISHED
@ 23,4 SAY 'XX'
@ 23,10 GET select
READ
LOCATE FOR &select
IF EOF
  @ 21,10 SAY 'NO MORE RECORDS CAN BE FOUND
  @ 22,10 SAY 'PLEASE PRESS RETURN TO CONTINUE
  @ 23,4 SAY ' '
  STORE  ' T '  TO select
```

Fig. 8-8. Search file for customer records. (Continued on page 247.)

```
      SET CONSOLE OFF
     WAIT
     SET CONSOLE ON
   ELSE
     DO CUSTOMER.OUT
   ENDIF
 ELSE
  STORE F TO Mmore
ENDIF  F
ENDIF  P
ENDIF  D
ENDIF  E
ENDDO  Mmore
RELEASE Mmore,Mmd
ELSE
    STORE F TO Gmore
ENDIF  M
ENDIF  P
ENDIF  N
ENDIF  S
ENDDO  Gmore
IF delete = 'Y'
    STORE 'N' TO answer
    @ 23,10 SAY 'WANT TO PERMANENTLY DELETE RECORDS(Y/N)'
    @ 23,49 GET answer
    READ
    IF answer = 'Y'
        PACK
    ELSE
        RECALL ALL
    ENDIF
        RELEASE answer
ENDIF  delete
RELEASE  command,Gmore,delete,select
 RELEASE mode
 RETURN
```

Here's a standard dBASE routine that sorts through a database, one record at a time, until EOF (the end of the file) is reached.

The **select** variable has previously been set, either to T, if we plan to print labels for the full list, or to the selection criteria we entered in the scan sequence. The command here uses the macro function to extract the instructions and select those labels which fit our specifications. If the specifications still read T, it will print the total list.

The next lines store the name and address information from each record into useful memory variables. This group is set up for a mailing list of commercial customers, using the **Contact** field to name an individual, and the **Name** field to identify the company. You can vary this to meet your needs; simply provide the number of lines you need. Just be sure you have matching sets of numbers here and in the printing instructions below.

The last line TRIMs the unused blanks from the **City** field and joins it to the state and ZIP code items. This produces a little better appearance—and a better impression on your customers.

```
SET PRINT ON
  ?  '  '+line1
  ?  '  '+line2
  ?  '  '+line3
  ?  '  '+line4
```

This is pretty straightforward: it turns on the printer and prints the four lines in order. One thing to remember in setting up the printer is to position the label at the point where you want the *first line* to appear. The next few program lines will add enough lines to cover the full label, but it will add them *after* the printed portion, not before:

```
  STORE 0 TO count
* IF LABEL IS LARGER, SKIP SOME LINES
  IF size >    4
   DO WHILE count < (size -    4 )
    ? '    '
    STORE count + 1 TO count
   ENDDO   count
  ELSE
  IF size = 0
   EJECT
  ENDIF   0
  ENDIF   >
  SKIP
```

Once the four lines of this particular label format have been printed, this routine starts a counter which runs on up to the number of lines in the full label, adding a blank line each time. Since we have a four-line listing on a six-line label, this procedure will give us two blank lines and take us to the starting point on the next label. The loop will then repeat itself until it reaches the end of the file.

Then comes the usual housecleaning, and our printer should hand us a list that looks like this:

```
PHIL PHILLIPS
UPTOWN DEMOLITION
21 HUDSON ST
BOSTON MA        02107
```

```
P. COMO
TOWN & COUNTRY MUSIC
241 CURRY RD
LEOLA PA        17540


BILL RHENQUIST
W O DOUGLAS LAW SCH
234 DUE PROCESS
WASHINGTON DC       20000


BILL KIDD
TYCOON SHIPPING
55 WATER ST
PORTSMOUTH KS       66666
```

If you meet the U.S. Postal Service's requirements, this program also can help you qualify for

```
* 	CUSTOMER.ED
* Editing program for customer files
STORE T TO Emore
 STORE  ' EDIT '  TO mode
* SET UP SCREEN VARIABLES
 STORE  custid  TO  Mcustid
 STORE  name  TO  Mname
 STORE  street  TO  Mstreet
 STORE  city  TO  Mcity
 STORE  state  TO  Mstate
 STORE  zip  TO  Mzip
 STORE  contact  TO  Mcontact
 STORE  phone  TO  Mphone
 STORE  type  TO  Mtype
 STORE  balance  TO  Mbalance
DO WHILE Emore
ERASE
* GET SCREEN INPUT
 DO  CUSTOMER.IO
 @ 21,10 SAY  ' ENTER ALL CHANGES '
 READ
 STORE 'N' TO command
 @ 21,10 SAY  ' ANY MORE CHANGES (Y/N)? '   GET command
 READ
* PUT SCREEN ENTRIES INTO FILE
 REPLACE  custid  WITH  Mcustid
```

Fig. 8-9. Edit customer records. (Continued on page 250.)

```
            REPLACE   name  WITH  Mname
            REPLACE   street  WITH  Mstreet
            REPLACE   city  WITH  Mcity
            REPLACE   state  WITH  Mstate
            REPLACE   zip  WITH  Mzip
            REPLACE   contact  WITH  Mcontact
            REPLACE   phone  WITH  Mphone
            REPLACE   type  WITH  Mtype
            REPLACE   balance  WITH  Mbalance
            IF  !(command)<> 'Y'
              STORE F TO Emore
            ENDIF
           ENDDO
           RELEASE mode,Emore,command
           RELEASE Mcustid
           RELEASE Mname
           RELEASE Mstreet
           RELEASE Mcity
           RELEASE Mstate
           RELEASE Mzip
           RELEASE Mcontact
           RELEASE Mphone
           RELEASE Mtype
           RELEASE Mbalance
           RETURN
```

Fig. 8-9. Edit customer records. (Continued from page 249.)

discounts on your postage. This system indexes the customer file in the ZIP code, so the resulting mailing list is produced in ZIP code order—the way the Post Office expects you to sort your volume mailings.

PREPARING THE MAILINGS

The next routine, Fig. 8-12, lets you translate the same customer mailing list into a set of personalized sales letters, using a standard word processing program. This particular routine is designed to work with MicroPro's WordStar, but it sets up the data in a standard format that can be used in other programs as well, including those you write yourself. You might put it to use in the "integrated program" routines described in the final chapter.

The program works this way:

```
STORE 0 TO count
STORE '                              '  TO select
STORE  'Y'  TO answer
STORE  '            '  TO datafile
DO WHILE datafile = '           '
 @ 21,10 SAY  ' NAME OF DATA FILE '  GET datafile
 READ
```

```
*       CUSTOMER.OUT
* Format file for output from customer file
@ 01,036 SAY mode
@ 02,000 SAY '===================='
@ 02,020 SAY '===================='
@ 02,040 SAY '===================='
@ 02,060 SAY '===================='
@ 03,032 SAY 'CUSTOMER RECORD'
@ 04,032 SAY '================'
@ 05,000 SAY 'ACCOUNT ID  CUSTOMER'
@ 05,021 SAY 'NAME         STREET'
@ 05,056 SAY 'CITY         STATE  ZIP'
@ 06,000 SAY '----------   --------'
@ 06,020 SAY '-----        ------'
@ 06,056 SAY '----         -----  ---'
@ 07,001 SAY custid
@ 07,013 SAY name
@ 07,034 SAY street
@ 07,057 SAY city
@ 07,068 SAY state
@ 07,075 SAY zip
@ 09,032 SAY '---------------'
@ 10,000 SAY 'CONTACT'
@ 10,024 SAY 'PHONE              OPEN'
@ 10,045 SAY 'OR BALANCE'
@ 10,065 SAY 'BALANCE'
@ 11,000 SAY '--------'
@ 11,024 SAY '-----          ----'
@ 11,044 SAY '-----------'
@ 11,064 SAY '--------'
@ 12,001 SAY contact
@ 12,025 SAY phone
@ 12,041 SAY type
@ 12,065 SAY balance
RETURN
```

Fig. 8-10. Output format for customer information.

   This group of commands initializes the variables the program will use to count records and reply to prompts. The first prompt is to establish a filename for the mailing. In doing this, remember that the same title will be used on both the text file of the letter and the data file that will contain the address list. Later in the program, dBASE will establish two files with this name: one with a **.Dat** suffix; the other with a **.Doc**. If files by these names are already on your disk, they will be *erased without warning*. Be careful.

```
@ 21,10
@ 21,10 SAY  ' DO YOU WISH TO SCAN FILE?  ' GET answer
READ
IF !(answer)= 'Y'
 @ 21,10
 @ 21,10 SAY  ' PLEASE ENTER SELECTION CRITERIA '
 @ 23,10 GET select
 READ
 @ 23,10
ELSE
 STORE  ' T '  TO select
ENDIF
```

This is comparable to the scanning functions in other files, including the label procedure. As usual, if you state any criteria such as a business type or ZIP code, those criteria will be listed in the variable **Select**. Otherwise, **Select** will ride through the program with a value of T, a signal to print everything in the file.

```
STORE TRIM(datafile) TO datafile
STORE datafile+'.DOC' TO docfile
STORE datafile+'.DAT' TO datafile
```

The filename you selected a few moments ago now is applied to the pair of files. First, dBASE trims off any unused blank spaces in the existing variable, then adds the suffixes to the chosen name.

```
@ 22,10 SAY  ' CREATING DOCUMENT FILE:  '+docfile
SET CONSOLE OFF
SET ALTERNATE TO &docfile
SET ALTERNATE ON
?'.OP'
?'.DF '+datafile
?'.RV '+' contact, name, street, city, state, zip'
SET ALTERNATE OFF
SET CONSOLE ON
```

Here, dBASE uses an alternate file to create a new file. The first is the heading for your form letter. After the three question marks are formatting commands used by WordStar and its MailMerge accessory. The first suppresses page numbers that otherwise would appear at the bottom of the letter, the second identifies the data file that contains the address list, and the third lists the variables that match the data file items. The first item in the data file will be read as **contact** the second as **name**, and so on.

If you use a different word processing program, replace these three lines with the commands that do the same jobs in your system. Next, the program sets up the data file in the same way:

```
@ 23,10 SAY  ' CREATING DATA FILE:  '+datafile
SET CONSOLE OFF
SET ALTERNATE TO &datafile
SET ALTERNATE ON
GOTO TOP
```

```
* REPEAT UNTIL datafile ENDS
DO WHILE .NOT. EOF
 IF &select
 STORE count+1 TO count
 ?
 ??   CHR(34)+ TRIM(contact) +CHR(34) +','
 ??   CHR(34)+ TRIM(name) +CHR(34) +','
 ??   CHR(34)+ TRIM(street) +CHR(34) +','
 ??   CHR(34)+ TRIM(city) +CHR(34) +','
```

```
X      MAILLIST.LBL
X Produces mailing labels from customer records
ERASE
USE CUSTOMER INDEX CUSTZIP
STORE '         '  TO mode
STORE  6 TO size
STORE  '                                        '  TO select
STORE 'Y' TO answer
@ 21,10 SAY 'DO YOU WISH TO SCAN? (Y/N)'  GET answer
READ
@ 21,10
IF !(answer)='Y'
 @ 21,10 SAY 'PLEASE ENTER SELECTION CRITERIA'
 @ 23,10 GET select
 READ
 @ 21,10
 @ 23,10
ELSE
 STORE 'T' TO select
ENDIF
@ 21,10 SAY  ' HOW MANY LINES PER LABEL?  '
@ 22,10 SAY  ' (ENTER 0 TO GET FULL PAGE EJECTS) '
@ 23,10 SAY  ' PLEASE INCLUDE THE SPACE BETWEEN LABELS  '  GET size
READ
GOTO TOP
@ 23,10 SAY  ' PLEASE SET UP YOUR PRINTER                        '
SET CONSOLE OFF
WAIT
SET CONSOLE ON
X REPEAT UNTIL FILE ENDS
DO WHILE .NOT. EOF
 IF &select
  STORE contact TO line1
```

Fig. 8-11. Mailing label command file. (Continued on page 254.)

```
      STORE name TO line2
      STORE street TO line3
      STORE TRIM(city)+' '+state+' '+zip TO line4
   ELSE
    SKIP
    LOOP
   ENDIF
  SET PRINT ON
   ? ' '+line1
   ? ' '+line2
   ? ' '+line3
   ? ' '+line4
   STORE 0 TO count
 * IF LABEL IS LARGER, SKIP SOME LINES
   IF size >     2
    DO WHILE count < (size -     2 )
     ? '   '
     STORE count + 1 TO count
    ENDDO  count
   ELSE
   IF size = 0
    EJECT
   ENDIF  0
   ENDIF  >
   SKIP
 ENDDO   NOT EOF
 SET PRINT OFF
 SET CONSOLE ON
 RELEASE size,count,answer,select
    RELEASE line1
    RELEASE line2
    RELEASE line3
 RETURN
```

Fig. 8-11. Mailing label command file. (Continued from page 253.)

```
 ??   CHR(34)+ TRIM(state) +CHR(34) +','
 ??   CHR(34)+ TRIM(zip) +CHR(34)
 ENDIF
 SKIP
ENDDO
SET CONSOLE ON
```

This routine pages through the customer file, taking the items that meet your selection criteria and setting them up in the data format MailMerge recognizes, the data items are strung together and separated by quotation marks.

CHR(34) is one way of creating a quotation mark, and at first it may seem like it's doing so by way of East Rotgut. But think about it for a minute: quotation marks signal an operating program to reproduce literally any material that's found between them. Were we to use them in this instance, we would unleash a true infestation of bugs—filling the data file with the instructions instead of the data. The method used here—the ASCII symbol for a quotation mark—keeps the punctuation in its proper place.

If we check the resulting document file it should look like this:

```
.OP
.DF TEST.DAT
.RV   contact, name, street, city, state, zip
```

```
X       CUSTOMER.WS
X  Sets up data and document datafiles for word processing program.
X Initialize variables for item counter and replies to queries
STORE 0 TO count
STORE '                                      '  TO select
STORE  'Y'  TO answer
STORE  '          '  TO datafile
DO WHILE datafile = '        '
 @ 21,10 SAY  ' NAME OF DATA FILE '  GET datafile
 READ
ENDDO
@ 21,10
@ 21,10 SAY  ' DO YOU WISH TO SCAN FILE?  '  GET answer
READ
IF !(answer)= 'Y'
 @ 21,10
 @ 21,10 SAY  ' PLEASE ENTER SELECTION CRITERIA '
 @ 23,10 GET select
 READ
 @ 23,10
ELSE
 STORE  ' T '  TO select
ENDIF
@ 23,10
STORE TRIM(datafile) TO datafile
STORE datafile+'.DOC'  TO docfile
STORE datafile+'.DAT'  TO datafile
@ 22,10 SAY  ' CREATING DOCUMENT datafile:  '+docfile
SET CONSOLE OFF
SET ALTERNATE TO &docfile
SET ALTERNATE ON
?'.OP'
```

Fig. 8-12. File to create data for customer letters. (Continued on page 256.)

```
?'.DF '+datafile
?'.RV '+' contact, name, street, city, state, zip'
SET ALTERNATE OFF
SET CONSOLE ON
@ 23,10 SAY  ' CREATING DATA datafile:  '+datafile
SET CONSOLE OFF
SET ALTERNATE TO &datafile
SET ALTERNATE ON
GOTO TOP
* REPEAT UNTIL datafile ENDS
DO WHILE .NOT. EOF
  IF &select
  STORE count+1 TO count
  ?
  ??   CHR(34)+ TRIM(contact) +CHR(34) +','
  ??   CHR(34)+ TRIM(name) +CHR(34) +','
  ??   CHR(34)+ TRIM(street) +CHR(34) +','
  ??   CHR(34)+ TRIM(city) +CHR(34) +','
  ??   CHR(34)+ TRIM(state) +CHR(34) +','
  ??   CHR(34)+ TRIM(zip) +CHR(34)
  ENDIF
  SKIP
ENDDO
SET CONSOLE ON
@ 21,10
@ 22,10
@ 23,10
@ 23,10 SAY STR(count,4)+  ' RECORDS WERE PLACED INTO DATA FILE '
GOTO TOP
SET ALTERNATE OFF
RELEASE datafile,docfile,answer,select,count
RETURN
```

Fig. 8-12. File to create data for customer letters. (Continued from page 255.)

There are the three MailMerge command lines we discussed earlier. They don't look like much, but they save some effort; the program has done the planning job of getting the list of variables to be read in the same order they appear in the data file. We've named that file **Test.Dat**, and it looks like this, quotation marks and all:

```
'PHIL PHILLIPS", "UPTOWN DEMOLITION", "21 HUDSON ST", "BOSTON", "MA", "02107"
"P. COMO", "TOWN & COUNTRY MUSIC", "241 CURRY RD", "LEOLA", "PA", "17540"
"BILL RHENQUIST", "W O DOUGLAS LAW SCH", "234 DUE PROCESS", "WASHINGTON", "DC", "20000"
"BILL KIDD", "TYCOON SHIPPING", "55 WATER ST", "PORTSMOUTH", "KS", "66666"
```

This is nothing more than the data in your customer file without the field labels that dBASE applies. Instead, they're separated by standard punctuation marks, and this file depends on the order listed in the

```
THIS IS YOUR COMPANY                              ================
At This Address                                       INVOICE
In This Wonderful Place                           ================

INVOICE NO ==>:          :     INVOICE DATE ==> :        :   CUSTOMER ID ==>:       :
                               DATE PAID ==> :          :
============== SOLD TO =============      ============ SHIP TO ============
 :                    :                   :              :
 :              :                         :          :
 :              :   :   :    :      :     :       :        :   :    :     :
============================              ===============================


ITEM        QUANTITY    DESCRIPTION                        PRICE        TOTAL
----        --------    -----------                        -----        -----
 :            :   :        :                                :      :    :      :
 :            :   :        :                                :      :    :      :
 :            :   :        :                                :      :    :      :
 :            :   :        :                      TOTAL ==> :     :     :      :
                                                  TOTAL ==> :     :
```

Fig. 8-13. Invoice display.

```
*       INVOICE.CMD
*   Set up program for invoice procedures
*   DATABASE NAME IS    INVOICE
*   DATABASE IS KEYED
SET TALK OFF
SET FORMAT TO SCREEN
STORE FILE('INVDATE.NDX') TO index
 ERASE
IF .NOT. index
        @ 21,10 SAY  ' FILE IS NOW BEING INDEXED '
        SELECT PRIMARY
        USE  INVOICE
        INDEX ON   invdate+ custid to INVOICE
ENDIF
SELECT PRIMARY
USE INVOICE    INDEX   INVOICE
SELECT SECONDARY
USE CUSTOMER INDEX CUSTOMER
RELEASE index
RETURN
```

Fig. 8-14. Command file for invoice display.

document file to keep every piece of data in its proper place. Many programs, including dBASE itself, use such a system internally.

Here it is made visible. Since the order and the punctuation are both so important to your success, the real value of the WS program is that it takes care of these vital details.

Of course, your document program still consists of only three lines. You must still decide how to place the data in proper format on the letter. With MailMerge you would do it like this:

```
&contact&
&name&
&address&
&city&,&state*,&zip&
```

Then you're off into the text of the sales letter no customer could resist. Your first letter would begin:

```
PHIL PHILLIPS
UPTOWN DEMOLITION
21 HUDSON ST.
BOSTON, MA 02107
```

And you're off, with a hearty "Dear Customer," or something like that. The mail merging program will produce a separate letter for each entry on the list—and in the same ZIP code order as the labels.

SENDING AND COLLECTING INVOICES

Some businesses do it the easy way—collecting cash over the counter. Other retailers and service businesses rely heavily on bank credit cards; with these in effect, few small businesses try to maintain their own revolving credit any more.

There are many lines of business, though, in which the invoice is a basic instrument for collecting receivable accounts. You prepare an invoice listing the items and charges in the customer's order, and you hope the customer in turn will prepare a check.

This procedure does two very simple but very important things: it prepares an invoice, and it checks up on those that haven't been paid. The procedure starts from this database:

```
STRUCTURE FOR FILE:    INVOICE.DBF
NUMBER OF RECORDS:     00000
DATE OF LAST UPDATE:  00/00/00
PRIMARY USE DATABASE
FLD        NAME        TYPE WIDTH      DEC
001        INVDATE      C    008
002        CUSTID       C    010
003        PDDATE       C    008
004        NAME         C    020
005        SHIPNAME     C    020
006        STREET       C    015
007        SHIPSTR      C    015
008        CITY         C    010
009        STATE        C    002
010        ZIP          C    005
```

```
*        INVOICE.ADD
* Prepare Invoices
STORE T TO Amore
DO WHILE Amore
* SET UP DEFAULT VALUES
 DO  INVOICE.FAU
ERASE
STORE ' ADD '  TO mode
* GET DATA TO ADD
DO  INVOICE.IO
@ 21,10 SAY ' ENTER INFORMATION FOR INVOICE        '
@ 22,10 SAY ' WHEN DONE ENTER BLANK FORM         '
READ
* ARE WE DONE?
IF Mcustid <> '              '
* PERFORM VALIDATION
 DO  INVOICE.VAL
 APPEND BLANK
* PUT SCREEN DATA INTO FILE
 REPLACE  invdate  WITH  Minvdate
 REPLACE  custid  WITH  Mcustid
 REPLACE  pddate  WITH  Mpddate
 REPLACE  name  WITH  Mname
 REPLACE  shipname  WITH  Mshipname
 REPLACE  street  WITH  Mstreet
 REPLACE  shipstr  WITH  Mshipstr
 REPLACE  city  WITH  Mcity
 REPLACE  state  WITH  Mstate
 REPLACE  zip  WITH  Mzip
 REPLACE  shipcity  WITH  Mshipcity
 REPLACE  shipst  WITH  Mshipst
 REPLACE  shzip  WITH  Mshzip
 REPLACE  part1  WITH  Mpart1
 REPLACE  q1  WITH  Mq1
 REPLACE  desc1  WITH  Mdesc1
 REPLACE  p1  WITH  Mp1
 REPLACE  part2  WITH  Mpart2
 REPLACE  q2  WITH  Mq2
 REPLACE  desc2  WITH  Mdesc2
 REPLACE  p2  WITH  Mp2
 REPLACE  part3  WITH  Mpart3
 REPLACE  q3  WITH  Mq3
 REPLACE  desc3  WITH  Mdesc3
```

Fig. 8-15. Write new invoices. (Continued on page 260.)

```
   REPLACE   p3  WITH  Mp3
   REPLACE   part4  WITH  Mpart4
   REPLACE   q4  WITH  Mq4
   REPLACE   desc4  WITH  Mdesc4
   REPLACE   p4  WITH  Mp4
ELSE
     STORE F TO Amore
ENDIF
ENDDO
RELEASE mode,Amore
X RELEASE INPUT FIELDS
RELEASE Minvno
RELEASE Minvdate
RELEASE Mcustid
RELEASE Mpddate
RELEASE Mname
RELEASE Mshipname
RELEASE Mstreet
RELEASE Mshipstr
RELEASE Mcity
RELEASE Mstate
RELEASE Mzip
RELEASE Mshipcity
RELEASE Mshipst
RELEASE Mshzip
RELEASE Mpart1
RELEASE Mq1
RELEASE Mdesc1
RELEASE Mp1
RELEASE Mpart2
RELEASE Mq2
RELEASE Mdesc2
RELEASE Mp2
RELEASE Mpart3
RELEASE Mq3
RELEASE Mdesc3
RELEASE Mp3
RELEASE Mpart4
RELEASE Mq4
RELEASE Mdesc4
RELEASE Mp4
RETURN
```

Fig. 8-15. Write new invoices. (Continued from page 259.)

```
*       INVOICE.GET
* Search and print program for invoices
STORE  ' T '  TO select
STORE T TO Gmore
STORE  'N'  TO Gdel
DO WHILE Gmore
ERASE
STORE  ' GET '  TO mode
* DISPLAY CURRENT RECORD
IF &select
 DO  INVOICE.OUT
ENDIF
STORE  ' '  TO command
@ 21,10 SAY  ' ENTER N FOR NEXT, P FOR PREVIOUS '
@ 22,10 SAY  '       S FOR SEARCH, M FOR MORE COMMANDS '
IF select <>  ' T '
 @ 23,4 SAY 'XX'
ENDIF
@ 23,10 SAY  ' PRESS RETURN WHEN DONE '  GET command
READ
IF !(command)= 'S'
STORE T TO Smore
DO WHILE Smore
 ERASE
 STORE  ' SEARCH '  TO mode
* GET FIELDS TO SEARCH FOR
@ 02,000 SAY 'THIS IS YOUR COMPANY'
@ 02,060 SAY '===================='
@ 03,000 SAY 'At This Address'
@ 03,066 SAY 'INVOICE'
@ 04,000 SAY 'In This Wonderful Place'
@ 04,060 SAY '===================='
@ 06,000 SAY 'INVOICE NO ==>'
@ 06,027 SAY 'INVOICE DATE ==>'
 STORE  '00/00/00'  TO Minvdate
@ 06,044 GET Minvdate PICTURE '99/99/99'
@ 06,058 SAY 'CUSTOMER ID ==>'
 STORE  '              '  TO  Mcustid
@ 06,073 GET Mcustid
@ 07,027 SAY 'DATE PAID ==>'
@ 08,000 SAY '============== SOLD'
@ 08,020 SAY 'TO ============'
```

Fig. 8-16. Search invoice records. (Continued on page 262.)

```
@ 08,044 SAY '============ SHIP'
@ 08,064 SAY 'TO ============='
@ 12,000 SAY '================='
@ 12,020 SAY '================='
@ 12,044 SAY '================='
@ 12,064 SAY '================='
@ 14,000 SAY 'ITEM          QUANTITY'
@ 14,024 SAY 'DESCRIPTION'
@ 14,060 SAY 'PRICE         TOTAL'
@ 15,000 SAY '----          --------'
@ 15,024 SAY '-----------'
@ 15,060 SAY '-----         -----'
 @ 21,10 SAY  '  PLEASE ENTER VALUES TO SEARCH FOR  '
 IF select <>  ' T '
  @ 23,4 SAY 'XX'
 ENDIF
 READ
* EXIT FROM LOOP IF FOUND
 GOTO TOP
 STORE TRIM(Mcustid) TO key
 IF select=  ' T '
  FIND &key
  IF # <> 0
     STORE F TO Smore
 ELSE
  @ 22,10 SAY  '  NOT FOUND  '
  @ 23,10 SAY  ' TRY AGAIN(Y/N)? '
  SET CONSOLE OFF
  WAIT TO retry
  SET CONSOLE ON
  IF !(retry) <>  'Y'
  STORE F TO Smore
 ENDIF  Y
 RELEASE retry
  ENDIF  # <> 0
 ELSE
  LOCATE FOR  custid  = Mcustid .AND. &select
  IF .NOT. EOF
   STORE F TO Smore
 ELSE
  @ 22,10 SAY  '  NOT FOUND  '
  @ 23,10 SAY  ' TRY AGAIN(Y/N)? '
```

Fig. 8-16. Search invoice records. (Continued on page 263.)

```
     SET CONSOLE OFF
     WAIT TO retry
     SET CONSOLE ON
     IF !(retry) <>  'Y'
     STORE F TO Smore
   ENDIF  Y
   RELEASE retry
    ENDIF EOF
   ENDIF  select=T
ENDDO  Smore
RELEASE Smore
RELEASE key
ELSE
IF !(command) =  'N'
 STORE T TO next
 DO WHILE next
    SKIP
    IF &select
      STORE F TO next
    ENDIF
    IF EOF
      STORE F TO next
      STORE ' T '  TO select
      @ 23,4 SAY ' '
    ENDIF
 ENDDO
 RELEASE next
ELSE
IF !(command)= 'P'
    STORE ' T '  TO select
    @ 23,4 SAY '  '
    SKIP -1
ELSE
 IF !(command)= 'M'
 STORE T TO Mmore
 DO WHILE Mmore
 STORE ' MORE '  TO mode
 STORE ' '  TO Mmd
 @ 21,10 SAY  ' ENTER E TO RECORD PAYMENTS, D TO DELETE,
 @ 22,10 SAY '         P TO PRINT, C TO SCAN FILE         '
 IF select <>  ' T '
  @ 23,4 SAY 'XX'
```

```
    ENDIF
    @ 23,10 SAY  ' PRESS RETURN WHEN DONE                              ' GET Mmd
    READ
   IF !(Mmd) = 'E'
       ERASE
IF select <>  ' T '
  @ 23,4 SAY 'XX'
ENDIF
X EDIT RECORD
       DO  INVOICE.ED
ELSE
IF !(Mmd)= 'D'
       STORE  'N'  TO answer
  IF select <>  ' T '
   @ 23,4 SAY 'XX'
  ENDIF
@ 23,10 SAY  ' ARE YOU SURE(Y/N)?
@ 23,28 GET answer
       READ
IF !(answer)= 'Y'
       DELETE
       STORE  'Y'  TO Gdel
ENDIF
RELEASE answer
ELSE
IF !(Mmd)= 'P'
  @ 23,10 SAY  ' PLEASE SET UP PRINTER
  STORE '        '  TO mode
  SET CONSOLE OFF
  WAIT
  SET CONSOLE ON
  SET FORMAT TO PRINT
  DO  INVOICE.OUT
  SET FORMAT TO SCREEN
ELSE
IF !(Mmd)='C'
  GOTO TOP
  STORE  '                                        '  TO select
  @ 21,10 SAY 'PLEASE ENTER SELECTION CRITERIA       '
  @ 22,10 SAY '    DO NOT PRESS RETURN!!!             '
  @ 23,4 SAY 'XX'
  @ 23,10 GET select
```

Fig. 8-16. Search invoice records. (Continued on page 265.)

```
        READ
        LOCATE FOR &select
        IF EOF
           @ 21,10 SAY 'NO MORE RECORDS CAN BE FOUND          '
           @ 22,10 SAY 'PLEASE PRESS RETURN TO CONTINUE          '
           @ 23,4 SAY '  '
           STORE  ' T '  TO select
           SET CONSOLE OFF
           WAIT
           SET CONSOLE ON
        ELSE
           DO INVOICE.OUT
         ENDIF
       ELSE
        STORE F TO Mmore
ENDIF   F
ENDIF   P
ENDIF   D
ENDIF   E
ENDDO   Mmore
RELEASE Mmore,Mmd
ELSE
      STORE F TO Gmore
ENDIF   M
ENDIF   P
ENDIF   N
ENDIF   S
ENDDO   Gmore
IF Gdel =  'Y'
     STORE  'N'  TO answer
     @ 23,10 SAY  'WANT TO PERMANENTLY DELETE RECORDS(Y/N)'
     @ 23,49 GET answer
     READ
     IF answer =  'Y'
         PACK
     ELSE
         RECALL ALL
     ENDIF
         RELEASE answer
ENDIF  Gdel
RELEASE  command,Gmore,Gdel,select
RELEASE mode
RETURN
```

```
* 	INVOICE.ED
* Records payments and corrects errors in invoice files
STORE T TO Emore
 STORE ' EDIT ' TO mode
* SET UP SCREEN VARIABLES
 STORE  invdate  TO  Minvdate
 STORE  custid  TO  Mcustid
 STORE  pddate  TO  Mpddate
 STORE  name  TO  Mname
 STORE  shipname  TO  Mshipname
 STORE  street  TO  Mstreet
 STORE  shipstr  TO  Mshipstr
 STORE  city  TO  Mcity
 STORE  state  TO  Mstate
 STORE  zip  TO  Mzip
 STORE  shipcity  TO  Mshipcity
 STORE  shipst  TO  Mshipst
 STORE  shzip  TO  Mshzip
 STORE  part1  TO  Mpart1
 STORE  q1  TO  Mq1
 STORE  desc1  TO  Mdesc1
 STORE  p1  TO  Mp1
 STORE  part2  TO  Mpart2
 STORE  q2  TO  Mq2
 STORE  desc2  TO  Mdesc2
 STORE  p2  TO  Mp2
 STORE  part3  TO  Mpart3
 STORE  q3  TO  Mq3
 STORE  desc3  TO  Mdesc3
 STORE  p3  TO  Mp3
 STORE  part4  TO  Mpart4
 STORE  q4  TO  Mq4
 STORE  desc4  TO  Mdesc4
 STORE  p4  TO  Mp4
DO WHILE Emore
ERASE
* GET SCREEN INPUT
 DO  INVOICE.IO
 @ 21,10 SAY ' ENTER ALL CHANGES '
 READ
* VALIDATE INPUT
 DO  INVOICE.VAL
```

Fig. 8-17. Edit invoice records. (Continued on page 267.)

```
   STORE  'N'  TO command
   @ 21,10 SAY  ' ANY MORE CHANGES (Y/N)? '   GET command
   READ
* PUT SCREEN ENTRIES INTO FILE
  REPLACE   invdate  WITH  Minvdate
  REPLACE   custid  WITH  Mcustid
  REPLACE   pddate  WITH  Mpddate
  REPLACE   name  WITH  Mname
  REPLACE   shipname  WITH  Mshipname
  REPLACE   street  WITH  Mstreet
  REPLACE   shipstr  WITH  Mshipstr
  REPLACE   city  WITH  Mcity
  REPLACE   state  WITH  Mstate
  REPLACE   zip  WITH  Mzip
  REPLACE   shipcity  WITH  Mshipcity
  REPLACE   shipst  WITH  Mshipst
  REPLACE   shzip  WITH  Mshzip
  REPLACE   part1  WITH  Mpart1
  REPLACE   q1  WITH  Mq1
  REPLACE   desc1  WITH  Mdesc1
  REPLACE   p1  WITH  Mp1
  REPLACE   part2  WITH  Mpart2
  REPLACE   q2  WITH  Mq2
  REPLACE   desc2  WITH  Mdesc2
  REPLACE   p2  WITH  Mp2
  REPLACE   part3  WITH  Mpart3
  REPLACE   q3  WITH  Mq3
  REPLACE   desc3  WITH  Mdesc3
  REPLACE   p3  WITH  Mp3
  REPLACE   part4  WITH  Mpart4
  REPLACE   q4  WITH  Mq4
  REPLACE   desc4  WITH  Mdesc4
  REPLACE   p4  WITH  Mp4
  IF  !(command) <> 'Y'
   STORE F TO Emore
  ENDIF
ENDDO
RELEASE mode,Emore,command
RELEASE Minvdate
RELEASE Mcustid
RELEASE Mpddate·
RELEASE Mname
RELEASE Mshipname
RELEASE Mstreet
```

```
RELEASE Mshipstr
RELEASE Mcity
RELEASE Mstate
RELEASE Mzip
RELEASE Mshipcity
RELEASE Mshipst
RELEASE Mshzip
RELEASE Mpart1
RELEASE Mq1
RELEASE Mdesc1
RELEASE Mp1
RELEASE Mpart2
RELEASE Mq2
RELEASE Mdesc2
RELEASE Mp2
RELEASE Mpart3
RELEASE Mq3
RELEASE Mdesc3
RELEASE Mp3
RELEASE Mpart4
RELEASE Mq4
RELEASE Mdesc4
RELEASE Mp4
RETURN
```

Fig. 8-17. Edit invoice records. Continued from page 267.

011	SHIPCITY	C	010	
012	SHIPST	C	002	
013	SHZIP	C	005	
014	PART1	C	011	
015	Q1	N	004	
016	DESC1	C	035	
017	P1	N	007	002
018	PART2	C	011	
019	Q2	N	004	
020	DESC2	C	035	
021	P2	N	007	002
022	PART3	C	011	
023	Q3	N	004	
024	DESC3	C	035	
025	P3	N	007	002
026	PART4	C	011	
027	Q4	N	004	
028	DESC4	C	035	
029	P4	N	007	002
** TOTAL **			00359	

The field called **Custid** is the key one here, because it serves as the link between this file and the customer record. The other fields are based on the form in Fig. 8-13. It serves both as a data entry form, to record invoices for new sales, and as the basis of the invoice itself. This particular program gives you room to list four separate items on a single invoice; you can call for more or fewer as your needs dictate.

The command file, Fig. 8-14, calls and indexes the databases. New entries are made using the addition program in Fig. 8-15. One feature here is a sequence that checks to make sure the invoice has not already been entered. It searches for the same combination of customer identification and invoice date. If it finds another record with the same combination, it will skip past the data entry part of the routine and present a message warning you of the duplication. It may be just a coincidence, but if in doubt, use the scanning facilities of the file maintenance sequence to call the similar entry and compare it with the one you

```
X       INVOICE.OUT
X    Format file for invoice output
@ 02,000 SAY 'THIS IS YOUR COMPANY'
@ 02,060 SAY '======================'
@ 03,000 SAY 'At This Address'
@ 03,066 SAY 'INVOICE'
@ 04,000 SAY 'In This Wonderful Place'
@ 04,060 SAY '======================'
@ 06,000 SAY 'INVOICE NO ==>'
@ 06,015 SAY invno
@ 06,027 SAY 'INVOICE DATE ==>'
@ 06,045 SAY invdate
@ 06,058 SAY 'CUSTOMER ID ==>'
@ 06,074 SAY custid
@ 07,027 SAY 'DATE PAID ==>'
@ 07,042 SAY pddate
@ 08,000 SAY '=============== SOLD'
@ 08,020 SAY 'TO ============'
@ 08,044 SAY '=============== SHIP'
@ 08,064 SAY 'TO ===========>'
@ 09,001 SAY name
@ 09,045 SAY shipname
@ 10,001 SAY street
@ 10,045 SAY shipstr
@ 11,001 SAY city
@ 11,015 SAY state
@ 11,022 SAY zip
@ 11,045 SAY shipcity
@ 11,065 SAY shipst
@ 11,073 SAY shzip
@ 12,000 SAY '======================'
@ 12,020 SAY '====================='
```

Fig. 8-18. Format file for invoices. (Continued on page 270.)

```
@ 12,044 SAY '=========================='
@ 12,064 SAY '=================='
@ 14,000 SAY 'ITEM          QUANTITY'
@ 14,024 SAY 'DESCRIPTION'
@ 14,060 SAY 'PRICE         TOTAL'
@ 15,000 SAY '----          --------'
@ 15,024 SAY '-----------'
@ 15,060 SAY '-----         -----'
@ 16,001 SAY part1
@ 16,013 SAY q1
@ 16,025 SAY desc1
@ 16,060 SAY p1
@ 16,069 SAY q1*p1
@ 17,001 SAY part2
@ 17,013 SAY q2
@ 17,025 SAY desc2
@ 17,060 SAY p2
@ 17,069 SAY q2*p2
@ 18,001 SAY part3
@ 18,013 SAY q3
@ 18,025 SAY desc3
@ 18,060 SAY p3
@ 18,069 SAY q3*p3
@ 19,001 SAY part4
@ 19,013 SAY q4
@ 19,025 SAY desc4
@ 19,060 SAY p4
@ 19,069 SAY q4*p4
@ 20,030 SAY 'TOTAL DUE ==>'
STORE (q1*p1)+(q2*p2)+(q3*p3)+(q4*p4) TO total
@ 20,069 SAY total
RETURN
```

Fig. 8-18. Format file for invoices. (Continued from page 269.)

are about to enter. Figures 8-16 through 8-18 list other modules for the program.

If you have an acceptable new invoice, you can type the appropriate entries into the form presented by the IO format (Fig. 8-19). You need enter only the basic information; any calculated values will be computed later before the invoice is printed.

The file maintenance program and input and output screens follow much the same patterns as in previous systems. It uses the editing program to record payments on the invoices. The **Val** program (Fig. 8-20) makes sure you have a valid customer record on file for any voucher entry. Figure 8-21 shows the default values for the invoice program.

Printing Invoices

The print option in the maintenance program is the means to print your invoices. It calls the data you entered in the invoice addition program and computes the calculated items. For each item, it multiplies the quantity times the unit price to get the full cost. Then it adds a grand total for every item on the invoice. The result looks like Fig. 8-22.

The Big Report

The report program in the last chapter (Fig. 7-25) will serve you for this program, too. Copy it under the name **Invoice.Rpt**, or alter the command file back at Fig. 8-2 to call it by its current name.

The report most important to most managers is the *ageing report*—the one that lists accounts that are one, two, or more months overdue.

There's an easy way to do this—and there's a hard way. We'll go with the easy one for now. Index the

```
*       INVOICE.IO
* Working screen for invoice functions
@ 02,000 SAY 'THIS IS YOUR COMPANY'
@ 02,060 SAY '======================'
@ 03,000 SAY 'At This Address'
@ 03,066 SAY 'INVOICE'
@ 04,000 SAY 'In This Wonderful Place'
@ 04,060 SAY '======================'
@ 06,000 SAY 'INVOICE NO ==>'
@ 06,014 GET invno
@ 06,027 SAY 'INVOICE DATE ==>'
@ 06,044 GET Minvdate PICTURE '99/99/99'
@ 06,058 SAY 'CUSTOMER ID ==>'
@ 06,073 GET Mcustid
@ 07,027 SAY 'DATE PAID ==>'
@ 07,041 GET Mpddate PICTURE '99/99/99'
@ 08,000 SAY '=============== SOLD'
@ 08,020 SAY 'TO =============='
@ 08,044 SAY '=============== SHIP'
@ 08,064 SAY 'TO =============='
@ 09,000 GET Mname
@ 09,044 GET Mshipname
@ 10,000 GET Mstreet
@ 10,044 GET Mshipstr
@ 11,000 GET Mcity
@ 11,014 GET Mstate
@ 11,021 GET Mzip
@ 11,044 GET Mshipcity
@ 11,064 GET Mshipst
@ 11,072 GET Mshzip
@ 12,000 SAY '====================='
@ 12,020 SAY '====================='
```

Fig. 8-19. Format file for invoice input. (Continued on page 272.)

```
@ 12,044 SAY '========================='
@ 12,064 SAY '================='
@ 14,000 SAY 'ITEM          QUANTITY'
@ 14,024 SAY 'DESCRIPTION'
@ 14,060 SAY 'PRICE         TOTAL'
@ 15,000 SAY '----          --------'
@ 15,024 SAY '-----------'
@ 15,060 SAY '-----         -----'
@ 16,000 GET Mpart1
@ 16,012 GET Mq1
@ 16,024 GET Mdesc1
@ 16,060 GET Mp1 PICTURE '9999.99'
@ 16,073 SAY q1*p1
@ 17,000 GET Mpart2
@ 17,012 GET Mq2
@ 17,024 GET Mdesc2
@ 17,060 GET Mp2 PICTURE '9999.99'
@ 17,073 SAY q2*p2
@ 18,000 GET Mpart3
@ 18,012 GET Mq3
@ 18,024 GET Mdesc3
@ 18,060 GET Mp3 PICTURE '9999.99'
@ 18,073 SAY q3*p3
@ 19,000 GET Mpart4
@ 19,012 GET Mq4
@ 19,024 GET Mdesc4
@ 19,060 GET Mp4 PICTURE '9999.99'
@ 19,073 SAY q4*p4
@ 20,030 SAY 'TOTAL DUE ==>'
@ 20,073 SAY total
RETURN
```

Fig. 8-19. Format file for invoice input. (Continued on page 271.)

report and call for subtotals for each customer. Since the index uses the invoice date as a secondary index, the listings for each customer will be printed in order of the invoice date. When specifying the criteria for the report, call for only those invoices for which the **invdate** = '00/00/00.' That will confine the report to the unpaid vouchers.

Here's a simple but useful ageing report:

```
. REPORT FORM AGEING
ENTER OPTIONS, M=LEFT MARGIN, L=LINES/PAGE, W=PAGE WIDTH
PAGE HEADING? (Y/N) Y
ENTER PAGE HEADING: ACCOUNTS PAYABLE; AGEING REPORT
```

```
DOUBLE SPACE REPORT? (Y/N) N
ARE TOTALS REQUIRED? (Y/N) Y
SUBTOTALS IN REPORT? (Y/N) Y
ENTER SUBTOTALS FIELD: custid
SUMMARY REPORT ONLY? (Y/N) N
EJECT PAGE AFTER SUBTOTALS? (Y/N) N
ENTER SUBTOTAL HEADING: CUSTOMER CODE:
COL      WIDTH,CONTENTS
001       8, invdate
ENTER HEADING: INVOICE DATE
002       7, (q1*p1)+(q2*p2)+(q3*p3)+(q4+p~~*p4)
ENTER HEADING: AMOUNT DUE
ARE TOTALS REQUIRED? (Y/N) Y
```

The small but useful result is shown in Fig. 8-23.

You may prefer a report that gives you a more specific breakdown, separating accounts that are more than 30 days overdue from those more than 60 days behind, and so on. This can be useful if you're dealing with volumes in which eyeballing the type of report we've just described would not be practical.

It involves some tricky programming; you can play around with it if you'd like. You'd use the substring function to extract the first two figures of the standard date listing; these are the two that represent the

```
*       INVOICE.VAL
* Checks invoices against customer file
STORE T TO Vmore
DO WHILE Vmore
SELECT SECONDARY
USE  CUSTOMER     INDEX  CUSTOMER
STORE  Mcustid  TO find
FIND &find
RELEASE find
IF # <> 0
    SELECT PRIMARY
    STORE F TO Vmore
ELSE
    SELECT PRIMARY
  @ 23,0 SAY  '
  @ 23,0 SAY  ' CANNOT FIND IN CUSTOMER FILE '
@ 06,073 GET Mcustid
READ
ENDIF
ENDDO  Mcustid
RETURN
```

Fig. 8-20. Validation file for invoice input.

```
*       INVOICE.FAU
* Default values for invoice program
STORE  '        '  TO  invno
STORE  '00/00/00'  TO  Minvdate
STORE  '             '  TO  Mcustid
STORE  '00/00/00'  TO  Mpddate
STORE  '                        '  TO  Mname
STORE  '                        '  TO  Mshipname
STORE  '                '  TO  Mstreet
STORE  '                '  TO  Mshipstr
STORE  '          '  TO  Mcity
STORE  ' '  TO  Mstate
STORE  '     '  TO  Mzip
STORE  '          '  TO  Mshipcity
STORE  ' '  TO  Mshipst
STORE  '     '  TO  Mshzip
STORE  '          '  TO  Mpart1
STORE  0  TO  Mq1
STORE  '                                             '  TO  Mdesc1
STORE  0.00  TO  Mp1
STORE  '          '  TO  Mpart2
STORE  0  TO  Mq2
STORE  '                                             '  TO  Mdesc2
STORE  0.00  TO  Mp2
STORE  '          '  TO  Mpart3
STORE  0  TO  Mq3
STORE  '                                             '  TO  Mdesc3
STORE  0.00  TO  Mp3
STORE  '          '  TO  Mpart4
STORE  0  TO  Mq4
STORE  '                                             '  TO  Mdesc4
STORE  0.00  TO  Mp4
STORE  (Mq1*Mp1)+(Mq3*Mp2)+(Mq3*Mp3)+(Mq4*Mp4)  TO  total
RETURN
```

Fig. 8-21. Default file for invoice input.

month. The command would look like this:

```
$(Date,1,2)
```

You'd then have to compare the results of this calculation for both the current date and the date of the invoice. But you aren't through yet. You then must find your way to:

```
$(Date,4,2)
```

to find out whether the invoice date calls for an earlier or later day of the month. If it's June 6 and the invoice was dated May 27, it's not yet nearly a month overdue.

```
THIS IS YOUR COMPANY                          ========================
At This Address                                        INVOICE
In This Wonderful Place                       ========================

INVOICE NO ==>              INVOICE DATE ==>  03/03/84   CUSTOMER ID ==> TYCOON
                            DATE PAID ==>  00/00/00
============== SOLD TO =============      ============= SHIP TO =============
TYCOON SHIPPING                          L.J. SILVER
55 WATER ST                              222 GULF BLVD
PORTSMOUTH    KS      66666              TR. ISLAND          FL      33706

===================================      ===================================

ITEM        QUANTITY     DESCRIPTION                    PRICE        TOTAL
----        --------     -----------                    -----        -----
 1            15         DEAD MEN'S CHESTS              25.50        382.50
 2            15         SHOVELS                        12.70        190.50
 3             1         TWO-MAN LIFEBOAT              875.00        875.00
 4            13         CASKETS                        35.00        455.00
                              TOTAL DUE ==>                         1903.00
```

Fig. 8-22. Invoice display.

Even after you've done all that you still have only determined whether the bill is so many *months* overdue. To reduce this to an accurate measure of 30, 60, or 90 days, you would have to resort to a date counting routine something like the "Star Trek" calendar. They exist—but before you get involved, ask whether it's really necessary for your purposes.

Many small businesses don't need this degree of sophistication. If it's July and your report shows that

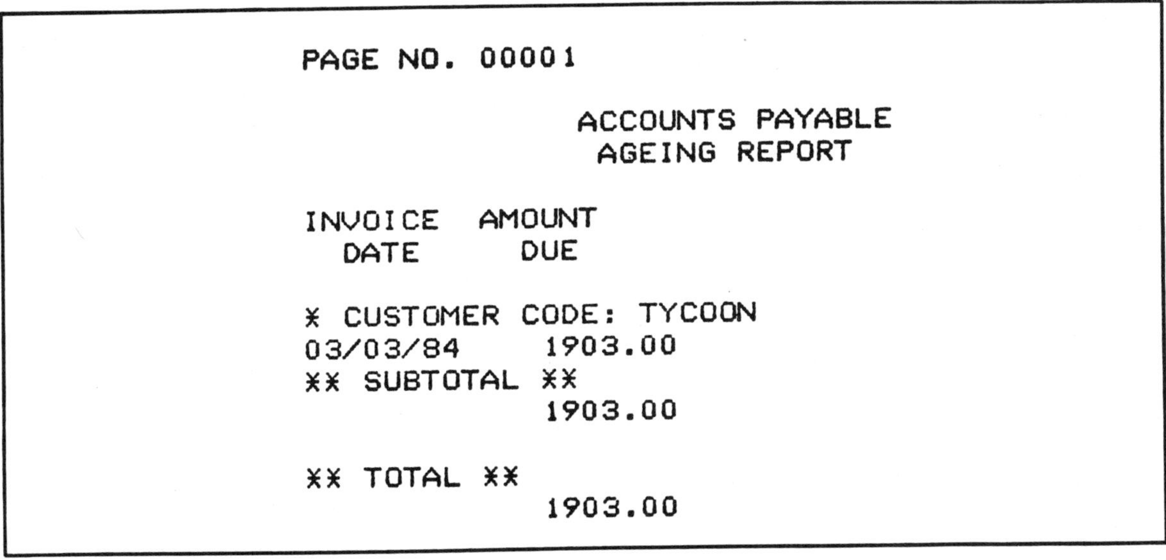

```
PAGE NO.  00001

                        ACCOUNTS PAYABLE
                        AGEING REPORT

INVOICE    AMOUNT
  DATE       DUE

X CUSTOMER CODE: TYCOON
03/03/84      1903.00
XX SUBTOTAL XX
              1903.00


XX TOTAL XX
              1903.00
```

Fig. 8-23. Accounts payable ageing report form.

you still haven't received payment for that odd shipment to Long John, it doesn't take a sophisticated program to let you know you have a problem. Even at the next higher level of sophistication, you can simply specify a date 30 days earlier than today and ask for all unpaid invoices that precede that date.

Then go back to the word processing file and work up a hard-hitting collection letter to these people.

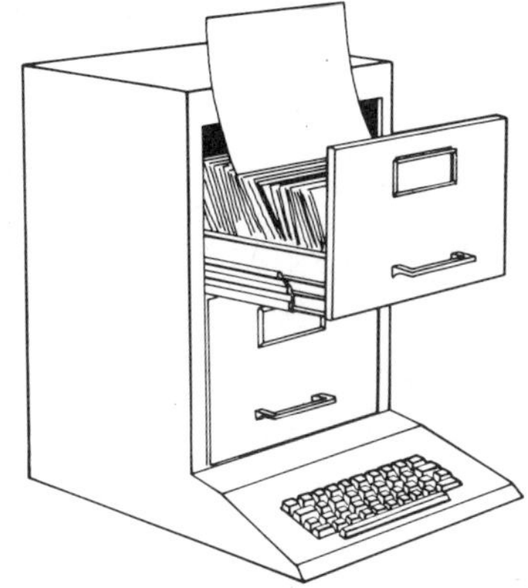

Chapter 9

Linked Files and Other Hazardous Substances

Some of you have probably reached this point with a vague feeling that there has been a gap between promise and performance. For others, the feeling may not be so vague.

In the early going, we talked about such dBASE ideals as proper database construction:

A database for everything and every database in its place.

You should be able to move freely between linked databases to retrieve the information in any of them.

Later, you may have seen these principles being violated. In the last chapter on receivables, for example, the invoice database is a flagrant violation, including data on both the customer and the transaction—information that properly should be in separate files.

The systems in this book also make only modest use of dBASE's ability to link one file with another. We've tied a few things together, but not to the degree of which dBASE is supposedly capable. Again an example from the previous chapter: wouldn't it be nice to sort out a list of customers whose payments are overdue, search the customer file for the same names, and automatically send collection letters to these people? It should be possible even to draft a polite letter to those over the 30-day mark, something more threatening for the 60-day group, and a referral to your lawyer for the 90-day crowd.

(Such boilerplate letter generation is possible, although it's more a MailMerge than a dBASE function. Prepare the standard letters in MailMerge format, then use dBASE to generate a data file of selected customers.)

PROMISE v. PERFORMANCE

Unfortunately, the way dBASE *should* work and the way it *does* work tend to be different, particularly where linked and indexed files are concerned. One glitch, which remains in some of the programs in this book, is that you will find yourself entering data for a paycheck or invoice while calculated data, and the items retrieved from other files, remain on the screen from a previous transaction. This can be disconcerting, but the file will update itself with the correct information before it prints the result.

Often, though, this problem is complicated by a tendency of dBASE's indexing system to get out of sync. Any number of things can throw off the indexing. When it happens, the command to search a second database may find something other than what you're looking for. The basic cure is to reindex the database; most of the systems in this book include easy means to do it. Technical bulletins from Ashton-Tate indicate that plenty of attention is being devoted to this type of problem.

Even so, troubles can persist. One unpublished legacy of this book: yards of printouts, representing dBASE routines that persist in issuing checks to the wrong people.

We're all familiar with this kind of mistake, and none of us wants to be either a victim or a cause. In fact, as this book was being written a household drama involving an automobile insurance policy was in progress. The insurance company's computer failed to recognize that we'd dropped the policy and continued to issue bills for the premium payments. Eventually it canceled the policy for nonpayment. Whereupon a computer in the state capital just as mindlessly spat out a notice that we were violating the state's financial responsibility laws, and were about to lose our licenses.

FOR HUMAN INTERVENTION

That experience probably helped to shape a major premise of this book: that a small business usually has the capacity to maintain human monitoring over what its computer does. The routines you see here are designed to make use of that capacity. (Even in larger institutions there are error-trapping routines available—such as finding out whether an insurance policy exists before canceling it.)

For those of you who want, or need, to go into more advanced dBASE operations, this chapter will look into some of the techniques. Just remember that once you pass this point you are in an area of questionable reliability.

Here's one routine you could call from any other program with the command:

. DO SEARCH

Use it to find the number of records that match a particular criterion. Let's say, for example, you want to search Nick Nader's inventory for all the Corvair parts that came from a particular supplier. The routine would go like this:

```
* Search.Cmd
USE STOCK INDEX STOCKVEN
ERASE
?
?
?
ACCEPT '      Field to Search ==>' to field
ACCEPT '      Item Wanted ==>' to key
* Establish a counter to keep track of the number of matches
STORE 0 to counter
* Find the first instance of a match
FIND &key
* If a match is found, display the record
```

```
IF # <> 0
    DO WHILE &field = key .AND. .NOT. EOF
         DISPLAY
         STORE counter + 1 to counter
         SKIP
    ENDDO
ENDIF
?
? '     TOTAL MATCHES FOUND:' counter
RELEASE field, key, counter
RETURN
```

This routine also could be used for such things as finding the records of your slow-paying debtors. It would not do much more, though, than counting and identifying them.

Listed in Fig. 9-1 is a routine that takes the next step finding a common item in a matching file. You could use it, for example, to update your customer records. One field in each record calls for the amount each customer owes. You could use this routine to update that amount with the figure from the latest

```
X UPDATE.CMD
SELECT PRIMARY
USE CUSTOMER INDEX CUSTOMER
SELECT SECONDARY
USE INVOICE INDEX INVOICE
SELECT PRIMARY
X Set up text file for audit trail
SET ALTERNATE TO UPDATE
SET ALTERNATE ON
X Proceed through invoice file and locate today's invoices
SELECT SECONDARY
DO WHILE .NOT. EOF .AND. invdate = Date()
     X Locate matching record in customer file
     STORE custid to &key
     SELECT PRIMARY
     FIND &key
     X If there is no match, make note of invoice recordir
     X    audit file
     IF # = 0
          SELECT SECONDARY
          X Converts record number (six digits) to string
          STORE STR(#,6) to recno
          ? 'ERROR &recno'
     ELSE
          X Print customer record in audit file
```

Fig. 9-1. Update command file. (Continued on page 280.)

```
            SET CONSOLE OFF
            X Update balance figure.  Total is a memory
            X   variable created in computing the invoice.
            REPLACE P.balance WITH P.balance + total
            X Sends updated record to audit file
            DISPLAY
        ENDIF 0
        SELECT SECONDARY
        SKIP
ENDDO
X Close out transaction files
SELECT PRIMARY
USE
SELECT SECONDARY
USE
X Call permanent audit file and add records from temporary
X    file
X USE CUSTAUD
APPEND FROM UPDDATE.TXT SDF
X Cleanup
X RELEASE key, recno
X Close temporary file
SET ALTERNATE TO NULL
SET CONSOLE ON
RETURN
```

Fig. 9-1. Update command file. (Continued from page 279.)

invoice. An added feature here: the program creates a separate listing of the update transactions, to serve as an audit trail.

This procedure transfers a record of the transaction to a text file for temporary storage, then at the end copies the information to a permanent data file called **Custaud.** If **Custaud** doesn't exist, of course we must invent it. That's not too difficult:

```
.   USE CUSTOMER
.   COPY STRUCTURE TO CUSTAUD
.   USE CUSTAUD
.   MODIFY STRUCTURE
```

There is one modification to make: as Field 1, add a new six-space field called **Record**; it will accept the record numbers of the invoice records that are transferred. Otherwise, the entries will follow the same structure as the **Customer** file, whose changes you are auditing.

There is one important difference. If there is no matching record, the temporary file—and eventually the audit database—will include an ERROR flag along with the record number in which the mismatch was found. Display the audit file, and you'll see where your problems might be.

```
*ZOOM.CMD
* Set up infinite loop
DO WHILE T
* Provide miniature menu
?
?
ACCEPT '                    Name File to Use ==>' to File1
STORE !(File1) to File1
USE &File1
* You now can use any dBASE command such as DISPLAY or
SKIP.
* The command Zoom will start the search for linked files.
?
ACCEPT '                    Your Next Command ==>' to command
DO CASE
CASE !(command) = ZOOM
* Find and display linking possibilities
SELECT SECONDARY
USE LINKUP
INDEX ON FILE, LINKFILE TO LINKUP
FIND &File1
IF # = 0
     ?
     ? '                         SORRY.  No Linkups Available'
ELSE
     ?
     ? '                         Links are available with:'
     ?
DO WHILE FILE = File1 .AND. .NOT. EOF
     ? LINKFILE
     SKIP
ENDDO
?
ACCEPT '              Which One Would You Like? ==>' to File2
STORE !(File2) to File2
* Find the second file and index
LOCATE FOR FILE = File1 .AND. LINKFILE = File2
STORE FIELD TO Mfield
STORE INDEX TO Mindex
* The second file becomes the first
SELECT PRIMARY
USE &File2 Index &Mindex
STORE File2 to File1
* Search for a matching record.
```

Fig. 9-2. Zoom procedure command file. (Continued on page 282.)

```
Find &Mfield
IF # = 0
          ? '        Sorry, no matching record found'
          ? '        You are now at the top of &File1'
          GOTO TOP
     ENDIF
ENDIF
OTHERWISE
     &command
ENDCASE zoom
ENDDO while T
```

Fig. 9-2. Zoom procedure command file. (Continued from page 281.)

A similar application of the text and audit files could be used to sort record the results of your earlier search through the Nader parts bin.

ZOOMING AROUND

The last idea—and the next—are based on the ideas of Adam Green, whose publications and seminars will be discussed a little more fully in the next chapter. These are the kinds of things he teaches his more advanced groups.

The next routine is used something like the zoom lens on a camera, to zero in on specific details of your records. It lets you start from one database, find out what other databases are related to it, and move to your choice of the related databases. From there, you can move to any other files that are lined with the new one.

You start by setting up database file which lists your database files, doing so in a particular way. Successive fields list the file in question, a file to which it can be linked, the necessary index file for the second field, and the field which holds the common data. Set up with some of the files used in earlier chapters, it looks like this:

```
STRUCTURE FOR FILE:    LINKUP.DBF
NUMBER OF RECORDS:     00003
DATE OF LAST UPDATE: 00/00/00
PRIMARY USE DATABASE
FLD        NAME        TYPE WIDTH      DEC
001        FILE        C     008
002        LINKFILE    C     008
003        INDEX       C     008
004        FIELD       C     010
** TOTAL **                  00035
```

The contents:

```
00001    EMPLOYEE  CAREER    CARRNO    SSNO
00002    CAREER    EMPLOYEE  EMPNO     SSNO
```

```
00003    PAYCHEK    EMPLOYEE   EMPNO      SSNO
00004    EMPLOYEE   PAYCHEK    PAYCHEK    SSNO
00005    STOCK      VENDOR     VENDOR     VENDOR
00006    VENDOR     STOCK      STOCKVEN   VENDOR
00007    VENDOR     VOUCHER    VOUCHER    VENDOR
00008    VOUCHER    VENDOR     VENDOR     VENDOR
00009    CUSTOMER   INVOICE    INVOICE    CUSTID
00010    INVOICE    CUSTOMER   CUSTOMER   CUSTID
```

The first item indicates that the **Employee** database is linked to the **Career** file, whose index file for this purpose is **Carrno.** The common field is **Ssno.** There's also a reverse linkage: **Career** is linked to **Employee,** with the **Empno** index file, and also on the basis of **Ssno.**

The file that zooms through these relationships is called, naturally enough, **Zoom.** It is listed in Fig. 9-2.

You can call up any database file that's on your disk. The menu prompt that asks for a command lets you do about anything you can do to a database. You might want to LIST it, DISPLAY a certain record, SKIP on to the next, or —SKIP to the one before. If you say ZOOM, that's when the action starts. Let's play with it for a few minutes.

For example, if you were in the **Employee** file you could search for a particular record or zoom to the **Paycheck** file. After searching for a matching record there you could come back to **Employee** and zoom to **Career,** perhaps to compare the pay level with the job evaluation and the employee's rating. Another part of the system that offers great opportunities for zooming around is the set of linkages between the inventory, the vendors and the accounts payable.

And, most of all, it's fun.

THE INDEXING PROBLEMS

A big restriction on using multiple files and indexes is in the dBASE indexing system. One type of compensation is a REINDEX command added to Version 2.4. It does the same necessary function as the Go and Command files used in this book.

Ashton-Tate acknowledges several difficulties, including problems when you try to use a multiple index in a data file. For example, if you are PACKing a database with more than one index open, it will only readjust one of them. Multiple indexing also adds greatly to the time dBASE needs to READ or REPLACE.

Seeing Double

One solution to the speed problem is to use a secondary database to do your updating, GETting and READing, using memory variables whenever you can. If you have a secondary database with only a single index it will work, since dBASE can scan through it much more rapidly than it can go through the heavily indexed version. Or, create a new database—like a transaction file—to do the manipulations. Then all you need do with the main database is APPEND or REPLACE from the secondary one.

You can't SKIP backward. Even if you're agile enough to perform this as a physical feat, you can't do it in an indexed data file. You can't INSERT a new field into the structure, either, without messing things up. For a similar reason, don't try to use the DISPLAY command directly before a REPLACE.

You also can create indexing problems, if you frequently modify the key field. The duplicate database again is a way around this. The basic sequence is this:

☐ COPY the database structure to a new file.
☐ SELECT the new file as a secondary database.
☐ APPEND a BLANK record.
☐ REPLACE the contents of that record with the
    comparable items in the main database.
☐ Make whatever additions and changes you have in mind.
☐ SELECT the original database as primary.
☐ APPEND the updated records from the secondary file.

Other no-nos include INDEX and FIND expressions of more than 98 characters, trying to index on a logical field, or trying to index on a pair of numeric fields. This could happen when, for example, you want to index first by a shelf number and then by a part number. If you say:

```
▪    INDEX ON shelfno + partno
```

dBASE will add the two numbers and then try to index on the result.

You can get around this by converting the numbers to characters:

```
▪    INDEX ON STR(shelfno,3) + STR(partno,6)
```

Out of Range

The error message RECORD OUT OF RANGE is a normal symptom of an indexing problem, but it can mean other things as well. It also can happen when the file count that appears in the record header when you display the structure gets out of sync with the actual number of records in the file. Among the causes, and their cures if any:

☐ Shutting down the computer while dBASE was still in use and the file still was open. That's one reason to make sure you quit every session with the QUIT command.
☐ Power interruptions, particularly while the PACK procedure is at work.
☐ Trying to SORT a file that has many deleted records.

The best solution is to try to avoid these situations. Short of that, try to APPEND a new record. The system may readjust in the process. Then again, it may not.

If that doesn't work, COPY the data to a new file. Beyond that you get into such things as debugging tools and BASIC programs to update the count in the record header.

But enough of this complaining. Like any product, dBASE has some flaws. They mainly serve to illustrate that there's still some distance between C. J. Date and Ashton-Tate—between the textbook author and a company executing many of his ideas on the open market—and in microcomputers to boot.

The fundamental fact remains that dBASE II is a first-rate product, and its shortcomings are . . . well . . . *short.*

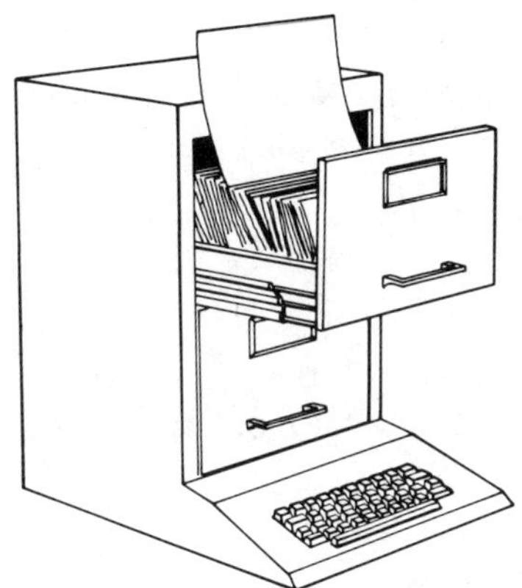

Chapter 10

Add-Ons, Training, and Information

For all its value and versatility, there are some things dBASE can't do. Its mathematical capability is grade school at best. So is its ability to produce graphics. It also has some features that are not well described in the dBASE manual. In the instructions for Version 2.3b, for example, the valuable DO CASE command appears only in a loose-leaf addendum.

Then, too, not everyone wants to spend time typing long lists of code or wrestling with dBASE's query language. The frustrated writer who tries to index articles and sources with dBASE will soon learn that it is sharply limited for that kind of work.

In spite of its lacks, dBASE has been a popular program. The combination of its popularity and the many other jobs it *could* do has made dBASE a prime candidate for enhancement, books, training programs, and a host of other "optional accessories." Some make dBASE easier to use, some make it more useful, some overcome shortcomings, and some do a combination of these. There has been a booming market lately in dBASE accessories, and here are some of the offerings.

MORE dBASE FOR YOUR dBASE

One particularly useful and inexpensive accessory for dBASE comes from Ashton-Tate and is called dBASE II. Most dBASE owners who bought their programs in 1983 or earlier have dBASE Version 2.3. The most recent version is numbered 2.4. If you have 2.3, Ashton-Tate will sell you an upgrade to 2.4 for $75. Given the price and the added capacity the newer version provides, if you have a 2.3 dBASE, the 2.4 upgrade must rank as a valuable accessory.

A major improvement in 2.4 is more flexibility in using memory variables, particularly if you want to save them in a .MEM file for future use. Under the old version of dBASE this was an all-or-nothing proposition. Either you saved *all* the variables then on record, or you saved *none* of them. It is possible to specify the types you want to save by listing them individually, but if you have any significant number to be listed, this can regress your computer quickly to the pencil-and-paper age.

Even more important to many users, you suffer the same lack of selectivity when you want to release variables to clean up your program and save valuable space. Again, you can't just release a selected handful without listing them all.

The new dBASE comes to the rescue. It gives you the options of saving or releasing selected types of variables. The trick is to specify the variables so you later can identify the types.

Let's say, for example, you have a list of variables that looks like this:

empname   empno   payrate   payamt   emptrans

Emptrans is a temporary variable used to transfer data from one location to another. Now that the switch has been made, you're through with **emptrans**. In the spirit of good computer housekeeping, you'd like to get rid of it. With 2.4 you could use this command:

. RELEASE ALL LIKE *trans

where the "*" character is a *wild card*—a signal to the computer to release any variable that ends in-trans.

Or, you would like to save just the payroll-oriented variables to a memory file for that kind of data. You could say:

. STORE ALL LIKE pay* to PAY.MEM

Put This Feature to Use

The best way to make use of this feature is to name your variables to take advantage of it. The use of the **pay** and **emp** prefixes is one example.

Another common situation is this: you have a mixed list of variables in a long routine. Some are *global*, serving you throughout the operation. Others are *local*, useful only during one of the individual modules that make up the routine. Since a long program can strain dBASE's 64-variable limit, you'd like to clear out the unneeded local variables as you're through with them.

With dBASE 2.4 you can precede the local variables with the letter L. At the right time you can command:

. RELEASE all like L*

Behold: the unneeded local variables have been cleared out; the useful global ones remain.

With this kind of capacity—if you make good use of it—there's no longer any reason the 64-variable limit has to be a limit at all. It's only a limit of 64 variables *currently in use*: you should never find yourself up against that kind of limit.

For Text Handling

Many writers and students have looked at dBASE with visions of electronic term papers dancing in their heads. There must be some way, they figure, to assemble notes like they used to do on the little index cards, then call on dBASE to assemble them in the proper order. A little editing on the word processor, and *voila!* there's your master's degree thesis or a best-selling book assembled for you, footnotes and everything.

An inner sense of reason tells us dBASE *ought* to work that way, but in the real world of practical experience, you'll soon find out that it doesn't. dBASE can assemble a well-organized outline and a neat bibliography, but you still must put the article together yourself.

The main restriction is the 254-character limit on the length of a dBASE field. That's enough to hold a very long name or address, or even the bottom line of the federal budget, but when you are working with text you'll find it's too short to be useful at all.

The character limit is necessary. dBASE must work within specified lengths and dimensions; among other things, it uses the stated field length as a guide to organizing your files. If it didn't have these fixed-length files, dBASE would have to sacrifice some of its other features to accommodate a different system.

The 2.4 upgrade, though, offers some relief for electronic writers. It has a new TEXT command that lets you compose a free-form block of text and call it to be inserted in a stated place in the file.

For example, you might write a block of text on memory variables and wild card commands, another on the TEXT command, and so on. With the right dBASE commands you then could assemble this chapter.

There is one major restriction: the text files cannot have formatting characters in them. You must use the WordStar "N" option, or its equivalent in other word-processing programs. You can format and edit the text once dBASE has assembled the notes in order.

Send Out the Search Party

An extension of this feature is the ability to have dBASE search for designated key words within your blocks of text. It requires that you load the text file into a database file—and the process is slow—but it does give you the means, for example, to search out notes on a specified subject. Other features of Version 2.4 are:

- ☐ A HELP command to guide new users, including a feature that can help trace the errors in a command file.
- ☐ A SET DELETE ON command makes the system behave as if items marked for deletion were already gone. One possibility here: work with selected portions of the file by deleting those items you don't want to use, then restoring them when you are done. You might mark a departing employee for deletion from the payroll file, leave it that way for the rest of the year, and then restore the name when it's time to issue W-2 forms.
- ☐ You can have more than one DO CASE in effect at the same time, assuming they are nested correctly. This was not possible under the old version.
- ☐ For users of the IBM PC, you now can set the function keys and get a greater variety of colors and reverse images in the screen display.

PROGRAM GENERATORS

Another users dream may be of the day you can sit down at the keyboard, call up a form on the screen, and fill out the blanks to enter data. Then, you can use another similar form to generate reports.

There now are several dBASE program generators on the market. Some will take you about a quarter of the way toward that goal. Some will get you about half. One or two may make the three-quarter mark. None will get you all the way.

Ashton-Tate also has an entry in the first of these groups. It's called ZIP, and it comes as an addendum to the 8-bit CP/M versions of dBASE. (At this writing VIP, an adaptation of ZIP for 16-bit machines, was reported in the works, but it was not yet available.)

ZIP can produce a form for the screen or printer, along with the basic commands for entering and retrieving the data. Once you've designed the screen, though, you probably will have to go back to dBASE to write the commands that organize and process the material. The process goes as follows.

Call up ZIP and check out the list of default values it presents. If you want to change the form size or the character used to draw ruler lines, this is a chance to do so. You'll next be prompted to enter the filename for your finished form, and will be presented with a blank screen for your design. Laying out the form is as simple as typing it in; the planning part can be difficult, but the typing part is easy.

ZIP has a couple of notable features: if you want to rule off areas of the form, it has easy commands to draw both horizontal and vertical lines (of sorts). Also, in a manner similar but not identical to the @ SAY command, you can specify the items you want to appear on the screen. If it's a label, like your company name or a column heading, just type it in. Use @ to retrieve a variable from the program and a # to indicate information you enter from the keyboard. You also can work some commands of your own into the screen by enclosing them in square brackets like this:

[SET DEFAULT TO B]

You will probably find, though, that space for these commands is tight, and you'll have to enter most of them later.

Files and Commands

When you save the completed form, you'll bring on another series of prompts. You'll be asked whether you want a command file or just a format file to be called from within another program. ZIP also will ask whether the form is to be used on a printer.

A potentially useful command, although it may not seem so at first, is the question of whether to change the filename. You can use this to pick up an existing screen, use ZIP to modify it into a companion screen in a similar style, then save it under a different name. Your program then will have two screens that look, as they should, like parts of the same system.

ZIP will generate three different files. If you chose, for example, to save the screen under the file-name ENTRY. ZIP would produce:

- ☐ ENTRY.ZIP, a version of the newly created screen.
- ☐ ENTRY.ZPR, the same thing in a version you can edit on a word processor, then recall as a modified version of the ENTRY form.
- ☐ ENTRY.CMD or ENTRY.FMT, depending on the option you've chosen. Either is a command file with all the @ SAY and other statements that make up the screen. The .CMD version also includes enough commands to execute the screen, but little else.

In Practical Use

Many of the screens and forms in this book were designed on ZIP—but not quite in the way its authors intended.

As a regular WordStar user, I found it easier to draw the screen with that familiar program, using the nondocument option. If I call the file ENTRY, I would save it as ENTRY.ZPR.

Switch to ZIP. With the right answers to the prompts, ZIP will load an (O)ld file known as ENTRY.ZPR. Make any last-minute changes, including this important one: insert a line at the top of the ZIP screen so the format begins on Line 1, not on Line 0. dBASE used to let you use Line 0 in your screens, but not any longer.

Saving the program from ZIP again will generate the three files. For examples of how ZIP translates the screen layout into command files, compare some of the .FMT files earlier in this book with the screen layouts they create.

More from the Source

Ashton-Tate also maintains a variety of publications and programs related to dBASE II. They include:

- ☐ dBRUN, an abbreviated version of dBASE you can use with your own application programs in the dBASE language.
- ☐ Friday! is a simplified database manager based on the dBASE model.

EXECUTING QUICKCODE

After the Tampa Bay Buccaneers had suffered a particularly bad defeat, coach John McKay was asked what he thought of his team's execution.

"I think that would be a good idea," the coach replied.

Sometimes I think QUICKCODE has the same attitude toward me. Even after a fair amount of experience I am greeted too often with the message "Execution Ended." It reminds me of the McKay quote because the message invariably means that a painfully constructed system had been put to death.

That's my main problem with QUICKCODE. Some of the simplest typographical errors can suddenly send you back to the operating system, at the expense of any work you have not yet saved. And since saving the file is nearly the last step in the normal QUICKCODE operating sequence, the chances of loss are great. I would feel much better about QUICKCODE if it could handle a small mistake with something less than capital punishment.

A QUICKCODE user should heed this advice: once you have drawn the input screen for your planned set of programs, or even once you have developed a good preliminary design, save it immediately. Save it again after every significant change or addition. Otherwise, you increase the risk of loss at every keystroke. For example, Control/Dash, the delete signal in my computer-word processor combination, (and a sequence I sometimes use from force of habit) is an instant way to bring out the QUICKCODE executioner.

Other Than That . . .

QUICKCODE has a few other quirks, most of them peculiar to—or at least made worse by—the Osborne version of the program. (See the separate comments on that experience.) Even so, it is a dBASE user's valuable accessory. It generates programs—not great programs, but good programs. If you're looking for a quick and simple application program for your own use, punch a few buttons (making sure you avoid the wrong ones), and QUICKCODE will create it. If you'd rather spend your time doing more creative things than hacking out lines and lines of conventional code, QUICKCODE will do the dirty work and leave you more time for the good stuff.

In fact, this book was prepared in just that way. The programs here have been tailored and adapted to serve their particular functions, but most of the basic coding is straight out of the QUICKCODE parts bin. In his review of QUICKCODE, Adam Green suggested that the instructions could use some good examples of practical applications. This book might serve that purpose.

The main benefit to the author is that QUICKCODE can fill a disk with programs in a matter of two or three minutes (although after several hours of planning and preparation). The benefits to the reader are that the code is conventional, proven, and (nearly) error-free. (The QUICKCODE literature indicates that a few errors have been corrected along the way, and I found one more. An unadorned version of the GET

Owners of the orphaned Osborne 1 must deal with a little weirdness once in a while. Their machines require more than the usual quota of adaptation. This is particularly true of the early versions, with their tiny screens and tinier disk capacities.

QUICKCODE is no exception. In fact, if your Osborne has undergone a double-density/big-screen conversion, you're in for a double dose of adaptation.

To accommodate the limited disk capacity of the original Ozzie, the Osborne QUICKCODE comes on three separate disks. As you work your way through the process, you'll be prompted to change disks as necessary. That isn't too difficult. The big problem is that it's ridiculously easy to put in the wrong disk by mistake. When you do, a call goes out for the QUICKCODE executioner.

If you have a double-density Osborne, things are better—and worse. You can copy any two of the original QUICKCODE disks onto a single working disk, but there's not quite enough room to squeeze in the third one. I finally settled on a combination of 1 and 3, useful for the original setup, switching to a combination of 1 and 2 when prompted midway through the program generation. That would have reduced it to a single disk change except .

. . .

The Osborne QUICKCODE works in reverse. You put the QUICKCODE disks in Drive B and the disk to receive your programs in Drive A. The A disk indeed receives most of the generated programs. However, just after you've made the midstream disk switch, QUICKCODE stubbornly tries to record the database file on the B drive instead. Since that disk has just been changed you get a Bdos error and, again, the executioner's song.

Sometimes it works right, so you can al-

ways hope to get lucky. Probably a better solution is to omit the database file when you set up the original list of files to be produced. You can come back later, reboot the disks, and use an option off the help screen that lets you generate the DBF file individually. It still probably will land on the wrong disk, and you must copy it from there, but at least it works.

QUICKSCREEN's sensitivity to proper screen alignment makes it particularly tricky with an Osborne. As most owners know, the original small screen actually shows 52 columns of an 80-column screen. The Quickscreen instructions tell you to use the Osborne setup program to specify the 80-column screen—it's probably set up that way already.

In an Osborne with the 80-column screen conversion, the setup program calls for both physical and logical screen sizes. After some experimentation I determined that the Quickscreen instruction refers to the logical size. But that brings on another complication.

The trouble is, the Osborne instructions for the 80-column conversion make it clear that the logical screen size should be larger than the physical one. If you want the 80-column display for which you paid the extra bucks, you must specify a larger figure for the logical size— contrary to the Quickscreen instructions.

You can, and probably should, set both size indications at 80 for QUICKCODE, observing the Osborne instructions for your other programs. This still entails a sacrifice, though: I like to prepare my QUICKCODE (or ZIP) screen layouts with WordStar, a versatile program whose commands (cynics please take note) have become second nature. With varied screen sizes between the WordStar and QUICKCODE disks, this doesn't work—or at least it doesn't work right.

---

sequence, which searches for data within a file, contains a reference to a phantom variable, MQ:SLCT in QUICKCODE language, used only in a more elaborate version of that program. It's in the first few lines and is easy to remove.)

Firing Up

The first-time user of QUICKCODE should be warned that, while it is definitely quick to create programs, the full process of using the program to its full advantage demands a significant amount of time, care and, most of all, planning. It can be a thrill of sorts to press one key and watch half a disk full of code roll out in a couple of minutes, but those few moments of enjoyment should properly be the reward for some long and careful preparation. QUICKCODE will produce the programs, all right. It's up to you to make sure they're good programs.

The first important stop within QUICKCODE is at the installation procedure. In my experience (and that of at least one other reviewer) QUICKCODE's screen display is particularly sensitive to a proper initial setup. Any deviation will produce misaligned gibberish. The time you devote to getting this part exactly right will be repaid later.

The next stop is at QUICKCODE's help menu and command center. Here you designate the title of your command files and exit to the first step in the design process, the "Quickscreen" mode. There you design the screen and print format for your system, designating lines and words to appear on the screen, fields for the database file, and items from other sources such as memory variables.

Setting the Limits

The screen design determines the appearance of your work, but it's really the next step that determines how your programs will work. It's the so-called "Fields" mode, and here you can designate some important things like:

- ☐ The length and type of each field.
- ☐ On which keys to index the file.
- ☐ A default value for any item.
- ☐ A range or list of permitted values, plus an error message to be displayed when they fall outside the limits. Another variation is to check the item against another data file.

Between the screen and fields modes you can specify whether the fields will be characters, numbers, or logical values. QUICKCODE also offers special designations for dollar amounts, dates, and telephone numbers. dBASE will read those items as one of its three standard forms, but QUICKCODE will automatically direct their length and format.

Plan Ahead

These early phases of the database design are important, because it is here you determine the actual shape of your system. The database variables and a host of other details are determined in these early stages. Take time to think of what you want to accomplish, and take just as much time to make sure the design you put together will do that job.

Back at the help screen, the planning and design process continues. You will leave again, in turn, to three separate setup screens. The first, which you may use only rarely, lets you vary the default commands for drawing the screen and other functions. Another lets you decide which of more than a dozen QUICKCODE programs you do—or don't—want to create. These include the basic addition, searching and editing programs, the screen layouts, and other utilities, and special programs such as the label printer and word-processor link.

The third screen is important to the planning process. You can decide, for example, whether you want to set up an alternative design for a report, or to reduce a customer or personnel file to a set of mailing labels. You also have an on-off switch for the Auto Pilot, which determines the level of sophistication on which QUICKCODE works.

With the Pilot on, QUICKCODE will generate a full, complete set of application programs. You could go to dBASE, command it to DO the program you've just created, and it would do exactly that. Without the

Pilot, QUICKCODE produces blocks of basic code, which programmers can work into their own applications.

The use of the Auto Pilot is the difference, for example, between the plain and fancy versions of the GET routine. One searches for records that meet the criteria you type in; after that, it's up to you to do something with what you've found. The other offers two different ways to search, plus options of editing, deleting, or printing the records.

It's Not *That* Quick

In spite of its name and function, don't get the idea that you can just sit down and start cranking out dBASE programs. To get the best from QUICKCODE—or even to get worthwhile programs—you must first use its many initial options to establish the kind of system you want. It can be a long, painstaking process—*and remember to save your work often.*

Then press the button and watch QUICKCODE roll.

Some Druthers

QUICKCODE's instruction manual appears to be an everchanging document, undergoing revisions and additions as Fox & Geller improve their product. There have been many since the first version but QUICKCODE could stand a couple more.

☐ A way to make good use of calculated values, such as multiplying the price times the quantity to get the total cost. There's a way to call a calculated value while you are creating the screen, but there's no good way to specify the formula for calculating it.

☐ A way to call data from a second file, and to update such a file with the material developed in the main program. QUICKCODE has the bare bones of such a technique in one of its validation program modules. It calls a secondary file and checks to see if entered data matches something in that file. The right small extension of that technique, and a better place to plug it into the QUICKCODE-generated system, would turn it into a more versatile instrument.

Other critics have said QUICKCODE needs a better way to produce reports—that it relies too heavily on the also-criticized dBASE report generator.

I agree, but only to the extent that the output side appears in general to be dBASE's most neglected aspect. There are plenty of ways to get data into a database. What we need are more ways to get it out in useful, meaningful forms.

The dBASE report generator is indeed weak, although it will do more than many people believe. QUICKCODE's label generator also has possibilities that go well beyond its initial function.

OTHER CODE GENERATORS

A close competitor of QUICKCODE is Autocode 1, developed by the British firm of Stemmos Ltd. and marketed by the Axel Johnson Corporation, of San Francisco.

Like QUICKCODE, Autocode can generate a limited list of basic types of programs. The main difference appears to be that Autocode does not have its own screen-image generator like the Quickscreen portion of Fox & Geller's offering. Whether that is a serious drawback is for you to decide; you still can create the screens with ZIP, a word processor, or even dBASE's MODIFY COMMAND. Autocode also has a lower list price.

The Autocode user works, as usual, from screen forms and menus. The first step is to design the screen, remembering the Autocode won't do this part. You then can fire up Autocode and will be presented with these menu choices:

```
<1> MENU GENERATION

<2> FILE MAINTENANCE GENERATION

<3> REPORT GENERATION

<4> EXIT
```

If you're setting up your own menu for a payroll system, select Option 1, and Autocode will display:

```
Menu File Name ?
Menu Title
No. of Options


OPTION NO.        OPTION MESSAGE                FILES TO EXECUTE
```

A filled-in version of the screen:

```
Menu File Name ?      B:PAYMENU
Menu Title            *** PAYROLL MENU OPTIONS***
No. of Options        3


OPTION NO.        OPTION MESSAGE                FILES TO EXECUTE

    (1)           ? UPDATE                      ? B:PAYUP
    (2)           ? REPORT                      ? B:PAYRPT
    (3)           ? EXIT                        ? EXIT
```

It all seems simple enough: this screen will generate a menu command file with the indicated title and the options of updating, reporting, or leaving the system. It also lets you indicate the files to be executed when you call each option.

Maintaining the Files

Autocode's file maintenance function displays your predesigned screen, along with the fields—this time it's Autocode, not dBASE using that term—through which you will enter and retrieve data. Further prompts will ask you to identify the dBASE fields, called *key fields* in Autocode, on which the file will be indexed. Autocode then asks you to set up the formulas for calculated fields, such as multiplying a wage rate by total hours, or subtracting deductions from gross pay. This is an area where QUICKCODE is weak, and Autocode appears to have an advantage.

Reporting

Again like QUICKCODE, Autocode relies heavily on the dBASE report generator. If you've set up dBASE reports, the Autocode screen will look familiar, asking the same questions in a somewhat different language.

Autocode does offer one big advantage over the dBASE generator: should you need to modify your report format, Autocode will walk you back through the question and answer sequence; dBASE has a frustrating trick, displaying your answers without indicating the questions to which you responded.

Autocode also has a means to let you specify the scope and conditions of the report.

One Generator That Combines Files

The common criticism of most report generators is that they do not produce sophisticated products. In particular, neither QUICKCODE nor Autocode 1 are designed to make use of more than one file. You can get around that by first writing your own program to combine the files into a form the code generator can use, but that cuts into the ease of use for which you would buy such a program in the first place.

One generator that does let you combine files is dBASE Window, from Tylog Systems of Miami. Window's main claim to fame is that it will handle any number of files and up to five indexes each. The window in the title refers to the area where the databases are linked to each other.

Like the other generator programs, Window works from the input or output screen you design. Also in similar fashion, but in a different language and format, it asks you to identify the files, fields, and links you intend to create.

Window's report format also is more flexible than the others. It can use two databases at once, with accumulators for counting and subtotaling, and your choice of a variety of formats. There's also a provision for installing passwords.

Now, the Bad News

All this comes at a price. The retail list price is not out of line with the other report generators, but Window has other ways to prove the old saying that you get what you pay for.

The more functions and flexibility a program offers, the more it demands of your operating time and disk space. Reviewers have commented that Window demands copious amounts of both. That's the real price you pay for its extra functions.

ARE GENERATORS WORTH IT?

Program generators are marketed for two distinct types of users. The first is the beginner who can use them to produce basic, useful programs that can be used right away.

The second is an advanced user. This person can use a program generator to produce all the routine code in minutes that might otherwise take a day or two for even an expert to write and debug. The user then can concentrate on parts of the program that demand advanced skill and effort, letting the program generator handle the routine stuff.

A program generator can save time for either type of user. It's important to remember, though, that most of their products are elementary and do not make anything like full use of dBASE's potential. Keep that in mind when you make a decision.

Another point that might be important is also related to the generators' lack of sophistication. An expert programmer can produce "tight" code that operates at maximum speed. A program generator's code is a little looser and may not run quite as fast.

As dBASE expert Adam Green points out, though, the looser code actually may be an advantage. It's easier for a human to read and modify the program, should that be necessary, and Green prefers such a program to one that is fast but hard to understand.

ADVANCED REPORT GENERATORS

The limits of the dBASE report generator also are the limits of report generators that make heavy use of it, but in true mother-of-invention fashion, several products have been created to overcome those limits.

For example, Tylog also has created dBASE Door, which might be called an add-on to an add-on. It is particularly designed to give users of more conventional program generators some of the advanced relational and reporting features of its own dBASE Window.

Like its companion product, Door can produce calculated fields from one or two databases and can provide a variety of formats, counting, and mathematical operations.

Not Just for dBASE

If you're looking for something to extend dBASE's capacities or cover one of its shortcomings, you may find the answer in a product that isn't specifically designed for dBASE alone. One such product is the Friend report generator, which is designed for use on any standard data file, including the type dBASE produces.

You might know Friend as Access/80; the name was changed recently in a clash of trademark rights. It has been derived from mainframe report generators, and it offers most of their advantages—and drawbacks.

One particular advantage is cross-tabulation, the ability to break down survey responses by age group, for example, or categories of expenses by their monthly totals.

Let's say, for example, you want to tabulate your expenses by quarters. Only a sophisticated report generator—or a separate spreadsheet program—could produce a table like Fig. 10-1, based on the Friend brochure.

dBASE alone can't touch something like that. It shows what a well-designed add-on can do. Friend also can work with unlimited numbers of variables, do advanced mathematics, sort its own files, and do other jobs normally available only on the mainframe products from which it is derived.

All this versatility comes at a price. As Sandra Gey of Friends Software candidly puts it:

ACCOUNTS	TOTAL	1ST QTR	2ND QTR	3RD QTR	4TH QTR
Total	25412.55	9789.06	4532.23	6065.00	5026.26
Shipping	5598.33	4208.17	599.91	346.61	443.64
Supplies	3218.88	613.95	1149.64	1187.87	267.42
Equipment	7176.55	2607.37	867.57	2306.93	1394.68
Phone	7604.26	1781.03	1503.22	1845.30	2474.71
Travel	1814.53	578.54	411.89	378.29	445.81
Percentages					
Total	100.00	38.52	17.83	23.87	19.78
Shipping	100.00	75.17	10.72	6.19	7.92
Supplies	100.00	19.07	35.72	36.90	8.31
Equipment	100.00	36.33	12.09	32.15	19.43
Phone	100.00	23.42	19.77	24.27	32.54
Travel	100.00	31.88	22.70	20.85	24.57

Fig. 10-1. A limitation of dBASE.

Since it came from the mainframe world and is similar to RAMIS, (Friend) is generically different and more powerful than other micro software. Its disadvantage is the lack of some of the user-friendly features built into some recent micro software. The Friend user must type accurately and use the Friend manual. We do not have a menu-driven system or indexing. Not having these features, however, leaves space in memory for the magnificient functionality of Friend.

What Is Friendliness, Anyway?

Ms. Gey raises a good point, appropriate to much more than this single product. Just what is user-friendliness, anyway? Is it a product that's easy to use, but limited in its capacity? Or is it one that makes its user work a little bit in exchange for "magnificent functionality" or some other desirable feature? The choice is yours, but it's one you should make before you consider any dBASE accessory or application—or any piece of software, for that matter. Always remember, you probably will not remain forever at your present level of skill.

A PAIR OF UTILITIES

Shifting quickly from the magnificent to the mundane, let's turn our attention to a pair of the least spectacular—but potentially the most important—accessory programs available for dBASE. These are *utilities*. They don't make dBASE do anything it isn't already inclined to do, they don't particularly make dBASE any easier to use, and they don't even make it more fun. These are important add-ons, though, because they can help dBASE serve you in the best possible way.

dUTIL. From Fox & Geller, this is an inexpensive program whose sole purpose is to help you get your files in order. No doubt you've noticed all the indenting that's necessary to help make sure all your DO and IF loops are closed properly and in the right order. dUTIL will take care of the indenting and make sure you didn't leave a hanging IF somewhere. It will also capitalize the dBASE commands and place other names in lowercase, in the normal style of dBASE programming.

Other advantages: a list and diagram of how your programs link together, a means to neatly link files together, and a variety of options for inputs and reports.

If code and program generators are the lathes and power saws of programming tools, dUTIL is more like a screwdriver: simple, basic, and highly useful. It's an important tool, for beginners and experts alike.

DBPlus. This also is a utility, but it's the kind of utility that, as its name suggests, adds a little something to dBASE's performance. This program, from HumanSoft of Arlington, Mass., has three major functions:

- ☐ The Compress function squeezes a dBASE file to about a third of its original size. This can be useful if you're trying to save disk space; it also can save time and expense if you have to transmit the file by modem. There is a companion Decompress function that restores the file to its original form for use.
- ☐ A Sort feature greatly expands dBASE's sorting ability. dBASE lets you sort on only one field at a time. DBPlus will sort on multiple fields and do it much faster.
- ☐ The Transform function lets you modify a database structure without going through the clumsy routine of copying files to keep them from being erased.

EXTENDING YOUR REACH

Programs like Friend and DBPlus stand as evidence of the dangers of any kind of pigeonholing system. Friend is more than a report generator, and DBPlus is something more than a pure utility. Both cross the line into the area generally known as dBASE *extenders*. These are programs that add new capacities to dBASE itself.

One such program is ABstat, from Anderson-Bell of Canon City, Colorado. It performs statistical operations on dBASE files or, like Friend, on any other kind of standard-format data file.

ABstat can handle standard deviations, analysis of variation, frequency distributions, t-tests and U-tests, cross tabulations and chi squares, regression analysis, and probability functions, among other things. If you understand what all those are, you probably have use for something like ABstat. It also includes an editor for your data and a flexible report generator which, among other things, lets you add a prewritten text file to your statistical report.

Reviewers have given ABstat generally high marks for performance and ease of use, but it does have some limits. It won't accept the sheer volume of data a mainframe statistical program can handle, and it is designed for use by knowledgeable statisticians.

Other dBASE add-ons include dGRAPH, another Fox & Geller product, which adds some graphics capacity to dBASE, translating data files into graphs and charts. dBRx, from Gryphon Microproducts, adds advanced mathematical functions including logarithms, square roots, and trigonometric functions. dB/Ra overcomes another dBASE shortcoming by letting you set up arrays of up to three dimensions.

Figure 10-1 gives the addresses of manufacturers or distributors for all the dBASE add-ons mentioned.

READ ALL ABOUT IT

If there's anything surer than the proverbial death and taxes, it is this: any program as successful as dBASE is sure to spawn an outpouring of books on the subject. After all, you're reading one right now.

<table>
<tr><td>

Anderson-Bell
PO Box 191
Canon City, CO 81212
(303) 275-1661
    ABstat

</td><td>

Gryphon Microproducts
PO Box 6543
Silver Spring, MD 20906
(301) 946-2585
    dBRX, DB/RA

</td></tr>
<tr><td>

Ashton-Tate
10150 W. Jefferson
Culver City, CA 90230
(213) 204-5570
    dBASE II; Friday; DBrun

</td><td>

Humansoft
661 Massachusetts Av
Arlington, MA 02174
(617) 641-1880
    DBPlus

</td></tr>
<tr><td>

Axel Johnson Corp.
PO Box 7067
San Francisco, CA 94120
(800) 262-8800
    Autocode 1

</td><td>

Softwarebanc
661 Massachusetts Av
Arlington, MA 02174
(800) 451-2502
    dBASE Seminars

</td></tr>
<tr><td>

Fox and Geller
604 Market St.
Elmwood Park, NJ 07407
(201) 794-8883
    QUICKCODE, dUTIL, dGRAPH

</td><td>

Tylog Systems Inc.
9805 SW 152 Terr.
Miami, FL 33157
(305) 252-5942
    dBASE Window, dBASE Door

</td></tr>
</table>

Fig. 10-2. Source directory for add-on programs.

Other books also can help you learn about dBASE or expand and apply your understanding. Here are some of them:

☐ *Everyman's Database Primer*, by Robert A. Byers. (Ashton-Tate/Reston, 1982.)

This is ostensibly a book using databases in general: it is copublished by Ashton-Tate, so guess which program is used as an example. Byers has put together a good book for the beginner who wants to gain a quick, simple understanding of the system. He gets into some more advanced material, too, but the strength of this book is in the fundamentals. If you want to learn just enough about dBASE to put it to good use, this book can help. You can also gain an understanding of its more advanced features, although not a detailed knowledge. It's a nonfrightening way to get to know dBASE.

☐ *dBASE II For the First Time User*, by Alan Freedman. (Ashton-Tate, 1984.)

This book still was "forthcoming" at this writing, but the title indicates it would be even more fundamental than Byers' volume.

☐ *Using dBASE II*, by Carl Townsend. (Osborne/McGraw Hill, 1984.)

Townsend starts about where Byers leaves off. Unlike most other books on dBASE, he leaps almost directly into programming while continuing to discuss other aspects of dBASE use. It is suggested for gaining a more advanced understanding of dBASE, particularly its programming aspects.

☐ *dBASE II Users Guide*, by Adam B. Green. (Softwarebanc, 1983.)

Adam Green is undoubtedly the leading dBASE teacher in the country today. The founder of Softwarebanc, he tours the country conducting seminars on dBASE, and this book covers much the same material as the first two sessions of his three-day course. What Green has to offer is his mastery of both dBASE and instructional technique—he's an expert in his subject who also is an expert teacher.

This is one book you definitely should not judge by its cover. It has that distinctive "instant print shop" look, and the best thing you can say about the typography is that it was done, at least, on a letter-quality printer. One other thing about the cover that might throw you back is the listed price of $29.

Spend the money. The contents are well worth it.

☐ *Report Writing in dBASE II*. (Softwarebanc, 1984.)

The weakness of the dBASE report generator has often been criticized. Here's a book that reports on its strong features. Cynics might say there aren't enough strong points to fill a book—and this volume *is* thin. Still, it fills a need.

Most dBASE instruction books are so anxious to get past the report writer and into painted-screen programming that they pass over many of the system's useful features. In this book, three Softwarebanc staff members have gone back to check out those features—and have found more than you might expect. The report generator still is a dBASE weakness, but as the authors point out, it isn't nearly as weak as you might have thought.

A book doesn't have to be specifically about dBASE to be useful to a dBASE user. One notable example is

☐ *Database: A Primer*, by C. J. Date. (Addison-Wesley, 1983.)

298

Chris Date is one of the nation's leading experts on database use and design, and the primer is a nontechnical description of fundamental database techniques for the individual or small-business user. Many of this book's ideas on proper database design were found in Date's volume.

Most of Date's examples are in SQL, a query language for a mainframe database. It's close enough to the dBASE language that you can follow along, and in one chapter Date does describe his principles in dBASE terms.

For really serious readers, Date also is the author of the two-volume *An Introduction to Database Systems*, also from Addison-Wesley. These standard textbooks describe the same kind of material on a much more detailed and technical level.

☐ *Business Systems Analysis and Design*, by Gary B. Shelly and Thomas J. Cashman. (Anaheim Publishing Co., 1975.)

As computer books go, this is an oldtimer. It's about as long in the tooth as the office clerks in some of its pictures are short in the skirt. What's more, it presents its material in a traditional corporate data processing environment. You'd need a computer just to keep track of all the multipage memos that go flying around in the process of developing a new program.

No small business can afford to bury itself in the amount of paperwork this book suggests, but if you can get past that part, the book has something to offer. It apparently was written as a textbook, and it can teach you something.

It does a particularly good job of walking you, step by very slow step, through the development of a payroll program. Ignore the involved procedural steps and concentrate on the thought process that goes into planning and developing this program. These ideas are as valid today as they were when written, and they're good for businesses of all sizes.

BACK TO SCHOOL

When Adam Green describes his teaching techniques he uses sophisticated terms like "information density," the number of information items he presents per minute. He knows how much we can absorb, and how much our capacity varies with time, temperature, and diet. That means one of his dBASE seminars is a slick, tightly controlled presentation.

When Green teaches one of his three-day seminars, it will be in a climate-controlled room in a location that may have been selected for how well his books sell in the area. He brings the same kind of detail to the teaching of dBASE.

Green's students tend to be mid-level applications development people. One typical group included two people who were developing dBASE applications for their companies, a small business software consultant, and a Navy doctor who wanted to develop a computerized system for his coming switch to private practice.

The first day starts with dBASE fundamentals, and Green tailors this material as much for experts who will become training instructors as for raw dBASE beginners. The second day gets into programming, and the third deals with advanced techniques.

Another sponsor of dBASE seminars is the Center for Advanced Professional Education (CAPE), which holds a series of two-day sessions.

YOUR OWN "INTEGRATED SYSTEM"

If you shopped for your dBASE program recently, you probably considered—perhaps you strongly considered—one of the integrated business programs like Lotus 1-2-3 or the Context MBA. These combine database programs with spreadsheets and word processors to give you a full-featured business program that can readily swap data from one mode to another. The tradeoff is that none of these three elements offers as many features as a good database program like dBASE, or a comparable word-processing or spreadsheet program.

There is a way, though, that you can have it all—or at least most of it. You can use dBASE with other programs, and you can move data from one program to another via the standard data format, or SDF.

For example, you could link a dBASE file with MicroPro's WordStar, the popular word-processing program, and Sorcim's SuperCalc, one of the leading spreadsheet programs available. The techniques used to link these three programs can be adapted to most other spreadsheets and word processors as well.

Two Options for WordStar

There are two ways to link dBASE and WordStar. The first was used widely to prepare this book. The text of this book contains many screen displays and snatches of code, placed there to illustrate the topic of the accompanying text. The technique: as the dBASE routines were run, a separate text file captured the action. This file then was copied into the appropriate place within the text of the book. The technique: fire up dBASE and enter this sequence:

```
. SET ALTERNATE TO TRANS
. SET ALTERNATE ON
```

With those commands, nearly everything that came across the screen (GET commands are the major exception) also was captured in a file called TRANS.TXT.

As a program was run, its workings would be captured in the alternate file. Once finished, I could transfer to WordStar (I copied dBASE and WordStar onto a single disk for the occasion) and begin writing the text to accompany the programs. As I reached the point where I wanted to print a screen or part of a program listing I would copy the TRANS file (using WordStar's CTRL/KR command) to the bottom of my text and bring up the various bits and pieces I needed. I then could take advantage of the word processor's formatting techniques to organize and display the dBASE material within the manuscript.

If you own dBASE 2.4, you might find even greater potential, combining this technique with 2.4's superior text handling facilities.

The second technique is the one in the accounts receivable chapter. You use the names on a selective mailing list, processed with dBASE, to address and print form letters through WordStar's MailMerge option. The list of suppliers at the end of this chapter was done in this way.

I originally entered these listings as a dBASE file, using the INDEX feature to put them in alphabetical order. I then used a DELIMITED option to copy these files to the form used by MailMerge.

What's delimited? As you may know, MailMerge uses a version of the standard data format in which the individual fields—name, address, ZIP code and so on—are separated by commas. (You can use double quote marks if there are commas within the fields themselves.)

The command to create such a file:

```
. COPY TO TRANS.TXT DELIMITED WITH ,
```

This produced exactly the type of data file MailMerge uses. I then instructed MailMerge to print the listings on what it thought was a series of eight-line pages. You could use the same technique, of course, to print a series of six-line address labels, as well as placing the names and addresses at the tops of your letters.

COPY . . . DELIMITED normally will use a single quote mark as the delimiter unless you specify some other punctuation. That's what the receivables program was doing when it used CHR(34) to generate double quotes.

In Reverse

dBASE also will accept files delimited with the single quote mark. To go in this direction you use APPEND instead of COPY. Perhaps more usefully, it will accept files set up in fixed record length like dBASE itself uses.

With WordStar, use the tab key to set up a table-like arrangement of the data. The last name could start in column 1, the first name in column 11, the middle initial in column 21 and so on. Then set up a dBASE file that uses the same lengths, in this case 10 characters each for the first and last names. Then say:

```
. APPEND FROM (your filename) SDF
```

dBASE will put the first 10 characters, whatever they are, into the last name field, the next 10 into the first name and so on, according to your specifications. Obviously, the field lengths in both files must match exactly.

The SuperCalc Matchup

Matching up the field lengths is reasonably simple when you are transferring a SuperCalc file to dBASE. The width of the columns in the SuperCalc spreadsheet can be set to correspond exactly with the field length in the dBASE file.

To get from one to the other your data must again pass through an intermediate text file. When the SuperCalc spreadsheet has been completed, use the Border command to get rid of the column and line numbers. Then call for an Output, and at the forthcoming prompts send the Display to a Disk file, which can be the always versatile TRANS.TXT.

Switch to dBASE, and if you haven't done so already set up your fields to match the SuperCalc columns. You then can APPEND the material in TRANS.TEXT just as you did with the earlier file.

One Yawning Gap

Unfortunately, there was no way to transfer a standard data file *to* the original version of SuperCalc. This cuts out what some of you may have been dreaming about: setting up your files in dBASE base, then switching them to the spreadsheet for the mathematical operations that are a dBASE weak point.

Two newer versions, SuperCalc^2 and SuperCalc^3, now have the capacity to load SDF files, much like MailMerge. If you're looking for a spreadsheet, it would pay to ask about its ability to pick up foreign files. Even if you don't want it now, you may want it later.

HOW GOOD IS dBASE—REALLY?

By the time you gain much experience with dBASE, you'll also gain experience with its frustrations. Whether you're a user anxious to make dBASE do a particular job—or an author trying to show you how—there will be inevitable times when you find that dBASE stubbornly resists doing what you want it to do.

At the very least, peak performance requires some sophisticated programming. As a small business manager, you probably have all the work you can handle trying to keep the business running smoothly and profitably. You don't have a lot of time to learn to be a programmer, and you shouldn't have to. That's why this book has concentrated so heavily on techniques that work with only minimal programming effort.

dBASE does an excellent job of collecting and organizing data. You should seldom run up against its size limits, and if you do there are ways to get around it.

Where dBASE falls short is on the output side. While its report generator is better than it is generally given credit for being, it still is sharply limited in comparison with some of the add-on products available. Its mathematical ability is below that of an inexpensive desk calculator.

Add-ons can help overcome some of these shortcomings, of course, but that raises the question of why you must buy a second program to make the first one do the job you expected of it.

Focusing on these shortcomings, though, is a good way to forget one point: dBASE II is an excellent product with at least one bookfull of practical uses. There's a reason for its popularity.

Index

Index